THE
Unfinished
Revolution

Learning,
Human Behavior,
Community,
and Political
Paradox

JOHN ABBOTT and TERRY RYAN

ASSOCIATION FOR SUPERVISION AND CURRICULUM DEVELOPMENT

Alexandria, Virginia USA

Association for Supervision and Curriculum Development
1703 N. Beauregard St. • Alexandria, VA 22311-1714 USA
Telephone: 1-800-933-2723 or 703-578-9600 • Fax: 703-575-5400
Web site: http://www.ascd.org • E-mail: member@ascd.org

The 21st Century Learning Initiative
3 Grosvenor Place
London Road
Bath BA1 6AX
UK

Phone/Fax: 44-1225-333376

The 21st Century Learning Initiative
11084 Saffold Way
Reston, VA 20190
USA

Phone: 703-787-4020
Fax: 703-787-4024

E-mail: info@21learn.org
Web site: http://www.21learn.org

This book was first published in the United Kingdom by Network Educational Press, Ltd., © 2000 by John Abbott and Terry Ryan.

ASCD publications present a variety of viewpoints. The views expressed or implied in this book should not be interpreted as official positions of the Association.

Printed in the United States of America.

ASCD Product No. 101062   s3/2001
ASCD member price: $21.95   nonmember price: $25.95

Library of Congress Cataloging-in-Publication Data
Abbott, John, 1939–
   The unfinished revolution : learning, human behavior, community, and political paradox / John Abbott and Terry Ryan.
      p.   cm.
Includes bibliographical references (p.   ) and index.
   ISBN 0-87120-513-0
1. Learning, Psychology of.   2. Community education.   3. Educational change.
I. Ryan, Terry, 1968–   II. Title.
   LB1060 .A25 2001
   370.15'23—dc21

                                                    2001000175

07 06 05 04 03 02 01   10 9 8 7 6 5 4 3 2 1

The Unfinished Revolution

Acknowledgments

First, our thanks to our wives and families for tolerating us as we struggled with ideas that absorbed far too much of our time and attention. Special thanks, also, to Emi Ryan for helping us design the cover (for the United Kingdom edition) and the graphs, and to Anne Abbott for her many editorial suggestions.

As the Endnotes testify, we have called upon the experience and wisdom of many people from several countries. We know some of these people personally and have communicated with them at great length, while others are known to us only through their writings. They, together with countless practitioners and innovators who, month by month, communicate with the 21st Century Learning Initiative from as many as 50 countries worldwide through our Web site, have contributed to our understanding of just why this has been an "unfinished revolution." But their help and experience have shown us just why and how things can now change.

We are deeply grateful to the trustees of Education 2000, and more recently, the 21st Century Learning Initiative, for their steadfast support, encouragement, and financial help. We especially thank David Peake, formerly chair of Kleinwort Benson; Tom Griffin, formerly chair of G.T. .Management; Christopher Wysock Wright; the Rt. Reverend Bishop of Ripon; Dr. Bruce Farmer, chair of Morgan Crucible plc; Dr. Stephanie Pace Marshall, president of the Illinois Mathematics and Science Academy; Ted Marchese, vice president of the American Association of Higher Education; Dr. Paul Cappon, director general of the Canadian Council of Ministers of Education; Dr. Ash Hartwell of the University of Massachusetts (Amherst); and Bill Gorham, president of the Urban Institute in Washington, D.C.

We would especially like to record our thanks to the late Dr. Al Shanker, who died in 1997 as president of the American Federation of Teachers; to the late Sir Keith Joseph, British politician and one-time president of Education 2000; to Ray Dalton of Cambridge for his many years of patient encouragement; to Charles Bray, formerly director of the Johnson Foundation in Wisconsin; to Dr. Aharon Aviram of Ben-Gurion University in Israel, who helped us think about not just learning but also unlearning; and to Wiktor Kulerski, former Polish member of Parliament and Solidarity

iv

leader, who made it possible for the two authors to meet and become collaborators.

Many people have generously contributed their professional time in sharing with us research that we might not normally have been aware of. Many of these have been powerful theoreticians, while others have been down-to-earth practitioners more concerned with outcomes than the search for "underlying principles." The juxtaposition of such people has given energy to the book.

Many people, from Europe and the Americas, to South Africa, Israel, Australia, Japan, and the Far East, have attended lectures and workshops on the ideas developed in this book; their questions and observations have shaped the structure of the argument set out here.

We are especially grateful to all those who have provided editorial support, especially Ted Marchese, Wendy Varley, Paul Fisher, and the editors of ASCD.

To all these people we are, indeed, most grateful, though the final responsibility for what is written here is very much ours.

Introduction

John Abbott

How children learn, and why some adults carry on learning for a lifetime (and others don't), has fascinated me for years. As director of the Education 2000 Trust in England, I was fortunate in the early 1990s to meet and work with educators, researchers, and policymakers from many countries. In early 1995, I approached several English businesses to sponsor the 21st Century Learning Initiative in Washington, D.C. The group we set up comprised some 60 educational researchers and practitioners from England, the United States, Canada, Germany, Israel, Australia, Poland, Venezuela, Ethiopia, Colombia, Denmark, Lebanon, Scotland, and Scandinavia. Between 1995 and 1997, we held six conferences at the Johnson Foundation's Frank Lloyd Wright mansion in Racine, Wisconsin.

The Initiative focused on learning, not schooling, for the obvious reason—at least to us—that if we weren't clear about how people learned, we couldn't begin a proper consideration of educational reform. Our standpoint was that the crisis in education stems from misunderstandings about how humans learn rather than any generalized failure of schools and teachers. In other words, we quickly realized we were dealing with a crisis in childhood, not simply a crisis in schooling. The conferences echoed the more widespread problem of how society at large can convert disparate new findings on learning into useful maps for the future of education.

We found many of the Initiative's more academic delegates were stronger at setting out the details of their own specialization than finding any agreement on what the totality of their combined work might mean. When an array of esoteric opinions surfaced, I began to understand why politicians and the general public find it so difficult to understand professional educators and researchers. I also understood that within the mass of discussion were ideas that would influence children's learning if properly articulated and understood. It was left to me and my colleague, Terry Ryan, to synthesize all the conference proceedings into something that could be useful to people wanting to transform the way their communities educate their young people.

I am a one-time geography and religious studies teacher at Manchester Grammar School; head master of an old grammar school being reorganized into a comprehensive school in the 1970s; and, for a dozen years, director

1

of the Education 2000 project in the United Kingdom. I have a passionate interest in improving youngsters' ability to take control of their own learning. I often repeat the Catholic doctrine of subsidiarity that states that it is wrong for a superior body to take to itself the right to make decisions that an inferior body is well qualified to make for itself. That doctrine has to apply to students as well as teachers. It also applies to those with the power to direct local communities when those communities already contain untapped resources that could regenerate community life and lift academic standards beyond anything conceived and delivered by outsiders. All this I wrote about in my earlier book *The Child Is Father of the Man: How Humans Learn and Why*. This subsequent book explores these issues in greater depth and focuses on setting out their possible strategic and resource implications.

I met Terry at an international conference he organized for the Polish Ministry of Education on education in a democracy. He is an American half my age and is an ideas sleuth who loves to try and understand all things political and economic. He is passionate in his search for understanding why things work (or don't) the way they should or could. After getting his master's degree in political economy, he received a fellowship from the American Federation of Teachers to work with educational reformers and students in Poland from 1994 to 1995. His mentor was the former Solidarity leader Wiktor Kulerski, whose family did as much as any during the 20th century to create a free and independent Poland. His next book is a collaborative work on 20th century Poland with Kulerski entitled *From the Shadows of the Past*.

Both Terry and I are as conscious, if not more so, of our roles as parents as we are as interpreters of educational policy. Both of us are much concerned, as citizens, with the increasing fragility of our communities and our planet.

Over the past five years we have grown from a master/apprentice relationship to an equal partnership where each of us brings a different generational, national and cultural perspective. Our fundamental shared view—and one that informs every word in this book—is that there should be a constructivist and apprenticeship-based approach to learning that takes full account of recent neuroscientific research. These leitmotifs are enlarged upon in the first chapter and returned to throughout, so it's enough to say here that constructivism expands on an old idea expressed by a Chinese philosopher who, more than 2,000 years ago, said: "Tell me and I forget. Show me and I remember. Let me do and I understand."

We draw heavily from our direct experience of living and working in both the United States and the United Kingdom. In a book intended for an international audience, we make no apologies for this fact. What is currently happening in English schools puts them at the forefront of conventional school reform movements. We believe that the world in general would benefit from a better understanding of the unintended consequences of these efforts. The United States leads the world in its commitment to uninhibited economic expansion, and again we believe that citizens of other countries need to understand the impact this has on social structures and, in particular, on those that are central to children's learning. Our extensive involvement with other countries, especially Canada, makes us realize just how beneficial it is for policymakers and educational practitioners alike to use international experience to temper their own more parochial strategies.

Our five-year study of the science of learning and the biological nature of the brain has revealed a massive mismatch. The nature of learning is very different from the political mantras driving educational reform in most countries. This is a potentially dangerous disconnection because the welfare of individuals and communities—especially when set against rapid, social, technological, and economic changes—is increasingly dependent on the ability to continuously learn and adapt. The shift in our understanding of learning has already started but is all too frequently frustrated by people's attempts to fit it into pre-existing systems.

Schools as we understand them now are a product of political and economic compromises informed by assumptions about learning with their roots in the late 19th and early 20th centuries. The historical chapters of this book show how the institutionalization of learning has led to the trivialization of community as a key component of people's lives and, in particular, the bond between generations. The relationships within the community need to be so strong that you don't need top-down solutions because there is such strength within ordinary people that they can sort out their own problems. Each person has a role and a responsibility.

We're not repeating the old "school is dead" slogan; nor are we saying that schools should just keep up with the times. We have to consciously shape the future. What is recommended in this book—from the specifics in our graphs on intellectual weaning and current expenditure to our broader observations on the open-ended nature of learning—is predicated on fresh understandings. This book is our attempt to chart a course across disciplines that goes well beyond just what happens in the decontextualized setting of the classroom. We realize we have risked making fools of ourselves yet, if one accepts the constructivist model of learning as we do, then it becomes imperative to see learning as too interconnected to be left to schools and educators to handle alone.

1 The Biological Nature of Learning

Thus, the task is not so much to see what no one yet has seen, but to think what nobody has thought about that which everybody sees.

SCHOPENHAUER

We will start with two simple assertions: Humans are born to learn, and learning is what we are better at than any other species. These old and essentially intuitive insights are now supported by the new biological understandings yielded by brain-imaging technologies developed since the late 1980s. Noninvasive brain mapping has enabled researchers to watch learning occur as specific patterns of activity within the brain light up on a computer screen. The brain is revealed as a more flexible, self-adjusting biological system that grows and reshapes itself in response to challenge or withers through lack of use. The mass of evidence now emerging about learning and brain development has spawned a movement towards educational practice that confirms that thinking skills (metacognition) can be learned, and significant aspects of intelligence developed. The brain is now seen as a collection of specialized and complex systems, each engineered by natural selection to aid our species in decision making. Humans are predisposed to learn from and adapt to their environment.

So why does today's environment seem antithetical to productive learning? Why do schools need more controls and incentives than ever before to get children to learn those skills and values that civilized, democratic society holds dear? The biology of learning is providing some powerful answers that, in turn, raise serious questions about our largely unlimited faith in schools being able to prepare children for life in the open, free, dynamic societies of the 21st century.

The last decade of the 20th century saw a convergence of insights from the evolutionary sciences with findings from the cognitive sciences, neuroscience, linguistics, and psychology. They have helped researchers understand why our brains are as they are and what they might shortly become. Robert Sylwester, the University of Oregon professor of education, remarked of these opportunities in 1995 that, "We [educators and policy people] don't have to apologize. What you have to realize is that the medical profession is at least 50 years ahead of us in theory and research. We started maybe 10 years ago in terms of the biology of learning. In terms of the speed at which our knowledge is emerging, it is simply phenomenal. . . . [C]onventional wisdom used to have it that 90 percent of what we knew about the brain was learned in the last 10 years. Because of the development of fMRI two years ago, 90 percent of what we will know about the brain in three years will have been learned in the last three years. What is happening is simply a phenomenal influx of new information. It is happening on our watch. We don't have to apologize for the last 50 years, but we are sure as hell are going to have to apologize to our grandchildren if we drop the ball at this point."[1]

What Sylwester and many other researchers are starting to make clear is that it is now possible to begin mapping models of learning that go far further than what we've inherited from the limited science of behaviorism and the needs of industrialism. Central to such models is constructing a bridge between the dichotomy of the mind as an inflexible biological product (the position of IQ-test advocates) and the mind as an endlessly malleable social product (the position of behaviorists). Such a bridge is possible by merging findings from the brain and cognitive sciences into an evolutionary framework. "If the evolutionary perspective is simply set aside, the data collected by psychologists and neuroscientists are likely to be grossly misinterpreted,"[2] argued Dartmouth cognitive neuroscientist Michael Gazzaniga in 1998. The point here is that if those working to improve the direction of education don't have a good grasp of where we come from as a species, then it will indeed be difficult to chart an effective course for where we want to go. Each generation is not simply starting from scratch.

Today's evolutionary perspective argues that nature plays a far more important, and complementary, role than behaviorists believed. However, the evolved nature of the brain does not so much constrain as it creates or enables.[3] Evidence has accumulated to show that for education to go with the inherited basis of brain function, then the learning needs of young people must be seen in terms of both the culture and the accumulated evolutionary experience previous generations found useful to their survival. This means that we need to focus as much on trying to understand the internal structures and processes of children's minds as we do on the knowledge we wish to share with them through the curriculum. For those of us trained in the social sciences, this is a radically different way of viewing human development. Culture (which curricula are designed to support) is critically important, but culture has to be seen in light of human evolution. Ask yourself, "If culture creates the individual, what then creates culture?"

Philip Tobias, the director of the University of Witwatersrand's paleo-anthropology unit in South Africa, captured the balance when he wrote: "The brain-culture relationship was not confined to one special moment in time. Long-continued increase in size and complexity of the brain was paralleled for probably a couple of million years by long-continued elaboration and 'complexification' of the culture. The feedback relationship between the two sets of events is as indubitable as it was prolonged in time."[4] Smarter models of learning require an implicit balance between our evolutionary inheritance and the culture that education is designed to support. "Each brain not fully utilized is two billion years of evolution wasted."[5]

Evolution, we now understand, has provided humans with a powerful tool kit of predispositions that go a long way in explaining our ability to learn language, to cooperate successfully in groups, to think across problems, to plan for the future, and to empathize with others. Predispositions provide individuals with a whole range of skills that enable them to relate flexibly to their environment. Yet, because for most of human history humans tended to live in relatively small groups, these skills have to be developed collaboratively, as very few people ever possess all these attributes. The speed with which our predispositions evolve seems to be incredibly slow, and it is thought there have been no major changes in the last 30,000 years.

The Language Predisposition

Human nature matters enormously in learning. For the vast majority of time, Homo sapiens' experience of living as a wandering tribe in the ancestral environment shaped the broad structures of our predispositions (which encapsulate various successful evolutionary adaptations). These subsequently have been recreated in the brains of every succeeding generation. Thus, what served the purposes of our ancestors is still with us. Both with regard to language and social skills, the young child who could not talk effectively, or empathize with other children, would not have been able to survive when the group moved around; the child's genes would simply have perished. Language and social empathetic skills therefore need

7

to be seen in a survival context. The critical lesson from the evolutionary sciences is that all human development is an intricate interplay; "nature and nurture don't compete, they cooperate."[6]

For reasons that are still not totally clear, the human brain started to grow very rapidly about 100,000 years ago.[7] Some evolutionary biologists and linguists have advanced the theory that there is a direct connection between our ability to develop symbolic thought and use language and the growth of the prefrontal cortex, the frontal part of the brain that processes language and abstract thought.[8] As the brain has grown, so has the skull. This has produced a biological "bind." The child's head has increasing difficulty passing down the mother's birth canal. Because of this, human babies, unlike the young of most other species, are born with their brains incompletely formed. Much brain development, which in other species takes place in the womb, has to take place postbirth. It is for this reason that the human infant is far more vulnerable for a longer period of time than the young of other species. Nature has compensated for this dependency by equipping every newborn child with an amazing set of predispositions to learn. The full understanding of these predispositions is critical to our appreciation of the human potential to learn.

In the 1950s the linguist Noam Chomsky argued that language was simply too complex for each individual brain to learn it from scratch. Without a stumble, the average person can produce 150 words a minute, each word selected in milliseconds from as many as 50,000 possibilities and arranged in a meaningful sequence dictated by an elaborate mental stylebook of grammar and syntax. It is amazing. Work on the nature of language development from Chomsky onward contends that each brain is born with the predisposition to learn language in a particular, natural way. Our brains owe their basic design to our genetic program. Thus, language is hereditary, and the brain is no clean slate as regards language development. A more appropriate analogy is closer to an old-fashioned gramophone record, which needs a layer of wax removed from its surface before it reveals its preformed structure.[9] Subsequently, virtually every child born today has the innate capability of recognizing about 100 sounds, quite enough to combine in various forms to create all the alphabets in each of the earth's 5,000 plus languages.[10] The neurological structures that make the acquisition of language possible are identical to all human beings, regardless of culture.

Newborn babies can tell the difference between "pah" and "bah." By 4½ months of age, an infant "understands" the significance of clauses. At 10 months the infant understands how the ordering of noun and verb phrases fits in sentences. Below 18 months babies learn the meaning of new words at about one-third of a word a day; from then onward it speeds up to about 10 words a day. By listening to the language spoken around them, children set the rules appropriate to their own language by 18 months of age, and in many instances earlier.[11] Bénédicte de Boysson-Bardies, Director of Research in the Experimental Psychology Laboratory at the Centre Nationale de la Recherche Scientifique in Paris notes, "The child is therefore born with an implicit knowledge of the universal principles that structure language and with a genetic program for its acquisition. But for this program to operate, the child needs to hear speech. Human newborns must acquire their language; without linguistic information, their initial biological abilities remain unexploited."[12]

What this means is that, "All humans of normal intelligence can learn any language provided they start at a very young age. After the age of five or six, a child can almost never become perfectly fluent in a language, and the ability to learn it can completely disappear soon after that. After puberty, it is almost impossible to perfect the pronunciation of a second language."[13] The Italian geneticist Lugi Luca Cavalli-Sforza calls on educators to take advantage of this fact when he argues, "This is an excellent reason to begin foreign language instruction in elementary school, but few governments seem to have noticed this virtually absolute rule."[14]

The brain is essentially economic. What is not needed in one generation is replaced by a more appropriate function. A native-speaking Japanese will not have the equivalent of an *L* or *R* sound in his or her own language. Attempting to learn to speak English at the age of 15 or 20 will present a Japanese person with an almost impossible task of correctly articulating these sounds. The ability has just disappeared.

Collaboration Is a Survival Skill

Another predisposition that researchers are beginning to understand far better is that of social skills. Even though it may seem counterintuitive to those of us living in an era that glorifies individualism and cutthroat competition, it seems that we humans are predisposed to friendliness and cooperation. Human survival is almost totally dependent on relationships with other people. Faced with a hostile environment, our ancestors banded together to achieve as a group what they could not do alone, just as our communities, businesses, and nations are tied together in networks of mutual cooperation and dependency today.[15]

Our Stone Age forebears survived by cooperating with one another in relatively small groups. They found safety in numbers, but only to a certain extent. Today among tribes in the Brazilian rain forests, groups of over 12 or 14 fighting men (with women, children, and dependent relatives, that means a group of 50 or 60 people) either divide of their own peaceful volition or split through bloody rivalry.[16] Evidence from England in the thousand years before the industrial revolution suggests that most people lived within groups of less than 12 or 13 people.[17] Psychologists state that no one is ever likely to grieve deeply for more than 12 people in a lifetime; it is as if there is a ceiling beyond which our hearts don't break anymore. As any musician, actor, or team athlete can attest, we work best in relatively small, self-supporting groups.

Children reflect strongly the predisposition to be social, collaborative, and problem solving in groups through play. It was an intriguing early insight that created the word "toy," for this linguistically is the diminutive for the word "tool." Without the proper stimulation of social skills, individual children found survival difficult in earlier times. For if they couldn't empathize they would have been left behind when the tribe moved along. Evidence is accumulating to show that the predisposition toward such empathetic activity is at its strongest below the age of 6. If collaborative skills are not valued by that stage, then the networks are better replaced with "other" skills that could be useful, such as the behavior of the isolate and the dependent, or a simple regression toward violence.

With all this evidence available it seems curious that education systems still place children in classes of 25 or 30 students at the age of 5, and high school students are collected in schools of 1,500 pupils or more. Young people react to this impersonal scale by immediately forming into more cohesive units of friends with similar views and interests. Go to any high school and you will see packs of athletes, scholars, and beauty queens along with numerous other subgroups and cliques. Children find out about themselves by measuring themselves against the standard of their group mates. They come to think well or poorly of themselves by judging how they compare with the other members of their own group.

The U.S. commentator Judith Rich Harris takes this point even further when she argues, "The culture acts upon children not through their parents but through the peer group. Children's groups have their own cultures, loosely based on the adult culture, and it's impossible to predict what they'll include. Anything that's common to the majority of kids in the group may be incorporated into the children's culture, whether they learned it from their parents or from the television set."[18] Rich Harris's point adds a new twist to the old adage "it takes a village to raise a child." Her research argues that individual parents are greatly limited in how much influence they have on adolescents, while adults as a collective are vastly influential. Rich Harris also asserts, "Although individual parents have little power to influence the culture of children's peer groups, larger numbers of parents acting together have a great deal of power, and so does society as a whole. Through the prevailing methods of child rearing [society] fosters, and through influences—especially the media—that act directly on peer-group norms and values, a society shapes the adults of the future. Are we shaping them the way we ought to?"[19]

Ronald Kotulak, in his Pulitzer prize-winning series of articles on violence and young people for the *Chicago Tribune*, adds a neurological spin to the importance of developing young people's social predispositions when he warns that, "By failing to provide young children with the supportive and nurturing environments in which they can develop their predispositions towards social, collaborative, and team-building skills, young children's brains react with astounding speed and efficiency to the violent world they experience around them by rewiring trillions of brain cells that literally create the chemical pathways for aggression."[20] If Kotulak is right, aggression, rather than conciliation, becomes the action of first response. "He dissed me in front of my homeboys so I popped him," is the sort of explanation police officers across the United States have grown accustomed to hearing as the reason for why a young person kills. Nurture (in this case a peer group that has a complete disregard for human life) has the power to modify nature in each succeeding generation.

Even if we don't study the extremes that Kotulak did, there is much evidence to worry us deeply. It is highly likely that there is a direct connection between the child who was not encouraged to use his or her innate desire to collaborate in the earliest years of life and the young graduate who is the despair of his first employer, an employer who is staggered to find that after 16 years of formal education this employee can't work in a team and has to be told what to do. Developing such collaborative higher-order skills at the age of 23 or 24 is infinitely harder, and more expensive, than developing them with the "grain of the brain" at age 5 or 6. Isolation is a learned behavior, and in the world of hypermedia, and in particular the World Wide Web, it is considerably easier than at any other time in history to live as a loner completely disconnected from the physical world of other people.

In light of this evidence it is disturbing that at the beginning of the 21st century, a time when the richest countries are richer than ever, more than 22 percent of children under the age of 18 in the United States live in relative poverty, while 1 in 5 children in England live below the poverty line.[21] This is not, however, to argue for the expansion of the "nanny state" where young children spend most of their waking hours in formal institutions at ever younger ages; rather, we reason that children need the time of their parents and other adults in neighborhoods and communities that care. This requires a shift in societal values. It calls for dealing with not just issues related to the school but to those of the family, community, housing, health care, and, most profoundly, spirit. In the very recent past young parents were supported by extended family and neighbors, and in hindsight this was a much more effective system of inculcating children into a culture and set of shared values than any subsequent formal government program. How can intergenerational human support networks be encouraged and supported in the 21st century is what those concerned not only about improving the learning skills of young people, but also keeping civilized society together, need to ask themselves.

Formal education has a role to play. As children enter primary school there are great advantages in allowing them the opportunity and space for productive play and social interaction. Consider the Japanese approach to early education. According to Catherine C. Lewis, a U.S. educator who lived and worked in Japan while her two sons attended Japanese schools, the high academic achievement of Japanese students is not a result of their highly regimented secondary schooling; rather, it is due to Japanese society meeting younger "children's needs—for friendship, for belonging, for opportunities to shape school life." Lewis wrote:

• Japanese kindergartens center on free play, not academic instruction. Japanese kindergartners spend almost four times as much time in free play as their U. S. counterparts.
• Japanese elementary schools emphasize kindness, collaboration, and persistence—not test scores. Without ability grouping or tracking, Japanese children cooperatively master a challenging academic curriculum.
• Japanese students assume much authority. Even 1st graders quiet their classmates, help solve disputes, lead class meetings, and shape class rules and activities.
• Small groups are at the heart of elementary school life. The four or so members of a group together pursue a wide range of activities, from art to lunch to science. Only when small groups become "like families" do teachers expect learning to occur.[22]

There are other innate predispositions that are informative. We know, for instance, that there are critical periods for the development of numerical skills,[23] and for different forms of musical appreciation.[24] It is a fascinating fact that two of the countries that most stress the teaching of music for young children—Japan and Hungary—consistently score well in mathematics on the International Mathematics and Science Survey. As a guiding principle for those working on more effective models of learning, it is likely that the more we come to understand these predispositions, the more we will come to appreciate how different evolutionary traits from long past have shaped our preferred ways of doing things. Among these has to be the recognition of the significance of emotion in providing a short circuit in the way in which the brain responds to those things of high emotional interest, a vastly different set of innate responses to those of more logical and abstract significance. The role of the amygdala will receive increased attention. This almond-shaped section of the limbic system within the brain regulates our aggression, emotions, and sex drive by intentionally bypassing the brain's carefully constructed logical functions. The existence of an override mechanism is an important clue to the nature of learning for it indicates a primacy of emotion above logic in driving attention spans, shaping action, and aiding memory retention. We must also heed notions of "spiritual intelligence"[25] and the work of Danah Zohar and Ian Marshall, which we consider in greater depth later on.

The Motivation Behind Learning

The link between emotions and intrinsic motivation should surprise no one; consequently, the sterility of emotionally drained and aesthetically neutered learning environments has to be understood as contributing to low learning achievement. A successful childhood and adolescence is to a large degree defined by learning how to control and channel one's emotions to positive ends. The former basketball star Michael Jordan calls this the positive use of energy. To provide opportunities for young people to harness their emotional energy requires expanding the opportunity and range of extracurricular activities available to children and adolescents.

The significance of emotional outlets for exceptional performance helps to explain why many adults are so taken by the achievements of high school students on the athletics field or, still far too often in many countries, on the battlefield. A model of learning that focuses on the needs of all children will have multiple outlets beyond athletics for high performance that integrates intellect and emotions. Far too many young people do not know the success of the playing field, the stage, academic competitions, or the music hall. In fact, they know no success at all. Policymakers, educators, and parents need to consider seriously the downside of cutting extracurricular activities in order to focus on those with academic ability. Young people need more outlets for success, not fewer.

This link with intrinsic motivation is an important one. There are many definitions for creativity, but in the literature from psychology and cognitive science there is one concept that is in almost every effort to define how people develop it: intrinsic motivation. According to their review of the research on creativity, the U.S. psychologists Hennessey and Amabile observed that, "People will be most creative when they feel motivated primarily by the interest, enjoyment, satisfaction, and the challenge of the work itself—not by external pressures."[26] No one has ever enjoyed science as much as Einstein.

The *Washington Post* carried some anecdotal evidence about the significance of motivation on creativity with the following story. "Enter just about any elementary or middle school," it reported, "and you'll find that for doing well, students constantly are rewarded with stuff: McDonald's fries for good grades, pencils if they show up for standardized tests, a chance for a restaurant lunch if they do a good deed." The reason the *Post* gave for relying on extrinsic rewards was "educators rely on such incentives at a time when studies show it is harder than ever to motivate students. There is no fix on why teachers are grasping at ways to engage children, but commonly cited culprits include busy parents who don't demand much or don't pay attention, more family and societal problems, rife consumerism, and scanty Nintendo-era attention spans."[27]

Teachers are doing what they can to make learning happen in their classrooms, and central to creativity is a base of knowledge on which children can build new ideas and connections. Good schools and teachers help children acquire such knowledge. But for children to develop creativity and a passion for excellence there are yet other factors that must come into play. These are persistence, commitment, and a sense of purpose. It is purpose (meaning) that drives all human activity. The most creative and successful people in any endeavor seem to get extremely involved in a problem. They become so immersed that they stick to the problem, and the problem sticks to them. This sort of dedication comes from an internal desire to succeed. It is the result of intrinsic motivation.

Yet, increasingly even educators in good schools see the need to use external rewards and punishments to try and develop a desire within children to learn and take control of their own mental faculties. On both sides of the Atlantic teachers make the point that there just isn't time for children to explore what they are good at because the curricula must be covered. Howard Gardner wrote in 1993 that, "The greatest enemy of understanding is coverage. As long as you are determined to cover everything, you actually ensure that most kids are not going to understand. You've got to take enough time to get kids deeply involved in something so they can think about it in lots of different ways, and apply it—not just at school, but at home and on the street and so on."[28] Gardner's insights have been known by good teachers since the ancient Greeks, but they have rarely been listened to by education systems. In 1941, the president of Corpus

Christi College Oxford, Sir Richard Livingstone, told the English government that, "The test of successful education is not the amount of knowledge that a pupil takes away from school, but his appetite to know and his capacity to learn. If the school sends out children with the desire for knowledge and some idea of how to acquire and use it, it will have done its work. Too many leave school with the appetite killed and the mind loaded with undigested lumps of information. The good school master is known by the number of valuable subjects which he declines to teach."[29]

Consider the words of Gardner and Livingstone in light of the following from the late 1990s: "The Third International Mathematics and Science Survey (TIMSS) criticized curricula that were 'a mile wide and an inch deep' and argued that this is much more of a problem in America than in most other countries. Research on expertise suggests that a superficial coverage of many topics in the domain may be a poor way to help students develop the competencies that will prepare them for future learning and work."[30]

How is it that the brain is predisposed to learn and take responsibility for it, yet so many young people seem completely apathetic about learning and education? Educators increasingly deal with this dilemma by using extrinsic rewards to bribe children to learn and the fear of failing standardized tests as the stick to punish those who've become completely turned off to education and, for far too many, much of life generally.

The motivator of much student achievement is the vision of a good job and a decent income. According to Geoffrey Colvin of *Fortune* magazine, "Financial incentives will get people to do more of what they are doing. Not better, just more. . . . If you want to speed up the assembly line and you're not too particular about quality, workers will speed it up for a financial incentive. That's what the evidence shows. . . . But this is exactly what employers today don't want. If they want to speed up the assembly line, they rewrite the software. From employees they want imaginative thinking about how to solve problems that didn't exist yesterday (e.g., those problems you can't be taught to deal with beforehand). Can you get this kind of thinking by offering to pay for it? What would you guess? You're right, of course. Trying to pay for it doesn't necessarily do it. The evidence on this is so overwhelming that it's amazing anyone thinks otherwise, but plenty of people do."[31]

The significance of Colvin's comments for those concerned about children's learning is clear. If we want all students to work smarter, more creatively, and with more purpose, then it will take more than just material rewards and punishments. This is a staggering thought and one that seriously needs to be addressed for those who care about equal educational opportunity for all. The economic imperative by itself cannot motivate all children to successfully tackle the challenges of responsible lifelong learning.

Constructivism

Within cognitive science, constructivist theories of learning are predicated on the progressive construction and deepening of meaning. The emphasis is on understanding as a process that is considerably more involved than transferred information or even knowledge. Constructivists argue that, by definition, a person who is truly passive is incapable of learning. With a constructivist form of learning, each child structures his or her own knowledge of the world into a unique pattern, connecting each new fact, experience, or understanding in a subjective way that binds the child into rational and meaningful relationships to the wider world. This constructivist view of learning has been strengthened by recent findings emerging from the neurosciences. Rather than thinking of the brain as a computer, the brain is now seen as a far more flexible, self-adjusting, ever-changing organism that grows and reshapes itself in response to challenge, with elements that wither through lack of use. Constructivist learning is a dynamic interaction between the environment and the individual brain.

Such learning, by drawing on the full range of a learner's experience, strengthens the individual's ability both to find novel connections and to harness peripheral perception. Contrast this with the political mantras of outcome-based education, which all too easily becomes a highly focused closed process based on performing to a test on prescribed material. Constructivism is open-ended, as is the neural structure of the brain. In contrast, the alternative is a structured and closed process that leads to high performance in encyclopedic type recall. We argue that national curriculum targets, for all their achievements, are essentially specific and do not support the genuinely creative or entrepreneurial.

This does not mean, however, that students can be left to discover everything for themselves, because real understanding means overcoming personally held naive theories.[32] For true understanding to occur, process and knowledge must be integrated in an effective partnership, and this requires an initial source of valued information. (This is where the curriculum and the school come in.) Understanding is related to the ability to make valid connections between existing knowledge and experiences with that of new knowledge and experience.

David Perkins of Harvard has observed that "understanding is a multilayered thing. It has to do not just with particulars but with our whole mindset about a discipline or subject matter. . . . If a pedagogy of understanding means anything, it means understanding the piece in the context of the whole and the whole as the mosaic of its pieces."[33] In the words of Jerome Bruner, "The person who understands is capable of 'going beyond the information given'." Perkins builds on Bruner's definition by showing that understanding is not a state of possession but one of enablement: "When we understand something, we not only possess certain knowledge about it but are enabled to do certain things with that knowledge."[34]

Constructivists see learning as a highly energetic, personally motivated, problem-solving activity that leads inescapably toward understanding. Understanding requires a balance between knowledge and process. Lauren Resnick of the University of Pittsburgh Learning Research and Development Center spoke for many cognitive scientists when she wrote: "First, we know that human memory for isolated facts is very limited. Knowledge is retained only when embedded in some organizing structure. Thus, students who learn many separate facts are unlikely to retain their knowledge beyond the current period of test taking—a much noticed, worrisome feature of the current educational system. Second, we now recognize that skills and knowledge are not independent of the contexts—mental, physical, and social—in which they are used. Instead, they are attuned to, even part of, the environments in which they are practiced. A new challenge for instruction is to develop ways of organizing learning that permit skills to be practiced in the environments in which they will be used (i.e., outside the classroom). Such contextualized practice is needed both to tune skills and knowledge to their environments of use and to provide motivation for practicing abilities that in isolation might seem purposeless or meaningless."[35]

A Chinese philosopher captured the essence of what cognitive science is saying when he observed, "Tell me and I forget. Show me and I remember. Let me do and I understand." Successful learning and its application are too complex and multifaceted to be constrained within the walls of a school. In summarizing the research into the nature of human learning in the 1990s, researchers working on behalf of the Santa Fe Institute, a multidisciplinary graduate research and teaching institute formed to nurture research on complex systems such as the brain, wrote, "The method people naturally employ to acquire knowledge is largely unsupported by traditional classroom practice. The human mind is better equipped to gather information about the world by operating within it than by reading about it, hearing lectures on it, or studying abstract models of it."[36] The researchers went on to observe, "Nearly everyone would agree that experience is the best teacher. What many fail to realize is that experience may well be the only teacher."[37] It is not enough to just give children information; they need to work at making connections in the real world with the information they receive. This means appreciating the balance between in-school learning and out-of-school activities.

Apprenticeship

Such comments on the limitations of schools may be hard for educators, politicians, and others to accept, but they make more sense when one considers the way humans have traditionally shared knowledge and developed the talents of young people. The education of children has traditionally been associated not with the decontextualized setting of the classroom but with the more integrated process of learning called apprenticeship. Apprenticeship learning put young learners into situations where they learned by doing. It was a form of learning that utilized their natural learning predispositions. Apprenticeship learning built functional skills through experimentation, explanation, and story construction. Apprenticeship teaching provided instruction reactively, in response to the learner's action.

Remember, and this may sound harsh to some educators, much of schooling during the course of the 19th and 20th centuries was really little more than custodial care. Education was primarily about keeping children off the streets while their parents worked. Whatever learning teachers managed to encourage in their charges was a bonus and reflected the dedication of the teacher more than the focus of the system. In contrast to the child-minding of the industrial age, learning through apprenticeship taught children rituals: how to grow crops, craft tools, and create weapons and how to understand their place in the larger community. Children learned by being shown how, by doing, and then ultimately by taking responsibility for it by themselves.

Apprenticeship integrated learning, working, and living into a single seamless web. This form of community-based learning was as central to the health of the community as it was to the induction of young people into adulthood. Apprenticeship was far more than just skill acquisition. At its heart it was a process in which the young learned to take full responsibility for finding appropriate solutions to novel problems. This was possible for learners because they had earlier developed the ability to look at new problems from a variety of perspectives. Apprentices aspired to become independent craftsmen, and a craft was more than a job: It was a way of life. The artifact was a demonstration of their personality. It provided status in society and the recognition of being significant within the community. In short, young apprentices saw that what they learned mattered and would actually be applied to situations that brought benefit to themselves and others. The lesson for the early 21st century is that a successful education should create in all young people a similar sense of ownership and pride in their practical and intellectual proclivities.

Apprenticeship describes a set of eons-old processes that people with few resources to spare used to induct the next generation into the skills and values already practiced by adults. It assumed that children are inquisitive and, if initially fascinated by some mighty works, do not find it difficult to practice whatever subtasks are first needed. The Russian psychologist Vygotsky wrote about this in the 1920s when he described in academic terms what ordinary people had known of long before people started to theorize about learning and education. Such apprenticeship recognized four stages. The first stage of apprenticeship involves an older person modeling a subtask, so that the learner sees the significance of this to the final product. For example, a master artist shows a young apprentice how to properly prepare one's brushes and the paints on a palette. This subtask is done while the young apprentice is fully aware of the master's finished work, and in fact has as the ultimate goal mighty works of her own.

Apprenticeship progressively built new skills onto earlier basic skills and took for granted that skills once learned and subsequently practiced were something that the individual learner would then assume full responsibility for himself or herself. Busy adults had only the time and energy to provide scaffolding, the second stage, for those tasks in which the learner was still uncertain. As the learner's confidence increased, the third stage—that of the "fading" of support—came into play, and the earlier scaffolding was progressively removed. The more proficient learners became, the more they became independent of the teacher. Apprenticeship was based on the process of "weaning" young people of their dependence on the master. This, from a survival perspective, was key because young people were greatly needed in societies where being in your 30s and 40s was considered "old."

Throughout the apprenticeship there was a fourth stage, and this stage encompasses what humans are incredibly good at doing: namely endless talking, or "dialogue." In those cultures that it has been possible to study, such talking is only partly about the nature of what has to be done in the task. Mainly the talking is about the circumstances and the culture in which the learning is being developed. It was intuitive, contextual learning that mattered. They applied what they learned as soon as they learned it. Learning had meaning because it was seen as a group activity where individual learners were indirectly teachers of their colleagues.

The English language has off-the-shelf expressions that describe this: "Jack of all trades and master of none" well describes the person who has only a rudimentary understanding and an incomplete set of skills. "Jack is as good as his master" was the ultimate compliment when Jack had completed a masterpiece to show that he was now outperforming his teacher.

From Traditional to Cognitive Apprenticeship: Making Thinking Visible

As we have entered the knowledge age where learning how to learn matters for everyone, it is not surprising that since the 1980s cognitive scientists looking to establish what could be seen as the brain's natural learning strategies have extensively studied apprenticeship. It is through the study of apprenticeship that it is possible to formulate a theory of natural cognitive apprenticeship.

Lauren Resnick argues that if children are to become independent problem solvers capable of understanding their own thinking and learning, then ways must be found to integrate the lessons of traditional apprenticeship into how children are educated. She says: "I looked for elements common to successful programs that could point cumulatively toward a theory of how learning and thinking skills are acquired. I found three key features. First, most of the effective programs have features characteristic of out-of-school cognitive performances (cognitive apprenticeship). They involve socially shared intellectual work, and they are so organized around joint accomplishment of tasks, so that elements of the skills take on meaning in the context of the whole."[38]

She continues, "Second, many of the programs have elements of apprenticeship. That is, they make usually hidden processes overt, and they encourage student observation and commentary. They also allow skill to build up bit by bit, yet permit participation even for the relatively unskilled, often as a result of the social sharing of tasks. Finally, the most successful programs are organized around particular bodies of knowledge and interpretation—subject matters, if you will—rather than general abilities."[39]

According to the seminal work on cognitive apprenticeship by Allan Collins, John Seely Brown, and Ann Holum, there are three differences between traditional apprenticeship and cognitive apprenticeship. In traditional apprenticeship, such as that of the aspiring artist above, the reasons for carrying out the subtasks are easily observable and understood. In cognitive apprenticeship, however, "One needs to deliberately bring the thinking to the surface, to make it visible, whether it's in reading, writing, problem solving. The teacher's thinking must be made visible to the students, and the students' thinking must be made visible to the teacher. That is the most important difference between traditional apprenticeship and cognitive apprenticeship."[40] This process of making thinking visible is known as metacognition. One can think of metacognitive skills as the ability to be critical of one's own problem solving.

The second difference between traditional apprenticeship and cognitive apprenticeship is in the fact that traditional apprentices see how what they are learning is situated in the real world: The young artist sees the mighty work and wants to create it for herself. In this case apprentices naturally understand the reasons for undertaking the process of apprenticeship. "But in school, teachers are working with a curriculum centered around reading, writing, science, math, history, etc., that is, in large part, divorced from what students and most adults do in their lives. In cognitive apprenticeship, then, the challenge is to situate the abstract tasks of the school curriculum in contexts that make sense to the students."[41]

The third difference between traditional apprenticeship and cognitive apprenticeship is the issue of transfer. In traditional apprenticeship it is obvious how the subtask learned (preparing the paints) transfers over to the broader task (production of a painting). However, it is not obvious to young learners how what they learn in history class, for example, transfers into their understanding of the real world. Transfer simply means applying existing knowledge in a setting sufficiently novel that it also requires learning new knowledge. Cognitive apprenticeship actively seeks to make thinking visible so that youngsters can see how what they learn in the classroom is actually applied to activities in the real world. This is where interaction with the community in the form of internships and the like becomes so important. This is also where the effective use of information and communication technologies can come into play. For example, a high school research project in the state of Illinois on the study of artificial intelligence can be shared on the school's Web site in order to receive feedback and criticism from students and scientists in other parts of the world. In this way young people feel responsible for generating knowledge that actually influences others.

Cognitive apprenticeship has shown to be an effective model of learning because it makes the processes of the activity visible to the learner. It is a process of nurture that has been practiced for so long that it appears to have influenced our natural processes. The apprentice learns by applying knowledge in an activity that matters to him and the group he feels a member of. The Institute for Research into Learning in Palo Alto, California, notes that, "What motivates people is their innate desire to belong. People are automatically motivated to learn whatever they need to become a member of the community to which they want to belong."[42]

There is, however, a real conflict between what motivates learning and many of our institutional arrangements for it. The Swiss researcher Etienne

21

Wenger captures this paradox when he writes, "Our institutions are largely based on the assumption that learning is an individual process, that it has a beginning and an end, that it is best separated from the rest of our activities, and that teaching is required for learning to occur. So we arrange classrooms where students—free from all the distractions of their participation in the world—can pay attention to a teacher or focus on exercises. We design computer-based training programs that walk students through individualized sessions covering reams of information and drill practice."[43] Not surprisingly, Wenger continues, "The result is that much of our institutionalized teaching and training is perceived by would-be learners as irrelevant, and most of us come out of this treatment feeling that learning is boring, arduous, and that we are not really cut out for it."[44]

The purpose of this chapter has been to show that the methods people naturally employ to learn are largely unsupported by traditional classroom practice. The traditional approach of those concerned about a crisis in education has been to point to deficiencies and it's easy to list the things people find wrong all over the world:

- Classroom discipline has broken down; children are out of control.
- We have to find better ways of motivating children; they're just not interested.
- We need better teachers with more qualifications.
- We need higher standards.
- We need a more detailed curriculum. No, we need a broader curriculum.
- We must stretch the gifted child more. No, we must stimulate the average child more.
- We need smaller classes and more computers.
- The parents are so irresponsible.

These are wrongs that can be put right, though not until reform movements abandon the existing paradigm of pupils/teachers/schools. What is needed is out-of-the-box thinking to unify new findings about the biological nature of learning and evolutionary predispositions with older wisdom embodied in constructivism and cognitive apprenticeship. We have it within our power to construct models of learning that go with the grain of the brain. Societies now stand at an evolutionary crossroads where the way ahead must be to capitalize on fresh understandings and remedy what the next chapters call an "upside down and inside out" education.

2

An Emergent Science
of Learning for
the 21st Century

*A great many internal and external portents (political and
social upheaval, moral and religious unease) have caused us all
to feel, more or less confusedly, that something tremendous is
at present taking place in the world. But what is it?*

PIERRE TEILHARD DE CHARDIN

Despite radical changes in economics, politics,
and technology, education in the United Kingdom and the United States at the beginning of
the 21st century would be familiar to anyone
who attended school before World War II. There is the same prevalence of
lecturing, drill, and decontextualized material and activities ranging from
basal readers to weekly spelling tests. Education and learning are still
largely defined by what happens in the closed environment of the classroom where tasks are prescribed for both teachers and students. The success of this interaction is measured by outside experts who set high standards and measure how well these are achieved by using standardized tests
across the system. Earlier generations of systemizers such as the behaviorist
Edward Thorndike (1874–1949) and the time-and-motion man Frederick
Winslow Taylor (1856–1915) would recognize such a system and give their
whole-hearted approval. Proponents of child-centered learning like John
Dewey (1859–1952), Friedrich Froebel (1782–1852), and Maria Montessori
(1870–1952) would be shocked.

When one studies the dialogue around educational reform, the language parallels that which would have been used in a boardroom discussion in the early part of the 20th century on how to improve the efficiency
of a production commodity or service. In such discussions, what is most
often mentioned are the mechanical concepts of improving production
(test scores) across the system, increasing standards (as if the standard is

not simply the lowest common denominator we'll accept for other people's children) across the system, or making certain that management is held fully accountable for everything that happens within the system. It sounds to be about the manufacture of products, not the nurturing of young minds for a world of opportunity and change.

In this chapter we will show that the human brain and children's learning are not as simple to define as the things that made a high-quality automobile at the apogee of the industrial age. In arguing this point we will also show that a new and more inclusive purpose for education is now available. This new purpose for education, in contrast to a singular focus on discussions about systemic issues around academic success, should actually focus on our best understandings of how the individual brain most effectively learns and takes control of future opportunities. This human-centered focus on learning reveals a growing discontinuity between our understanding of how to help individual young people maximize their creativity, personal responsibility, and intellectual potential and what schools are currently structured to achieve.

A Sweeping Shift in Orientation

It is becoming clear to a growing number of policymakers, businesspeople, educators, and the general public in North America, Europe, and elsewhere that successful education in the early 21st century requires helping all children to move beyond simply the traditional goals of literacy and numeracy. As a leading U.S. expert on computer information technology recently said: "It's not that literacy and numeracy aren't worthy goals, it's simply a fact that they alone aren't enough for children to be productive and satisfied citizens and workers in the digital economy."

Tony Blair, the British prime minister, touched on this theme of moving education beyond the factory goals of literacy for all during a speech at Oxford in late 1999. He urged an abandonment of the mindset that sees education as simply "offering a standardized, monolithic provision for pupils" in favor of moving toward a mindset and educational arrangements that operate under the premise that young people's learning "needs are highly diverse and individual."[1] The Organization for Economic Cooperation and Development (OECD) agrees and argues that, "A lifelong learning approach calls for a sweeping shift in orientation, from institutions, schools and programs to learners and learning."[2]

Many politicians and policymakers speak the rhetoric of such changes, but in their policies they are stuck fighting the battles of yesterday. They are stuck between what they know the future requires and the interests and influences behind current educational arrangements. It is as if we have a rubber-band education system that bends to changing realities when faced with political and social pressure to do so but then snaps back as soon as those applying the pressure move along to new problems or opportunities.

A forthright Chester Finn, Jr., former U.S. assistant secretary of education, described the political difficulties facing educational reformers in Washington D.C., when he wrote in 1999 that, "America is generally a hospitable environment for visionary thinking but Washington is by far the least suitable place for such ideas to find a receptive audience. Everyone here is caught up in programs, interest groups, institutional arrangements, legislative cycles, budgets, short-run politics, and other elements of the here-and-now. In fact, I believe you are presently living and working in a place that is incapable of grappling in any useful way with the important ideas you have been generating. . . . [Washington's] stock and trade is trying to alter today's education blunders tomorrow. We are all but incapable of dealing with the day after tomorrow."[3]

The reforms of the 1980s and 1990s simply shifted the balance of power within the system away from those who work directly with children without effectively questioning the underlying structure and purposes of the system itself. The politics of reform over the past two decades in education has resulted in an old model of education being coerced to work more efficiently, and in the best of circumstances toward higher academic standards. On the surface this may seem like a great success, but the sense of accomplishment quickly fades when it is measured through the lens of our current knowledge about learning and human development. It fades even more quickly when one contrasts where current systems of education are with what is emerging as today's challenges and opportunities.

In 1996, U.S. governors and CEOs launched an effort to rejuvenate public schools. Yet there was little discussion about how children learn or how systems of education could be revamped or integrated into the larger community to help all children develop their unique talents and skills. According to David Gergen, writing in *U.S. News and World Report,* "Each state was to set high standards for its students; the students would then be tested to the standards on a regular basis; and students, teachers, and schools would be held accountable for results. 'Standards, testing, accountability'—that was the mantra."[4]

This focus on systemic reform is also what has been happening in the United Kingdom, and when Gergen's quote was read to a group of English head teachers in early 2000, they jumped out of their seats and said, "David Blunkett [the Minister of Education] could have said that." Unfortunately for those seeking simple policy prescriptions, there is no direct

25

correlation between being good at taking tests and being thoughtful and creative. Nor is there even any evidence that being a good test-taker means a person is going to be a successful lifelong learner. In fact, according to Daniel Koretz of the RAND Corporation in the United States, the research on test scores show "characteristically simplistic use of test score data in the public debate" and the unfortunate tendency to believe that test scores alone really measure the effectiveness of education.[5]

The U.S. Secretary of Education Richard Riley noted the dangers of emphasizing exam results at the expense of other indicators of educational success during his 2000 State of Education address. He said, "If all our efforts to raise standards get reduced to one test, we've got it wrong. If we force our teachers to teach only to the test, we will lose their creativity. . . . If we are so consumed with making sure students pass a multiple-choice test that we throw out the arts and civics then we will be going backward instead of forward."[6]

Parents in the United States are starting to appreciate that raising test scores does not necessarily mean the same thing as improving their children's life chances. Clever parents, not having the time or the inclination to fight educational bureaucracies, go along with the mantras but make certain they provide their children with plenty of extracurricular activities and individual opportunities to travel, take private art and language classes, and use their home computers. It is interesting that in the high-tech corridor around Washington, D.C., the number of Montessori schools, all of them bastions of child-centered education, has more than doubled in the past few years.[7] Such parents understand that to excel in an economy that rewards creativity and personal responsibility, their children need considerably more than just the basics being promised by public schools.

An Opportunity to Go Beyond the Current Mantras

The British prime minister defined the larger purpose of education when he claimed in November 1999: "Our aim must be to create a nation where the creative talents of all the people are used to build a true enterprise economy for the 21st century—where we compete on brains, not brawn." However, such claims conflict with much of what his government's educational policies are calling for. Such contradiction is not unique to England because governments in many lands are struggling to figure out how to break away from the incongruity that affects many of their educational policies and initiatives. What sounds right may in fact be far off the mark.

Despite the political difficulties and inertia, an opportunity exists to expand the purpose of education and responsibility for it. Professor Ken Robinson, the man who headed up the British Department for Education and Employment's study on Creativity, Culture, and Education, captured the wisdom of moving beyond the singular focus on academic schooling and achievement when he asked where it leads. "What is a degree worth when we all have one?" he asked. According to Robinson, employers are already "saying that a degree is not enough, and that many graduates do not have the qualities they are looking for: the ability to communicate, work in teams, adapt to change, to innovate and be creative." To Robinson, "this is not surprising. . . . The traditional academic curriculum is not designed to promote creativity. Complaining that the system does not produce creative people is like complaining that a car doesn't fly. . . . It was never intended to. The stark message, internationally as well as nationally, is that the answer to the future is not simply to increase the amount of education, but to educate people differently."[8] It is not about simply working harder and more expensively but smarter and in new partnerships.

The lessons of the past couple of decades from business is that to work smarter it is necessary to build on a strong foundation of knowledge and technology. Science, best practices in business and training, and the power of information communication technologies now provide the basis for being smarter in the way we help young people learn. Later in this book we examine how the psychology of behaviorism, and the concept of intelligence as a static commodity, emerged as the intellectual basis for much that has happened in education. It is still behind much of what goes on in education, and is doing a great deal of harm. Let us explain.

To the behaviorists, external motivation was seen as the indispensable driver of behavior and, in particular, of learning. Behaviorists believed that learning was a simple cause-and-effect proposition where well-defined inputs (good instruction) led to well-defined outputs (achievement measured by test scores). It was all rather straightforward and simple, and the whole process of learning could easily be defined and measured. Education, once the parameters were defined, was like an assembly line where knowledge was packaged by experts, disseminated by teachers, and then tested for, and rewarded with, credentials. The behaviorist model of education argued that educational success involved:

1. Mastery of basic skills.
2. Largely solitary study.
3. Generally uninterrupted work.
4. Concentration on a single subject.
5. Much written work.
6. A high analytical ability.

The mantra of "standards, testing, and accountability" is based on these traditional views of education and learning. However, today's social and economic needs argue for a new model of learning that entails:

1. Mastery of basic skills.
2. The ability to work with others.
3. Being able to deal with constant distractions.
4. Working at different levels across different disciplines.
5. Using mainly verbal skills.
6. Problem solving and decision making.

Only one of these skills—the first—is common to both lists. Of these new skills, the vast majority of educational reforms will only effectively deal with the mastery of basic academic skills. To simply leave the rest up to chance is to unintentionally promote a society of haves and have nots.

But here is where the difficulty lies. The needs of an increasingly dynamic society and economy are supported by educational arrangements that reflect many of the ideas that educational progressives have argued for throughout the 20th century. This is an uncomfortable reality for many in the educational debate because it is completely counter to those who want to set up "progressive child-centered education" as a scapegoat for everything wrong in education. No doubt some students in the United States, the United Kingdom, and other English-speaking countries have been trapped by educational arrangements that gave students too few limits, too many choices, poor direction, and no structure. Yet, if education is to move beyond simply focusing on academic test scores, then it is essential to reappraise some of the insights offered by advocates of child-centered theories of learning.

A recent editorial in *The Guardian* shows how difficult it is for people to be genuinely objective and accurate about this history. "Who says the public sector cannot change?" asked the editorial. "A 25-year-old education cycle is coming full circle. Spurred on by the best of intentions, but producing the worst results, the Piaget era of child-centered primary education is drawing to a close. In the last five years there has been a switch from fuzzy topic work, to more use of direct whole-class teaching, and a greater readiness by teachers to group pupils by ability."[9] Such rhetoric is grossly misleading and misses the significance of much of the research that has gone on around learning and child development over the past few decades. There are powerful insights that cannot simply be ignored and dismissed if we want young people to be creative and personally responsible lifelong learners. Regardless of how politically incorrect this may seem at the moment, it is a cold, hard fact.

The research on learning comes from disparate fields and many countries and runs counter to those placing their faith in improving the life chances of young people by simply raising academic standards. Professor Robinson captured this tension when he observed that businesses "want people who can communicate, work in teams, and change direction as quickly as the landscape is moving around them. These qualities are not promoted by conventional academic education, nor are they meant to be. This is why so many graduates are turned away, or are hastily retrained to revive in them the qualities of creativity and communication that too often have been educated out of them."[10] The reality of politics means that once politicians invest a lot of their political influence—and indeed their futures—in a position, it is almost impossible for them to backtrack even when they want to. This results in an attitude of "damn the critics, we will simply work harder and get this to work."

A March Toward Folly?

The historian Barbara Tuchman described such self-assertive attitudes among the governing elite as "The March of Folly." Tuchman wrote in 1984 that "to qualify as folly the policy adopted must meet three criteria: It must have been perceived as counterproductive in its own time. . . . Secondly a feasible alternative course of action must have been available. . . . [A] third criterion must be that the policy in question should be that of a group, not an individual ruler, and should persist beyond any one political lifetime."[11]

On each of these three counts, using Tuchman's qualifications, the current mantras of education encourage a narrow view of education and learning that misses some of the key elements necessary for success in a society that is becoming increasingly dependent on individual creativity, responsibility, and entrepreneurship. There is a great deal of research and experience from many disciplines and countries that argues that much of what goes on in education is indeed counterproductive. There are also alternative courses of action available, albeit politically difficult to initiate, in the form of learning communities as identified by educational innovators in many lands (such as Education 2000 in the United Kingdom) since at least the early 1980s.

In both England and the United States, the current limited goals of educational reform have had the undivided support of leaders in both major political parties since the 1980s. But to continue marching forward without pausing to consider all that is now known about successful learning and human development is a march toward folly. Such folly is dangerous because the social, economic, technological, and political environments in which education systems were initially constructed to serve have changed radically. The accounting firm Arthur Andersen captured the significance of these changes when it observed in 1996: "Today's extraordinary state of flux in business and every aspect of political and social life is certainly owing to new technologies and increased economic competition; but on a deeper level, it also heralds humanity's passage into a new mode of thinking and working that offers a means of coping with ongoing turbulence and change."[12]

Yet this revolution will remain unfinished as long as education systems lag behind these larger transformations. Peter Drucker, the business management expert, caught the essence of this dilemma when he wrote: "So far no country has the education system which the Knowledge Society needs. . . [;] learning will have to permeate the entire society, with (organizations of all kinds) becoming learning and teaching organizations. . . . Schooling will no longer be what schools do. Increasingly it will be only one of the available teaching and learning institutions."[13]

The Balance Between Predispositions and the "Plastic Brain"

Education must also catch up with science, and the first step toward more effective learning arrangements is to develop a learning approach that exploits the findings in developmental psychology, cognition, the physiology of the brain, and evolution. Taken together, findings from these fields now offer a rigorous body of evidence that goes well beyond the limited assumptions of behaviorism that need to be put to sleep once and for all. By taking advantage of our intellectual and social predispositions, education can more effectively empower young people to take advantage of their God-given inheritance to be the planet's preeminent learners.

Argument rages, however, as to the relative significance of inherited predispositions and a constructivist theory of learning. Within neuroscience the constructivists build much of their case around the concept known as brain plasticity. The basic idea is simple: We make our brain as we use it. Its very shape and the efficiency of its processing are a measure of the way we operate. The more we use our brain, the more usable it becomes. A well-used brain actually gains weight. Even a brain at quite an advanced age can learn to do things that at an earlier stage were seen as quite impossible. What is most significant, however, is that the process of learning takes much longer than if it is being attempted during a window of

30

opportunity offered through inherited predispositions (e.g., learning a foreign language).

This concept of brain plasticity is advanced further by researchers at the Salk Institute in La Jolla, California. They argue that the way we use our neural networks at the earliest stages of childhood may literally shape the initial development of our brain and thus determine, in part, what we become as adults. From this perspective, early years learning guides later development and transforms the learning device itself. Thus, what has been learned can influence future learning. The brain, from this perspective, is seen as a highly malleable, self-adjusting organism in the earliest years, but over the course of a lifetime the brain's ability to learn is at least partially constrained and channeled by earlier life experiences.

The Hollywood children's advocate Rob Reiner has taken this evidence on brain plasticity and the significance of early years learning to lead a campaign that focuses on promoting early childhood development issues. Reiner claimed during a speech he gave at Harvard: "If we give children the right emotional supports during the first three years we can positively change their lives forever."[14] Reiner's campaign made it to the White House where President Clinton and the First Lady convened a conference on early years learning in April of 1997. Reiner told the White House gathering: "If we want to have a real significant impact, not only on children's success in school and later on in life, healthy relationships, but also an impact on reduction in crime, teen pregnancy, drug abuse, child abuse, welfare, homelessness, and a variety of social ills, we are going to have to address the first three years of life. There is no getting around it. All roads lead to Rome."[15]

This position is supported by Marian Diamond, a neurologist from the University of California, Berkeley, who says: "In the 1990s, researchers made remarkable gains in understanding how a child's brain develops, grows, and produces uniquely human capacities. . . . The emerging message is clear. The brain, with its complex architecture and limitless potential, is a highly plastic, constantly changing entity that is powerfully shaped by our experiences in childhood and throughout life."[16] Joel Davis, in *Mapping the Mind*, takes the opportunities of early childhood even further when he argues, "The great window of learning opportunity for the human brain clearly appears during the childhood years, especially up to about age 10." But he adds a point about plasticity: "That doesn't mean that we—or our brains—are over the hill after that point. . . . In fact, it doesn't matter how old our brains are—15, 25, or 50 years old, or more. As long as we stay healthy and active, the brain will retain some of its plasticity, growing more dendrites and axons and forging new connections among them."[17]

Ann B. Barnet, professor emeritus of neurology at George Washington University School of Medicine, adds, "Human babies are born helpless, and they stay helpless for a long time. They arrive expecting to be cared for and protected. They are born to learn, and their ability to learn—to make adaptive changes in their behavior on the basis of experience—is at its peak in the early years of life, when they are making the brain connections on which learning and living depend. To be sure the brain has remarkable capacities for self-protection and recovery. But the loving care and nurture children receive in their first years—or the lack of these critical experiences—leaves [sic] lasting imprints on young minds."[18]

The significance placed on the first few years of life has its critics. According to the cognitive scientist John Bruer, the prominence given by many in policy positions and public relations to the concepts of "early periods of development, windows of opportunity, or critical periods" is largely misplaced and in danger of leading to an ideology of infant determinism. Bruer believes such claims have led prematurely, at least in the United States, to "high-level justification for better prenatal, postpartum, and pediatric care; family planning; welfare reform; parent education; and high-quality day care and early childhood education."[19] Even further, Bruer fears, some believe that: "We need to change our child-rearing practices, we need to change the malignant and destructive view that children are the property of their biological parents. Human beings evolved not as individuals, but as communities. . . . Children belong to the community, they are entrusted to parents."[20] From this perspective, Bruer argues, there is a real danger of the emergence of a highly intrusive "nanny state."

Bruer argues that findings from the neurosciences do not support these efforts and are based on nothing more than "myth." In his book *The Myth of the First Three Years*, he says: "The jury is still out about the importance of the first few years of life. While the early years are no doubt important, it remains unclear just how important."[21] Bruer goes further: "The odds that our children will end up with appropriately fine-tuned brains are incredibly favorable, because the stimuli the brain expects during critical periods are the kinds of stimuli that occur everywhere all the time within the normal developmental environment for our species. It is only when there are severe genetic or environmental aberrations from the normal that nature's expectations are frustrated and neural development goes awry."[22]

The danger of infant determinism, argues a writer for *The New Yorker* magazine, is that it could lead to a justification for shortchanging the needs of older learners. "Why bother spending money trying to help older children or adults if the patterns of a lifetime are already irremediably, in place? Inevitably, some people will interpret the zero-to-three dogma to mean that our obligations to the disadvantaged expire by the time they reach the age of 3."[23]

The Pyramid Model of Education

In looking at the resources allocated to learning needs, the fears described above seem largely misplaced. It is a fact in the United States, and indeed across most of the world,[24] that there is a common pattern of educational spending. Expenditure per pupil rises sharply, like the shape of a pyramid, with the level of education and is dominated by personnel costs in a system where it seems perfectly natural that university researchers and professors make far more than 1st grade math teachers.

Between 80 and 85 percent of this expenditure is on salary for staff, with some 3 percent on books and 2 percent on other forms of learning technologies. The remainder goes to the maintenance of buildings and other overhead expenses. There is more money spent on secondary school students than on primary school students, and there is considerably more expenditure per college and university student than there is on secondary-level students. In the United States, for example, average annual expenditure per student in elementary schools is $5,371. In middle school and high school it rises to $6,812, and by the university years it is $16,262 per student.[25]

This funding structure is based on the assumption that the youngest children need less direct support and older children need more. It is just this sort of logic that has supported the model of education shown in Figure 2.1 (see p. 34).

A Biological Model of Learning

Even people who think the early years movement has gone to extremes would surely agree there is little evidence from the brain sciences to justify spending three times more on the learning needs of a 20-year-old than those of a 4- or 5-year-old. The fertile predispositions for learning in younger children, and what is now known about brain plasticity (whatever the balance between them), suggest that it is good public policy to develop a more balanced investment between the learning needs of younger children and those of older students.

We can take this argument a step further and make the case that it is not just about investing more in younger children but actually investing in such a way that would enable children, as they enter adolescence, to take more personal responsibility for their own learning. This increased

Figure 2.1 Current Relationship of Expenditure to Class Size

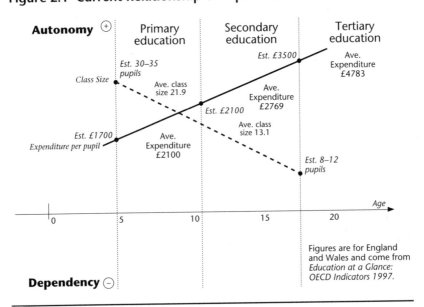

Figures are for England and Wales and come from *Education at a Glance: OECD Indicators 1997.*

responsibility would be in line with the adolescent predisposition to begin taking charge of their life. Such a view of learning is only realistic, however, if adolescents have developed the traditional basic literacy and numeracy skills in tandem with the higher-order skill of metacognition, thinking about one's own thinking. We call moving toward a brain-friendly model of learning turning the priorities of current systems of education "upside down."

Teenagers who are functionally literate and understand how they think and make themselves better learners actually need and want less direct formal classroom-based instruction. Many students in elite secondary schools have already gone beyond their dependence on teachers by accessing learning information online and through community-based resources such as museums, local universities, and businesses. Indeed, a group known as Schools Without Walls has developed an entire secondary educational experience around just this model of community-based learning resources. A model of learning, building on the skills children acquired during the primary years, that crossed an entire community would provide increased flexibility for older students and for education systems that increasingly face budgetary constraints and teacher shortages.

We will consider this idea more in Chapter 10, but let's first get deeper into the discussion about the biology of learning and why the learning skills of children need more than just classroom-based instruction to thrive. The argument advanced in these first two chapters shows that for the brain's predisposition toward a form of learning described earlier as constructivist to thrive, it is essential that all aspects of a child's learning environment be considered. Learning is open-ended, as is the neural structure of the brain. This is an important point because in no Western country do students spend more than 20 percent of their waking hours in a classroom.

Outcome-based education and national curriculum targets, for all their achievements, are essentially specific and focus exclusively on in-school learning, and thus a minority of children's time. Taken alone they do not support the genuinely creative or the entrepreneurial. In the light of what has been said about constructivism, predispositions, metacognition, motivation and the processes of apprenticeship, consider now Figure 2.2, which is a graph representing intellectual weaning.

Figure 2.2 (see p. 36) is based on what is currently known about normal human development. The graph would vary slightly for each child (e.g., some children might enter adolescence at age 11, while others may be closer to 13). The graph depicts the richness of predispositions in the early years of life and shows young children being highly dependent on other people to provide support and stimulation. Over the course of the millennia during which our species developed, this dependence on others was steadily replaced by a growing need to demonstrate that earlier skills had been mastered in such a way that the adolescent became increasingly responsible for his or her own development. It is easy to transpose onto this graph the cognitive apprenticeship model of learning where maximum support in the development of basic skills is given when children are very young. Subsequent external adult support takes the form of temporary scaffolding held in place only until the young learner is confident enough to move onto higher skills. Greatest adult support is given when the child is young so that as he or she grows, support diminishes and becomes more that of a facilitator.

In successful apprenticeship learning there is a continuous underlying theme. The more skills the learner acquires, the more the learner is responsible for using those skills. Learning therefore follows a strict weaning process. But note this: If the opportunity offered by the various predispositions is not seized when children are very young, then the young will struggle to deal with the challenges of adolescence. It is important to remember that in pre-industrial societies, weaning was a tough survival principle.

Figure 2.2 Intellectual Weaning Based on Normal Human Development

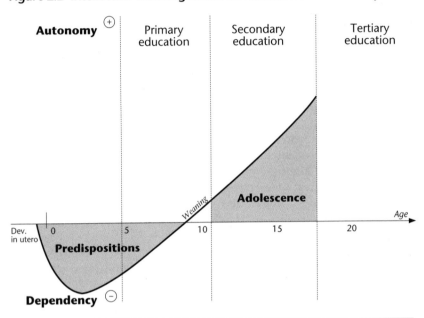

There was no way for those young people who were unable to graduate as autonomous learners to survive. In such societies there was no room for people who could not act to the benefit of themselves, their family, and their community. There is an obvious lesson here for our times. If we do a better job of maximizing the potential of young children and help them take control of their own learning, then we should begin to see adolescence as an opportunity rather than as a problem to be controlled.

Lifelong Learning Starts at Birth

The preparation for lifelong learning starts, whether we recognize it or not, at the very beginning of life. Ideally, children's learning should be supported by a loving and committed nuclear family reinforced by the extended family, neighbors, and the immediate community. This traditional arrangement is under threat (or has disappeared) for many. Nevertheless, if the goal of education is to extend the brain's natural inquisitiveness, then the youngest children need an environment that offers them the stability, challenge, values, and cohesiveness that we attribute to functional loving families. It is through constant support and appropriate stimulation that the learning predispositions of the youngest children are effectively nurtured. These predispositions are so powerful that children, if they are not in a degraded environment, are going to find things out for themselves. Children learn whenever and wherever they are stimulated; just what they learn is problematic.

A society that is careless about children's informal learning experiences has forgotten how children are inducted into adult society. By the time an American child is 11 years old, according to the American Psychological Association, he or she will have watched over 100,000 acts of brutality on television. In the United States, one-third of all children live apart from their fathers, and at some point during their childhood more than half will experience the absence of their fathers. The far too common occurrence of missing fathers has a particularly damaging effect on boys. A sense of direction and purpose is where the origins of intrinsic motivation begin for children. That is what keeps them going when times get tough. It is an inner strength. Without it youngsters all too easily get bored, cynical, and disillusioned. Children need to know where they belong. It is impossible to bring up children to be intelligent in a world that is unintelligible to them.

The Harvard psychologist Jerome Kagan has observed from his decades of studying children: "The concept of relative fitness in evolutionary biology assumes that the success of any one individual or species in a locale depends not only on its genes and biological-behavioral characteristics but also on the competences of the other individuals or species living in the same ecological niche with whom it competes." Note carefully the last part of that sentence: We do not live in isolation; part of our intellectual strength comes from others around us. Kagan goes on to explain what this means for children when he reasons "the quality of the school, the motivation of the teachers, the values of peers, the mores of the neighborhood, and the child's identification with his socioeconomic class will exert important influence during the childhood years."[26]

Ernest Boyer, former president of the Carnegie Foundation for the Advancement of Teaching, captured the significance of the whole environment on children's learning when he stated that, "To blame schools for the rising tide of mediocrity is to confuse symptom with disease. Schools can rise no higher than the expectations of the communities that surround them."[27]

The reasons for such a complexity of factors become clearer when one uses a constructivist view of learning. The premise of constructivism is that the human brain is driven to make sense of those things that matter to it by continuously relating new ideas to old assumptions. Therefore, by its very nature, constructivist learning has to be open and continuous. Learning is not turned on and off. Learning is the result of thinking; it can literally happen anywhere and at any time. The implications of this are profound. We argue that developing young people who excel as lifelong learners requires the involvement of the whole community; it has its own immediate feedback. Children and adults working together stimulate community regeneration as well. We call reconnecting community with the learning needs of children "turning education systems inside out" because the locus of learning has now to extend well beyond just the classroom.

3 The Economy and the Learning Needs of Children

The more sure one is that the world which encompasses human life is of such and such a character (no matter what his definition), the more one is committed to try to direct the conduct of life, that of others as well as of himself, upon the basis of the character assigned to the world.

JOHN DEWEY

Outside many schools we find Western societies where, for the first time in history, we have the time-poor rich and the time-rich poor. According to Jonathan Gerchuny's study in *Changing Times*, one in five British children suffers stress-related illnesses linked to the long hours their parents work.

These problems of time-poverty aside, many U.S. and English politicians and social commentators praise the dawning of a new economy where traditional limits to economic expansion are no longer relevant. Presidents and prime ministers proclaim the emergence of a new prosperity while directing education back to a singular focus on the basics, centralized control, and standardized tests. This is double talk at its worst. To its advocates the new economy is one where factors such as globalization and the influence of information technology have fundamentally changed the way the economy works. Thus, the United States and Britain can look forward to prolonged prosperity. Somewhere in all this optimism it must be acknowledged that the quality of the labor force will eventually have a major impact on whether or not the economy continues to expand. Even in a "new" economy, labor remains a key factor in economic growth.[1]

Along with technological changes, the worker/consumer has been central to the economic growth of the 1990s. For the average U.S. and British worker (many of whom are also parents) the new economy means working more hours. President Clinton's Council of Economic Advisers observed,

"The nation's labor market is performing at record levels: the number of workers employed is at an all-time high, the unemployment rate is at a 30-year low, and real (inflation-adjusted) wages are increasing after years of stagnation."[2] For politicians, economists, and stockholders, this is great news, but for workers, life has become increasingly synonymous with work. Adults in the United States now "put in more hours on the job than their counterparts in other industrialized nations. American adults work almost two weeks a year more than the Japanese and 14 weeks more than the Norwegians."[3] Taken together with an unemployment rate of less than 4.5 percent, this means that for economic growth to continue in the future, workers will not be able to simply work more hours; they will inevitably have to work smarter.

The economic growth and the increased working hours of the past couple of decades have enabled Americans and the British to go on a buying binge. The 1980s and 1990s were marked by most middle-class citizens on both sides of the Atlantic buying more consumer goods than any previous generation. At the close of the 1990s, the ambition behind the dream of a small suburban home with a family car and an annual vacation had expanded considerably. In the United States, houses have doubled in size in less than 50 years, and more people than ever before have a second home, multiple vehicles, boats, and other leisure "toys." The accouterments of the modern home now include several television sets, DVD players, stereo equipment, a personal computer or two updated every couple of years, and numerous other electronic goods and gadgetry. Designer clothes are now seen as mandatory not only for adults but also for teenagers and even little children. "At a minimum, the average person's spending increased 30 per cent between 1979 and 1995. At a maximum, calculating by taking into account a possible bias in the consumer price index, the increase was more than twice that, or about 70 percent."[4] For a vast swath of the middle class, much of this consumption has been facilitated by easy credit. Despite an expanding economy over the past two decades, the United States "borrowed approximately $5 trillion from the savers of the world, especially the Japanese, to finance their consumption and their investment. In the mid-1980s the United States went from its post-World War I position as the world's largest creditor nation to become its larger debtor."[5]

To appreciate just how ingrained the consumer society has become, consider that individuals now have lifestyles rather than lives. The U.S. author James Twitchell describes the new ethic. "For better or worse, lifestyles are secular religions, coherent patterns of valued things," he says. "Your lifestyle is not related to what you do for a living but to what you buy. One of the chief aims of the way we live now is the enjoyment of affiliating with those who share the same cluster of objects as we do. . . . One of the reasons terms like Yuppie, Baby Boomer, and GenX have elbowed aside such older designations as upper middle class is that we no longer understand social class as well as we do lifestyle, or what marketing firms call 'consumption communities.' Observing stuff is the way we understand each other. Even if no one knows exactly how much money it takes to be a yuppie, or how young you have to be, or how upwardly aspiring, everybody knows where yuppies gather, how they dress, what they play, what they drive, what they eat, and why they hate to be called yuppies."[6] And here is a critical implication of this philosophy: The more you earn, the greater is your credit rating and your range of choices.

The Age of Anxiety

These economic good times have an inevitable cost because a dynamic economy spawns unintended consequences and also breeds losers. That's the creative/destructive nature of capitalism, and the cost of the new economy is the decline of a century-long political culture that combined work, local social interdependence, and intergenerational continuity. As technological changes have freed the dynamic forces of economic individualism and the supremacy of individual consumers, these same qualities have emerged as the dominant ethic for success in an increasingly competitive and global economy.

The price of this new ethic is incurred disproportionately by children who now spend far less time with those adults who love them and more time with professionals whose job it is to educate them. The Organization for Economic Cooperation and Development (OECD) has noted that at the most basic level, children "compete with 'other' goods and services that limited purchasing power can provide. . . . The flood of options has induced a growing number of women to join the workforce in order to enlarge their purchasing power and take advantage of the increasing [economic] opportunities."[7] The average time U.S. adults spent per week shopping in 1985 was six hours. The average time they spent per week playing with children was just 40 minutes.[8] As a result of these economic and social changes, fewer children are being born in developed countries, especially to parents who have more than a high school education. Also, when adults do have children, they increasingly relegate the raising of their children to day care and educational professionals.

The *Washington Post* reported in late 1999 that, "Over the last two decades, American fathers' time at work has increased by 3.1 hours per week. . . [;] for mothers, it's 5.2 hours. Employed fathers with children younger than 18 now work an average of 50.9 hours per week; working mothers 41.4 hours."[9] This dearth of time is being filled partly by professional educators (who are asked to do more and more) and partly by the children themselves (latchkey kids) in time spent alone or with friends. The trade-off is simple: money over time. Kids are being born into more affluence, but they get less and less time with adults who love them.

In the context of this book's subject—human learning—we must ask ourselves if time with people who love them matters to the learning and developmental needs of children. This is an absolutely key question that has to be answered with a good understanding from evolution about our essential human needs. What are the implications of children spending increasing time in the structured settings of paid caregivers?[10] The psychologist Urie Bronfenbrenner says that "the one indispensable condition for a child's successful upbringing is that at least one adult must have a deep and irrational attention to him or her. In other words, someone must be absolutely crazy about that child. Children are put on this earth to be loved."[11] We need to ask ourselves honestly if there is truth in the old adage that children spell love T-I-M-E? Those of us who have children, or care about the future, should ask ourselves if we have gone so far down the path toward economic efficiency and individual fulfillment that a question about "loving children" no longer even really matters? Is all this too soft and value-laden to even raise in a debate about education? Before answering these questions remember the central theme of this book: Learning is far more than just schooling.

A "Tribe Apart"

It is not just young children who need the time of parents who love them. Adolescents are also predisposed to be social creatures who need the time of adults whom they can trust to tell the truth and ask difficult questions. Teenagers spend much of their lives dealing with people who really do not know them as individuals and under the control of formal institutions that strive to deal with people uniformly. When they leave the house, they are largely at the mercy of a battery of bureaucracies. Chief among these are public schools that have become increasingly large and impersonal.

The University of Chicago psychologists Mihaly Csikszentmihalyi and Reed Larson wrote in 1984, "That in all societies since the beginning of time, adolescents have learned to become adults by observing, imitating, and interacting with grown-ups around them. The self is shaped and honed by feedback from men and women who already know who they are, and can help the young person find out who he or she is going to be. It is startling how little time these teenagers spend in the company of adults."[12] In one of the largest surveys of young people ever taken, the New York-based Public Agenda Foundation noted in late 1999 that 42 percent of teenagers "feel bored every day or almost every day," and 74 percent spent their free time just getting "together with friends to hang out without anything specific to do."[13]

The word "teenager" did not enter the popular English language until just after World War II when prosperity started rising and adults in western society began defining adolescence as a problem rather than an opportunity. While modern parents and teachers find adolescents disruptive and even dangerous, earlier cultures directed adolescent energy in ways that benefitted the life of the community and strengthened those skills on which the community was dependent for its ongoing survival. Adolescents were needed, and in particular adolescent males were needed. In providing clear definitions of what was required of adolescents, adults of an earlier age ensured that young people learned, and practiced, what was seen as appropriate and useful social behavior.

At an international conference on Children and Families, Guido Walraven of the Netherlands noted: "Development to adult life is the emancipation of young people from their parents, earning their own place in the family and society at large. This process used to be more a matter of course than it is nowadays. Rituals denoting transition were culturally established (in French or in bilingual Canada this is called 'rites de passage'). Today's society offers young people much less opportunity to win a clear place. Compared to the old days, society no longer seems to need its young people. That has great effects on the emancipation process or the transition to adult life. For instance in some ways the period of adolescence is becoming longer, because becoming independent and having your own job and family tend to happen at a later age, while in other ways some children, especially children at risk, grow up at an early age, that means that by force of circumstances they have to stick up for themselves and to fight as adults."[14] The transition from childhood to adulthood is fraught with dangers, and this is especially true for young people who have not developed the ability to think for themselves.

So far, science knows far less about the neurological changes at this stage of life than it does about the predispositions that operate roughly below the age of 7. However, in the first study of its kind, researchers at McLean Hospital in Massachusetts used findings from functional MRI's of adolescent brains to show definitively "age-related physiological changes in the brains of adolescents which may help explain the emotionally turbulent teenage years. [From this they concluded that] adolescents are more prone to react with 'gut instinct' when they process emotions, but as they mature into early adulthood, they are able to temper their instinctive 'gut reaction' responses with rational, reasoned reactions. Adult brains use the frontal lobe to rationalize or apply brakes to emotional responses. Adolescent brains are just beginning to develop that ability."[15]

Effective models of education have traditionally taken advantage of these emotionally charged years by channeling this energy into powerful mental and physical challenges. In England's recent past, this meant international expeditions of groups of young people to rugged areas such as uninhabited islands or mountain regions. In the United States it has meant summers building schools, houses, and churches in less developed areas. Teenagers thrive in such challenging activities, and as any adult who has ever worked with such groups can attest, it is amazing how they can spend 12 hours on backbreaking work and still stay up half the night talking to each other. This is the energy of adolescence that is all too often wasted or, even worse, misapplied.

From an evolutionary perspective there must be a reason for the emotional surge in adolescent energy. Earlier societies saw adolescence as a period of great potential as well as one of turmoil. Such societies knew how to use the desire of adolescents to show mastery of certain skills to extend and improve the welfare of the community. The natural tendency of young people when they move into puberty is to reverse their dependency on adults. They want to be in control. This is not because they want to be bloody minded but because their newfound strength and emotional energy are pressing them to show that they can now use what they learned earlier to become fully functional, independent people.

In the advanced societies of the 21st century, those adolescents not equipped with the survival skills of basic literacy and numeracy, as well as the higher-order skills described earlier, are desperately ill-prepared to deal with the physiological changes of adolescence and end up mentally, emotionally and socially adrift. They quickly become "a tribe apart."[16]

The phrase "a tribe apart" belongs to the journalist Patricia Hirsch, whose book of the same title is an account of her time with a group of suburban U.S. adolescents between 1992 and 1997. (It was a suburb in northern Virginia in which, by coincidence, much of this book was written.) Hirsch wrote: "The most stunning change for adolescents today is their aloneness. The adolescents of the Nineties are more isolated and more unsupervised than other generations . . . not because they come from parents who don't care, schools that don't care, or a community that doesn't value them, but rather because there hasn't been time for adults to lead them through the process of growing up."[17]

We are not focusing on these changes in the way children grow up because we are modern-day Luddites or teary-eyed softies resistant to change; rather, if we want a bright future, economically and socially, for our children, then it is critical that learning and education are seen as being something too important to be left exclusively to formal institutions. The point, critical for the 21st century, is that creativity needs the challenge of whole-life situations combined with formal study. It requires balance. Or as professor Johnson-Laird of Cambridge contends in comparing creativity to murder, "Both depend on a motive, means, and opportunity."[18] Schools do a fine job of providing many of the means, and maybe even some of the motive, but they are greatly constrained in the opportunities they can provide for genuine creativity.

Should We Just Let the Professionals Handle It?

The promise of more schooling centered largely on the basics is argued by many as the key to the development of creativity and successful lifelong learners. The decline of the family and the community is leading to an increased emphasis on schools and formal institutions. This is not just true for adolescents but also our youngest children. This increased investment in formal education has not had a similarly increased rate of return. More money and political capital have gone into formal education systems in the 1990s than in any other decade, and yet standards as currently defined have not risen at the same level as the increased expenditure and political exposure.

Note the following: In 1989 President George Bush convened the nation's governors for the first education summit at which time they set goals for the year 2000 that included making the nation's students the world's highest achievers in math and science, wiping out adult illiteracy, and raising the high school graduation rate to 90 percent. After 10 years of increased investment and political attention, the *Washington Post* reported: "With 2000 a few months away, President Clinton and half the nation's governors gathered today for a third education summit with none of the eight education goals set in 1989 yet within reach. Despite a decade of reforms, efforts to meet those goals have generally failed."[19]

It may seem counterintuitive to argue that to improve children's learning we need to focus less on schools and more on what children do outside of it. "Surely schools are more important in the education of children than parents and the community," many people would reason. But consider the following piece of research from the Kellogg Corporation's Learning Now program. The "conclusion was based on research conducted in Michigan, which compared the relative influence that family, community, and other factors have on student performance. Amazingly, it concluded that factors outside of the school are four times more important in determining a student's success on standardized tests than are factors within the school. . . . [T]his reaffirmed, for those of us in business, the importance of becoming partners with educators, parents, and other institutions in our community dealing with the development and performance of young people. What this means is that business people cannot just sit on the sidelines and criticize but, rather, we must be involved."[20]

Despite such insights, based on decades of evidence,[21] the factors outside the school (family and community) are increasingly being minimized by economic and social forces. The political response in the United States and England has been the expedient path of facilitating such minimization by expanding the significance of formal systems of learning through a list you will well recognize: more schools, longer hours, more tests.

In analyzing the "time crunch," President Clinton's Council of Economic Advisers issued a report stating: "One of the most significant changes in the last three decades is the increasing amount of time women have devoted to market work—work that is performed for wages. Combined with hourly earnings increases among women, this means women's earnings have gone up substantially, while their time available in the home has declined. In contrast, men's average hours of paid work and earnings have remained relatively stable. As a result, families have higher incomes, but they have less time for other activities. In short, American families have been in the midst of change—change in time worked for pay; change in income and by whom it is earned; change in family size; and change in how household tasks are accomplished."[22] It has also meant changes in the range of activities children can have which aren't planned or organized days in advance. Spontaneity is out and with it so much of the stimulation to think creatively and divergently.

Parents are spending significantly less time with their children. However, the cryptic language of the presidential advisors seems to suggest that, despite the time crunch, parents are spending as much "quality time" with their children as they did in earlier decades. Are they really, or is this simply an example of convenient political speech? Picking up on the theme that you can have your cake and eat it, too, various expert groups in the United States and the United Kingdom are reassuring anxious parents that, "The evidence is fairly compelling now that the mere fact of having working parents doesn't create problems for children." So says Andrew Cherlin, a sociologist at Johns Hopkins University who continues: "We're clearly putting more structure in kid's lives, but there's not much evidence that it's hurting them."[23] Really? What matters, such experts try and persuade us, is not hours of time spent with children but quality time spent with children. According to a survey of 1,023 children, the Family and Work Institute in New York City discovered, "Most youngsters didn't say they want more time with their parents. Instead, they want better communication and more 'focused' time, with parents being less strained and tired." In a twist to the survey, the author notes that "Children may see more money as a way to lessen family stress."[24]

The Game of School

If one loses sight of the pressures facing families and communities, then the problems of stagnant school standards are easily placed solely on the shoulders of teachers and school administrators. Supporters of this view suggest the difficulties children face in their learning have nothing to do with the fact the rest of us are spending less time with our children or that children are no longer free to explore their neighborhoods because they are deemed unsafe. To appreciate what we are saying it is necessary to remember that learning is an intensely subjective, personal process that each person constantly and actively modifies in light of new experiences.

Learning is an open process, but schools by their very bureaucratic, rigid, and hierarchical nature are closed systems. Honestly ask yourself this question: How many hours did you spend in your formal education sitting in a classroom listening to a teacher drone on while you watched the clock move at a snail's pace and dreamed about your real interests? This is not a criticism of teachers but a realization that the closed, rigid, and decontextualized setting of a classroom is by its planned nature limiting.

It is for this very reason that much of what is taught in schools does not transfer over into the real world for many children. Consider this in light of the changes we've briefly described occurring in the economic and social environments that reward creativity and independent thinking. Lauren Resnick has observed that, "The process of schooling seems to encourage the idea that the 'game of school' is to learn symbolic rules of various kinds, and that there is not supposed to be much continuity between what one knows outside school and what one learns in school. There is growing evidence, then, that not only may schooling not contribute in a direct and obvious way to performance outside school, but also that knowledge acquired outside school is not always used to support in-school learning. Schooling is coming to look increasingly isolated from the rest of what we do."[25]

Yet, despite the limitations inherent in the "game of school" we continue to persist in preparing children for a rapidly changing world by requiring them to simply spend more hours working harder in schools that were themselves designed to fulfill industrial-age needs. The reason we do this is not because there is a lot of support from scientific research saying this is in the long-term interest of children's learning and development but because adults just don't have as much time for children as they did in the past. Unfortunately for children, this fact clashes with the reality that formal education makes sense to youngsters when they can connect what they learn in school to that which happens outside of it. When it doesn't, when what is learned in school seems static and conformist, then children pay only perfunctory attention to the "game of school."

Education and Learning in a Postfamily Era

It is to the detriment of children's ability to make connections that the public debate around education and learning seems now to be accepting the steady demise of parents and community in the education of children as a given fact of life. It is also to the detriment of parents. Parents themselves intuitively understand this. In one of the largest studies ever carried out in the United States about parental attitudes towards children and day-care, it was reported that, "At the most basic level, parents of young children believe that having a full-time parental presence at home is what's best for very young children (those under 5), and it is what most would prefer for their own family."[26] The August 2000 report continues, "In finding after finding, regardless of question wording or emphasis, parents of young children reiterate this heartfelt judgment. Two out of three strongly agree that 'if a family can afford it, it's almost always best for the kids to have a parent at home full-time'."[27] Parents, it seems, need children every bit as much as children need parents.

If we want young people who can function creatively and as successful lifelong learners, then it must be appreciated that institutions cannot do it alone. No matter how economically and politically convenient it would be to segregate learning and all responsibility for it to the professionals, it won't work. There must be a more realistic balance between the home, schools, and the larger community. Nowhere is this balance more critically needed than in the raising of very young children. The decrease in parental responsibility for learning and nurturing is most significant from the perspective of children's learning. The point we are pushing is that if a community can help parents provide for an open, loving, and stimulating learning environment for its youngest children, then it is easier for education systems and a culture to maximize the potential of those same children when they get older.

A financial analogy helps make the point: If you invest well early, you get a higher rate of return later. This doesn't mean you can't get a nice return on a later investment; it just means in all probability your return won't be as great. The question in the context of learning is this: For long-term growth and stability, is it better public policy to invest in parents so they can spend more time raising their youngest children? Or should we simply follow current market forces and respond by providing increased investments in daycare providers and facilities? Which investment will provide the higher rate of return over the long haul? Or, more fruitfully, from the perspective of the learning and developmental needs of children, what should the proper balance be between parenting and education? When do parents matter most, and when can schools and teachers be most productive? If we are to start thinking smarter about education and the learning needs of all our children, then these are some of the first questions that need to be asked. And for them to be asked fairly, we cannot take the increased working hours of parents as a given; nor should we take as a given the economic imperatives that so shape the way we now live. Both of these may well be part of the problem.

Many childcare experts who simply advocate more government spending on childcare often cite a 1997 study of 3,100 families in the United States by the American National Institute of Child Health and Human Development (NICHHD). The report noted that maternal stimulation and the home environment are critically important to a child's cognitive and language development, but "a young child in 'high quality' day-care, with 'positive caregivers and language stimulation,' is not at a disadvantage. . . . [W]hat matters most in day care for infants and toddlers is the children's relationship with caregivers."[28] One serious problem with increasingly farming children out to day-care, however, lies in the fact that the average day-care worker is poorly paid ($6.89 an hour in the United States). It is because they are poorly paid that it makes economic sense to many middle-class parents to work while paying day-care providers a proportion of their salary to play an important role in their child's intellectual and social development.

This simple economic logic helps to explain why six out of seven day-care centers are "mediocre to poor" in quality, according to a study cited by the *Washington Monthly* in 1998.[29] Some would see these statistics as evidence for why government should provide more resources for childcare. Many arguments are being advanced that suggest that as many parents do not understand their nurturing role very well, institutional provision with its emphasis on trained professionals could do this better. The economic attraction of the argument is strong. Such care providers are paid less than the wealth that working parents can contribute to the national economy. This in turn creates a niche market for unskilled women who could be trained as day-care workers.[30]

However, as with most complex problems, the simple solution is not necessarily the best one. Donald Cohen of Yale University has identified high quality care of children as simply "being there when (young children) need you. Sometimes when they need you is when they are upset and distressed. At such times, a lot of important work goes on between the parents, who are devoted to this child, whose primary preoccupation is this child. So, when the child is crying or is hungry or has fallen down or is disappointed, how the parent responds is critical. It makes an enormous difference whether it's your child, a child you really love and care about, or somebody else's child. It also makes a difference how awake you are, how stressed you are."[31]

The English psychologist Penelope Leach agrees when she argues: "The more parents are around, the better, and the younger the child, the more it matters. . . . The widespread Western cult of the professional teaches that 'expert' advisers and 'trained caregivers' often know better than parents because parents 'are too involved to be objective'." Leach insists that, "The last quality children require of the adults who care for them is objectivity: it is parents' unique tendency to consider their children uniquely wonderful that makes them so special." Benjamin Spock opened his famous childcare manual of the 1940s with the message to parents: "You know more than you think you know." More than half a century later, Leach tells parents: "You know more than you think you know and a great deal more than anyone else."[32]

There is no one best way of raising a child. Each family has to figure it out for themselves by balancing the pros and cons of their situations and opportunities. And, as many educators are quick to point out, "You're assuming children are actually part of families who care about them." In speaking with dedicated teachers from inner-city areas of the United States and the United Kingdom, we are constantly told about the "reality" of education in "a post-family era." The only answer we can give is that those who are dedicated to providing more opportunities to young people through education reform need to take the breakdown of the family as seriously, or even more seriously, as they do the needs of day-care centers, schools, and teachers.

Taking an evolutionary perspective, the eminent Harvard Biologist Ernst Mayr observed in 1997, "Throughout the hominid line, the family has been the foundation of group structure. . . . However, there is cohesion not only within the core family (husband, wife, children) but also among members of the extended family (grandparents, siblings, cousins, uncles, aunts). The extended family is important not just for mutual help but also for cultural cohesion and transmission to the next generation. The breakdown of the extended family is one of the basic roots of the cultural breakdown in inner-city slums."[33] Our point is this: It would be a dangerous paradox if the allure of economic growth were to extend the pathologies of dysfunctional families throughout society generally.

The Cost of Overinstitutionalizing Learning

Economically, nations gain in the short-term by getting parents into the workforce as soon as possible after the birth of their children. However, it has to be stressed that as children spend more time in structured learning environments they, not surprisingly, become successful in navigating and excelling in such closed environments. They feel comfortable in settings where things are structured and controlled. In contrast, a more open and risky environment intimidates them. They have learned to play life safe.

Two researchers for the Board of Governors of the U.S. Federal Reserve System wrote in 1997: "By identifying alternative means of accumulating human capital, we are able to show that an economy in the early stages of development may have too little education, but in later stages of development may have too much education. . . . When entrepreneurial human capital is more important than professional human capital in determining the level of technology, the steady state will have too many professionals and too few entrepreneurs. Thus, a reduction in education and an increase in entrepreneurial experience could increase per capita income."[34] Read this again: It says that a reduction in education and an increase in entrepreneurial experience could increase per capita income.

What this means is that in a developed country that needs a high number of entrepreneurs to sustain or expand economic productivity, it is important that young people have multiple opportunities to flex their intellect in the more opened environment of the larger community. In other words, for young people to thrive in highly flexible, changing environments, they need to have grown up in open and challenging environments that stimulate their ability to be creative and thoughtful. Such environments are most effectively supported by loving and caring family relationships and have been since the dawn of humanity.

Not surprisingly, these more open learning environments are very similar to the same sorts of environments where adults thrive as well. Arie P. De Geus of the Shell Corporation has written that a company that seeks short-term gains at all costs encourages lower employee loyalty and "reduced levels of trust, which then require a management style based on stronger hierarchical controls. Stronger controls reduce the space for innovation and lead to lower learning abilities of the company as a whole. Lower levels of learning in the post-industrial society reduce a company's life expectancy in a world in which success depends on the ability to maximize the use of the available brain capacity."[35]

Societies that do not invest in genuine, open learning situations ensure their own eventual stagnation.[36] Complexity theory summarizes this nicely: "If the dynamics of the system are too chaotic, no learning occurs because there is not enough stability to conserve information; if the dynamics are too static, no learning occurs because no change occurs in response to new information."[37]

In light of the above understandings, it is hardly surprising to note that as children's time in school and day-care have expanded, so have the number of young people who say they want the relatively closed and secure path of professional jobs. The Alfred P. Sloan Study of Youth and Social Development tracked and surveyed 7,000 teenagers from 1990 to 1995 and discovered that "90 percent of high school seniors expect to attend college, and more than 70 percent expect to work in professional jobs. In the 1950s, by contrast, only 55 percent of seniors expected to attend college and just 42 percent aimed for a professional career. Many teenagers set their sights too high. . . . Perhaps 56 percent become 'drifting dreamers' with grandiose visions of career achievements."[38]

These students learn in school that the path to success is not the risky path of entrepreneurs but the apparently safer path of professionals. This may be true in rich countries, but it is the entrepreneurs who add real value to the economy over the long haul, and it is an entrepreneurial attitude that individuals will need if they are to play their full part in the new economy.

Are We Rearranging the Deck Chairs on the Titanic?

The key to success and social stability in the 21st century therefore will be people working and living smarter than any previous generation. They will need to be more productive to help provide for an aging population[39] and will also need to be thoughtful enough to deal with a world where problems are increasingly global in scale and solution. If Einstein's statement that you will never solve the problems of today with the techniques of yesterday were ever true, it has to be now. The 21st century will be, even more than the previous one, the century of paradoxes, and to deal with it young people will have to be thoughtful and discerning.

The distinguished European political philosopher Nikolaus Lobkowicz has observed that democracies in the 21st century face a potentially dangerous paradox of how to balance tolerance without sliding into a world where all issues are relative. Lobkowicz says: "We live in societies with conflicting ideas on almost everything, from the most basic truths to the element of moral behavior. And, contrary to past societies, we seem to be able to bear it by insisting on tolerance and educating our offspring to accept this attitude. . . . Yet, tolerance ceases to be a virtue, indeed is in danger of becoming a vice, if it amounts to not caring for truth, ignoring what is morally good or not appreciating the values of the community. In order not to be accused of intolerance, people often refrain from being truly convinced of anything. In this way, the culture of tolerance characteristic of societies which take democracy seriously is in danger of turning into a culture of 'anything goes'. . . . In other words, the problem we face is how to be tolerant without succumbing to relativism."[40]

Despite the early 21st century imperative to think smarter, education remains firmly stuck in the problems and issues of the industrial age. We are not thinking at a deeper and more profound level about learning and education. We are still fighting the battles of yesterday; issues of school-based management, market incentives, more testing for students and teachers, high academic standards, and greater accountability of the current systems dominate the educational agenda. Is this systemic activity in danger of becoming analogous to rearranging the deck chairs on the Titanic as she plunged into the icy depths?

There Is No Conflict Here

To appreciate how stuck and polarized education is, consider the following incident. In August of 1999, researchers at the University of Durham in England studying the effect of homework on school-based test scores of 20,000 primary age pupils came up with a curious result. Contrary to the beneficial links that the British government wished to make between the quantity of homework and test results for very young children, the research actually showed that the highest test scores were achieved by students who had relatively little homework, while those who did most tended to get the lower grades. Since this finding seemed so counterintuitive, the British Department for Education immediately dismissed the research by saying that "homework backs up what is happening in the classroom. It should be properly set and marked. Children do regular homework in secondary school so it is sensible to prepare them for it at primary school."[41] This comment is an example of an educational official operating totally unaware of the different developmental stages of children. Anyone who has children, or who has worked with children, understands that primary age pupils are not simply miniature versions of secondary pupils; they are essentially different. Once again, work harder, not smarter, seems to be the mantra.

Several days later a strong statement by David Almond, when awarded the Carnegie Prize for Children's Literature, caught the Prime Minister and his Education Minister by surprise. In his acceptance speech, Almond accused the British Government of being obsessed "with tests, grades, and levels of homework which are killing joy and creativity in childhood. We are being asked to test children almost when they are still in nappies [diapers]. There is a ludicrous concentration on a noses to the grindstone, treadmill kind of work. The exhaustive chase after what we are told are higher standards has become a national obsession—an established religion. What children need is ten percent 'Eureka time.' When they can be left alone to use their own imagination; a time when target setting consists of maps of possibilities, where record keeping can consist of speculation, a time perhaps when we can admit that we haven't really got a clue what's going on in children's minds."

Almond continued, "What would the assessors and recorders have made of James Watson snoring in his bed as he dreamed the molecular structure of DNA? What indeed? Or of Isaac Newton and the apple, or of so many thoughtful people whose most original ideas tend to come when they are least expecting them. The pedants are triumphant and go about their task of disintegrating our world . . . [;] there is an arrogance at work, an arrogance that we know exactly what happens when someone learns something, that we can plan for it, that we can describe it, that we can record it and that if we can't do all these things then the learning does not exist. There is a madness here that will be laughed at in 50 years time."[42] In this condemnation of what seems an increasingly top-down education system, Almond illustrates the voice of a highly experienced teacher who, instinctively, understands children and how to respond to them.

David Blunkett, the English secretary for education, was immediate and extreme in his reactions. He accused Almond and the researchers at Durham University of "blatant elitism dressed up as well-intentioned liberalism." He went on to blame the "obsessive carping of educational researchers" who he said were "out of touch with reality." Blunkett continued: "Critics like these, in their various guises, tend to share one important characteristic. They would never apply their views to their own children, only to other people's children. They believe that it is right to read a bedtime story to their own child, but they think homework for other children is damaging."[43] This retort was curious not least because no one had ever suggested that parents should not read bedtime stories to their children. It appears that England has reached the stage where such natural, spontaneous, and gloriously informal activities now have to be classified against particular criteria on a government-directed curriculum.

Blunkett's response was followed immediately by criticism from the Prime Minister, who used a radio interview to say: "It is not unreasonable to expect children to write their own name and count to 10 by the age of 5. This is not about putting children under pressure, for if we didn't have such expectations, we would be letting the children down."[44] This is political scare-mongering, for who said that children should not be able to write their own name or count not simply to 10 but to 100 or more by the age of 5? Later Blunkett asked: "Do the critics believe that being unable to read helps you to become a better artist?"[45] Who said that they should not read or that creativity was simply a matter of becoming a better artist?

"What these critics really mean," said Blunkett, "was that there should be a return to the ill-disciplined anything goes philosophy that did so much damage to the last generation." The following day, Chris Woodhead, the chief inspector of schools, rushed to the defense of his minister. "These liberals believe that Mr. Blunkett has driven all fun and creativity from the primary classroom. . . . [H]e is thought to be obsessed with tests and targets and determined to impose his mechanistic philosophy on every energetic, inspirational and exemplary teacher noble or foolish enough to fight the good fight for progressive teaching. . . . [T]his is nonsense. . . . [I]n reality there is no conflict here. If we want creativity we must do everything possible to drive up standards of literacy and numeracy."[46]

"There is no conflict here." This is an extraordinarily simplistic statement. No one would ever deny that high levels of literacy and numeracy create better conditions for the human intellect to function, but these are processes, and processes need content on which to work. Creativity comes from the ability to indulge intelligently in divergent thinking. Divergent thinking meant for Archimedes that he was still learning when he spilled the bath water, and for Isaac Newton when he got hit on the head with an apple. How people most effectively learn and become productive human beings is too important to be misunderstood.

4 Learning and Schooling Are Not Synonymous

Most of the learning in use is of no great use.

BENJAMIN FRANKLIN

A search for an understanding of learning is enhanced by a history of how humanity has approached the transmission of collective wisdom. In delving into this history—and the philosophies that have informed it—the contrast between schooling and learning is what we are most interested in. This is the subject of the next few chapters, and, to summon up some very recent history, we'll return to the opening sentence of this book's introduction and ask, "How do humans learn?"

For that matter, how is it that some adults seem to carry on learning effortlessly throughout a lifetime, while others seem impervious to new ideas? How, in fact, do novel ideas originate? Just how did Pythagoras come to understand that the sum of the square of the hypotenuse is equal to the sum of the squares on the other two sides? By what process was he able to take all the wisdom of previous ages, presumably passed onto him by the wisest mathematicians of his day, and then go just that little bit further to earn a place in the minds of struggling young mathematicians more than 2,000 years later? How have our intellectual processes evolved over time, and what can we expect of that evolution in the future?

In recent years, archaeology and biomedical technology have started to extend our understanding of our distant ancestors' intellectual capabilities. So how can we now apply this to a better understanding of what we in our turn can achieve? Given the technologies of 3,000 to 4,000 years

56

ago, there are few artifacts that tell us just how our earlier ancestors actually thought; what they thought about; or how they shared their thoughts, ideas, and discoveries with younger generations. Records are even murkier about how people thought and transmitted ideas and values, say 10,000, 20,000, or 30,000 years before that. Yet, there are an increasing number of discoveries to be understood. The fascinating cave paintings, especially those in France as well as those in Australia and in Southern Africa, painted 20,000 years ago tell us of our ancestors' inquisitive and thoughtful nature.

A fascinating example is the shoulder blade of an ox unearthed in the 1980s by archaeologists investigating a stone-age encampment in the south of France (see Figure 4.1 on p. 58). Carbon dating showed this shoulder blade to be approximately 30,000 years old. The bone was marked with inscriptions that the archaeologists couldn't decipher. It was clear the markings were not a tally, a pattern, or any recognizable form of writing. Late one night one of the archaeologists noticed the moon, and something in its shape caught his curiosity. Then it struck him.

Here, on this fragment of a bone, was a lunar calendar complete with 72 observations made something like 1,600 generations ago. One of our common ancestors (statistically, all of us can claim a relationship to this thoughtful person) 30,000 years ago had the intellectual curiosity to watch the moon, night after night, and then transcribe these movements at scale onto the stone-age equivalent of a back of an envelope, as he (or she) attempted to "think it through." What makes us human is our ability to think, learn, and adapt to our changing environment. The story of the stone-age learner gets even better when you imagine a small community of people (adults, adolescents, children on laps) sitting around a campfire every night working out the meaning of the lunar phases together.

This story captures the essence of learning and teaching. Teaching is the sharing of knowledge between the generations, with the intention of this knowledge helping younger people to take responsibility for themselves and the world around them. But it's even more than this: Good teaching enables young people to see how it is that older people actually learn and think. Good teaching helps children develop methods in which they can take new information and use it to create new knowledge and understandings for themselves. This is exactly what Pythagoras did.

This form of teaching and learning probably had its roots as deep as the history of human language. If we are to construct the most effective learning models possible in the 21st century, then we have to understand how the brain works so that we extend its natural learning strategies beyond simply what comes naturally. The central point here is that successful

Figure 4.1 The Sequential Phases of the Moon

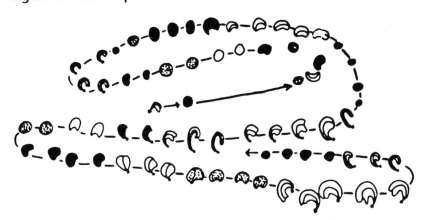

A bone pressure sketch from Blanchard, France, dating from about 30,000 years ago. The sequential phases of the moon have been engraved from observation over two and a quarter months. Nothing comparable for the next 10,000 years has been as yet uncovered. It is the first-known conceptual performance of Homo sapiens.

Source: Sir John Eccles. *Evolution of the Brain, Creation of the Self* (London: Routledge), 1989.

teaching and learning is a balancing act between nature (what our brains can do) and nurture (what the culture in which we live values and wants to pass on). This relationship is a central part of what this book is all about, for out of this comes the uniquely human capacity to be deliberately creative.

Learning to Go with the Grain of the Brain

We adults are able to learn, and help our young take responsibility for their learning, because as humans we have inherited remarkable brains. The essential purpose of the brain is to direct individual activity in ways that enable people to survive in an ever-changing environment. This is why we describe learning as a reflective activity that enables the learner to draw upon previous experience to understand and evaluate the present, so as to shape future action and formulate new knowledge.

Learning is a process of knowledge construction, not simply knowledge recording or absorption. Learning is knowledge dependent, with learners using current knowledge to construct new knowledge. Learning is context dependent and highly tuned to the situation in which it takes place.[1] "Learning is a dynamic interaction between a changing structured environment and neural mechanisms. The neural machinery is extensively shaped by activity stemming from the environment, while its intrinsic properties also constrain this modulation and play an indispensable role in shaping the resulting structures."[2]

The constructivist brain is a self-organizing system that is shaped by its interaction with objects and events in the world. In adapting to events, the brain's molecular mechanisms physically adjust to its environment. What this view argues is that perception is colored by experience. We neither see nor hear something in a totally objective form; rather, our receptive processes are colored by those environmental stimuli that have captured our interest in the past. We actually build the structure of our brains as we use them. This makes learning a highly personalized and interconnected cognitive and social process.

Such insights into learning and the brain are coming to the fore because new understandings are emerging through synthesizing disciplines of study and experience. For example, earlier findings from cognitive science (like constructivism) are actually supported by the more recent findings of neurology. This evidence is further supported by findings from evolutionary biology and psychology and, as noted above, even archaeology. Archaeology provides valuable supporting evidence to those seeking to understand human learning.

Archaeology helps fill in some of the blanks. For example, while brain tissue disintegrates rapidly after death, archaeologists have found skulls from different epochs of human evolution. By studying their internal shape and size they can draw reasonably firm conclusions about brain growth over the millennia. It's possible to go even further. By analyzing the artifacts left behind by our ancestors, and by relating these directly to the shape of their skulls, we can begin to plot the growth of the intellectual powers of early humans. For example, we know from skull size, bodily remains, and the number of artifacts left behind that Cro-Magnons of more than 30,000 years ago were, in terms of intellectual and physical capabilities, us. According to Ian Tattersall of the American Museum of Natural History, Cro-Magnons were physically "indistinguishable from living Homo sapiens; and, in its richness and complexity, the surviving material evidence of their lives indicates unequivocally that they were our intellectual equals."[3]

This evidence argues that humans have been learning and teaching each other for far more than 1,500 generations, and because of this fact we have thrived as a species. For the vast majority of time, learning and teaching took place through an arrangement we described in Chapter 1 as apprenticeship. Apprenticeship integrated learning, working, and living. This form of community-based learning was as central to the health of community as it was to the successful induction of young people into adulthood. Apprenticeship was far more than just skill acquisition. At its heart it was a process in which the young learned to take full responsibility for finding appropriate solutions to novel problems. This was possible for learners because they had earlier developed the ability to look at new problems from a variety of different perspectives. Apprentices aspired to become independent craftsmen, and a craft was more than a job: It was a way of life. The artifact was a demonstration of their personality. It provided a status in society and the recognition of being significant within the community.

This is an after-the-fact account, for numerous people in a variety of cultures over thousands of years never consciously thought of formulating what they were doing into a theory of learning. Yet when these different practices are studied one with another, they have a remarkable similarity. Invariably they are designed around the efficient use of an adult's time in inducting young people into taking evermore responsibility for their own activities, and so increasing their economic and social value. Learning has to be understood in a social problem-solving context.

During the past few years, scientists working with brain imaging technologies, such as functional MRI, have been able to "see" the ways in which ideas developed in different parts of the brain come together. This is close to providing a neurological base for appreciating why apprenticeship is such a successful model of learning. In other words, it is no coincidence that cultures worldwide evolved using apprenticeship; it simply goes with the neurological structure of the brain.

It is only in more recent times that modern societies have seen it advantageous to treat learning as something disconnected from the open experiential environment of the community and something that is transmitted through instruction by professionals in the isolated confines of a classroom. Because societies over the past 150 years (less than 8 generations) have put an increasing emphasis on learning in the decontextualized setting of schools, we now hear such comments as, "Oh, I was never very good at learning. That's why I left school at the age of 16." Too many people, at the dawn of the 21st century, see learning as something that is done to them by others and something over which they have little or no control.

This runs counter to our biological predispositions and to the goal of politicians, educators, and business leaders who see the need for all people to function as responsible lifelong learners. Aside from all the political claims and counterclaims, we have to stop and ask ourselves how is it that humans, the planet's pre-eminent learning species, can have their thinking so muddled as to believe that learning is something other people do to them? In order to answer this question, we must disentangle human learning from the baggage of schooling. This is not to say we should "de-school society" or that "the age of the school is dead." Instead, we seek to make the case that if we want a society of motivated, lifelong learners, we must find a better balance between the responsibilities of schools, families, the larger community, and information communication technology in the education of all children.

A History of Early Education Systems

The history of education systems in western countries is intertwined with the political, social, cultural, scientific, and economic ideas, interests, and needs of individual nation states as they have evolved over the last 150 or so years. The purpose of the following section is to outline, in general terms, how mass systems of education emerged; what ideas went into their development; what purposes they were meant to serve; what social environments they were created for; and, consequently, why it has become so easy for many people simply to assume that it is only in schools that legitimate learning takes place.

For most countries in Europe and North America, learning became irreversibly equated with formal systematic schooling sometime during the middle to late 19th century. This blurring of schooling and learning was a direct result of national governments using formal education to develop loyal, productive, and socially contented citizens. The English educational historian Andy Green captured the purpose when he wrote: "The national education system thus represented a watershed in the development of learning. It signaled not only the advent of mass education and the spread of popular literacy, but also the origins of 'state schooling'—the system which has come to predominate in the educational development of all modern societies in the 20th century."[4]

This conjunction of the needs of the individual with those of the state was not dissimilar to the way in which the Roman Empire took over Christianity under the Emperor Constantine in A.D. 330. This enhanced enormously the status of the Church, but it made Christianity forever dependent on political considerations. With the state taking responsibility for schooling, the various pressures that had previously existed on young people to hold themselves responsible for their own development diminished, and learning became what the state defined, not necessarily what individuals undertook for their own purposes. School systems across continental Europe arose in concert with the centralized, bureaucratic nation state, and in fact were central to the crafting of such states. For example, the Prussian system of education grew in tandem with Bismarck's unification of the German speaking people of central Europe under the banner of a single German state. Education systems played a central role in molding loyal citizens.

The U.S. Model of Education

In the United States, the education systems that evolved reflected the structure of the U.S. political system and were largely decentralized in comparison to the education systems of continental Europe. (The U.S. federal government, despite the rhetoric of Presidential politics, still has only a small role in educational policy.) By decentralized we mean local authorities control the tax base of schools and most educational spending. The actual systems of education that developed from state to state, and county to county, in the United States over the course of the 19th century were remarkably similar in form and even purpose to those in Europe.

By the close of the 20th century, the United States had a rather homogenized model of education familiar to students across the country for four primary reasons:

1. Teacher training colleges that taught the same basic curriculum.
2. The fact there are only two or three major publishers of school textbooks.
3. Teacher unions (there are only two) and associations that had national agendas, such as high standards for all.
4. The college entrance tests: ACT and SAT.

The late 20th century effort by politicians and educational policy makers in the United States to develop national standards and national testing regimes was, to a large degree, an effort to expand this standardized model from those who go on to college to those who leave formal education during or after high school.

From the beginning, the U.S. model of public education, like those in the states of Europe, was designed to nurture loyal citizens. This was a social, not an educational, agenda. The Stanford professor of educational history David Tyack captured this fact aptly when he noted that "the creation of efficient and uniformed police paralleled the movement to standardized schooling. Both were in part responses to the influx of the immigrant poor."[5] As Noah Webster (1758–1843), the creator of the U.S. dictionary of English, observed in 1790 during the early years of the U.S. experience: "It is an object of vast magnitude that systems of education should be adopted and pursued which may not only diffuse a knowledge of the sciences but may implant in the minds of the American youth the principle of virtue and of liberty and inspire them . . . with an inviolable attachment to their country."[6]

In Pennsylvania, Benjamin Rush (1745–1813), a signer of the Declaration of Independence, saw education as central to inculcating an overriding allegiance to the common good: "Let our pupil be taught that he does not belong to himself, but that he is public property. Let him be taught to love his family, but let him be taught at the same time that he must forsake and even forget them when the welfare of his country requires it." With the proper system of public education, Rush maintained, it would be "possible to convert men into republican machines. This must be done if we expect them to perform their parts properly in the great machine of the government of the state."[7]

Despite Webster's earlier urgings, it wasn't until the 1850s that the hodgepodge of religious and private schools that had made up formal education for an elite in the northeastern United States was largely replaced by government-supported common schools for all children. Initially these schools came in the form of elementary schools, and by the 1920s there was a more unified system incorporating both elementary and high schools. The common school reformers in Massachusetts, like Webster 60 years before, "believed that education could be used to assure the dominance of Protestant Anglo-American culture, reduce tensions between social classes, eliminate crime and poverty, stabilize the political system, and form patriotic citizens."[8] Such systems of common schools would be replicated later in other parts of the United States, with the south developing last.

In Europe and Elsewhere

The 1870 Elementary Education Act in England represented the creation of the modern education system for that country. The aim of the Act was to provide elementary schooling throughout the nation, filling the gaps in the existing schools established by the churches, private benefactors, and guilds.[9] A state-sponsored education system was able to develop later in England than in other countries because tradition provided the basis for being English that education systems had to provide in other less homogenous societies.

It is surprising to observe that educational reformers in the English-speaking countries looked to the state-sponsored school systems of continental Europe for a model that could be replicated at home. Early attempts at constructing national systems of education were pioneered by absolutist monarchs like Frederich V in Denmark, Maria Theresa in Austria, and Frederick the Great in Russia, but they floundered because they lacked the resources and centralized administration necessary for such a large-scale enterprise. The first functional state-sponsored school system was developed in Prussia. It was strictly formal; parents abrogated to the school full authority for all aspects of their children's learning.

By the 1830s Prussia had "a full national system of public elementary and secondary schools, which provided universal, compulsory schooling up to 14 years, and secondary education for the elite thereafter. . . . Decades ahead of any other nation, (thus winning wide international acclaim), Prussia had an integrated public school system which, not coincidentally, also exercised the most rigid control over what was taught."[10] Andy Green noted that it is "one of the great ironies of educational history that the more 'democratic' 19th century powers like France, England and the USA were forced to look to the autocratic German states for examples of educational reform to adopt at home."[11] It is interesting that few, if any, educators wanted to acknowledge any forms of education that were not strictly intellectual and provided for formally by academics. Rigorous mental gymnastics were thought to toughen the mind as physical gymnastics stretched the muscles.

The End of Apprenticeship: The School "in Loco Parentis"

The education systems throughout continental Europe, England, and the United States that had emerged by the late 19th century served various political purposes, but they all had roughly the same structural form. None, by the way, had goals remotely similar to those of helping children take control of their own learning and creativity. These were systems that were "carefully articulated, hierarchically structured groupings of schools, primarily free and often compulsory, administered by full-time experts, and progressively taught by specially trained staff. No longer casual adjuncts to the home and apprenticeship, such schools were highly formal institutions designed to play a critical role in the socialization of the young, the maintenance of social order, and the promotion of development."[12]

Such systems of education, and the professionalization of teaching they encouraged during the middle to late 1800s, came to dominate learning across Europe and the United States. As radical social, political, and economic changes overtook these rapidly industrializing nations, it was argued by 19th century educational reformers that education systems had increasingly to save children from the negative influences of parents and community. Parental authority and the traditional system of apprenticeship that had prepared youths for successful adulthood were collapsing under the pressures of long hours of factory work by parents, by urbanization and the vices that came with living largely in anonymity, and by the cultural breakdown spawned by large scale immigration. As the traditional bonds of authority and systems of learning fell apart, educational reformers argued that schools would have to replace parents and the community as the locus of learning and moral development.

In speaking about the teeming masses congregating in the cities of the eastern seaboard, Horace Mann (1796–1859), the American educational reformer who was secretary of the Massachusetts Education Board in the 1830s and 1840s, had no hesitation in recommending public intervention where the family and community were apparently failing: "No one at all familiar with the deficient household arrangements and the deranged machinery of domestic life of the extreme poor, and ignorant, to say nothing of the intemperate—of the examples of rude manners, impure and profane language, and all the vicious habits of low-bred idleness which abound in certain sections of all populous districts—can doubt, that it is better for children to be removed as early and as long as possible."[13] By 1848 Mann was referring primarily to the influx of Irish immigrants who threatened to overwhelm his Anglo-Saxon sense of civility, and, therefore, in his mind, public schools needed to succeed where the family and community had failed.

The purpose of schooling, said Mann, "was not so much intellectual culture, as the feelings and dispositions, the extirpation of vicious propensities, the preoccupation of the wildness of the young heart with the seeds and germs of moral beauty, and the formation of a lovely and virtuous character by the habitual practice of cleanliness, delicacy, refinement, good temper, gentleness, kindness, justice, and truth."[14] It is worth noting that the response of religious and social leaders in the Irish community to what they saw as an encroachment on their values was to create a separate system of parochial Catholic schools.

This shift from home and community-based learning towards mass schooling was a radical transformation in the history of how children acquired the skills, knowledge, values, and attitudes necessary for successful participation and membership in a community. Children's learning was no longer intricately connected to the adult world but became isolated in the realm of professionals.

England took longer to convince itself of the need for a mass education system, and when it finally did so it was largely for the practical reason of getting children off the streets. As one observer in Liverpool commented in 1867: "They [children] are idling in the streets and wynds; tumbling about in the gutters; selling matches; running errands; working in tobacco shops, cared for by no man."[15] The English educational legislation of 1870 was intended not so much to rescue children from exploitation as to corral them in schools as the Factory Act of earlier that year had prevented them from being employed in the mines or in the factories.

The ideas behind the English education system that emerged towards the end of the 19th century, much later than Europe's continental powers, had been well expressed by Adam Smith (1723–1790) some 100 years earlier. Smith had written in *The Wealth of Nations* that education could make craft workers more productive, moral, and socially thoughtful. He said: "The more they are instructed, the less liable they are to the delusions of enthusiasm and superstition. . . . An instructed and intelligent people besides are always more decent and orderly than an ignorant one[;] . . . they are more disposed to examine, and more capable of seeing through the interested complaints of faction and sedition, and they are . . . less apt to be misled into any wanton or unnecessary opposition to the measures of government."[16] For England, probably more than in any other western country, education of the masses was a form of social control totally separate from the education of the social elite. Learning for the masses was simply about instruction, an assumption that seemed obvious to those who saw social class as largely hereditary and who did not reflect on the nature of human inquisitiveness.

The School as the Secular Church

By the close of the 19th century, state-run systems of education had developed across the industrializing countries to define nationhood and moral, cultural, and political development of the nation. As the new secular church, it took upon itself the assimilation of immigrant cultures and the promotion of standard forms of the designated national language. Schools sought to inculcate new habits of routine and rational calculation, to encourage patriotic values, and to reinforce the hegemony of the dominant classes.[17]

Schooling and learning had become one in that the only real learning that was recognized as important was the academic learning that occurred in a formal classroom. An effect of institutional education was to almost completely displace apprenticeship. The first stage of the industrial revolution that had developed in England 100 years earlier had grown from the workshop upwards with workers making innovations to existing processes themselves. This steadily led to improved ways of manufacturing goods. Such a bottom-up process of innovation required that workers continually add to and improve the manufacturing processes they oversaw, but it did not require them to have knowledge of such abstractions as science and math. It didn't even require workers to be literate, and that fact helps explain why, during the first industrial revolution in England, literacy rates actually declined.[18]

This changed with the second industrial revolution that occurred largely after 1870 in which math and science in the form of engineering drove many of the technical advances that were at the heart of manufacturing, transportation, and communication. This latter revolution was primarily a U.S.- and German-led affair. Between 1859 and 1914, the value of U.S. manufactured goods increased 18 times, and by 1919 the value increased 33 times. This was the era of, among others, Edison, Bell, Rockefeller, and Carnegie in the United States; Krupp and Thyssen in Germany; and John Brown and Vickers in Britain. These were men who, for better or worse, literally changed the face of the world. This was also the era when science came to rule the manufacturing process, and by successfully doing so was seen as the panacea to many social problems, including how to most effectively educate masses of young people.

A Milieu of Big Ideas: Science Influences Social Affairs

It is important to point out in general terms what this science was and how it interacted with society. An industrial revolution, wherever it takes place, forces dramatic shifts of populations from the countryside to the city, from farms to factories. The resulting social, political, and economic changes shift the intellectual firmament, and Enlightenment societies looked towards mathematics and the natural sciences for methodologies and empirical support for their new assumptions and policies. The same spirit of rationalism that was harnessed to increase productivity was deployed in a search for understanding the uncertainties and disequilibriums of social structures and natural systems.

Sir Isaac Newton's *Philosophiae Naturalis Principia Mathematica* in 1687 provided, even as late as the 1930s, the Western world with the scientific foundations for how the world, and indeed the universe, appeared to work. Newtonian physics represented a reliable approximation of the behavior of ordinary material objects. It had accurately predicted the motions of planets and had enabled engineers to construct the internal combustion engine, steel bridges, and most of the other major technological advances that made up the modern society that generated the need for mass systems of education. So successful was Newtonian physics that its central principles were enthusiastically translated into a methodology for philosophy, politics, economics, and education.

By the late 19th century, according to Ian Marshall and Danah Zohar, the Newtonian concepts "of force, the reduction of any whole to a few simple and separate parts (atomism and reductionism), and the sense that events are determined by rigid laws of cause and effect (determinism) provided the central images and categories in terms of which people viewed their experience. People, and this was especially true of the learned, came to see themselves as separate, isolated islands connected to each other only by force or influence, their behavior all too often determined by biology, background, or conditioning. Newton's description of the universe as a vast machine, and the role of the machine in the new industrial revolution, gave rise to mechanism as the dominant metaphor for how people and organizations function."[19]

Newton's science was also a method for thinking about how complex problems are to be approached, and it was this feature of his work that had the most general effect on his contemporaries and on the scientific and philosophical thinkers who followed. The Newtonian method of scientific inquiry based on simplicity, determinism, objectivity, and predictability inspired John Locke's concept of the mind as a tabula rasa waiting for experience to shape it. It inspired, too, Descartes's dualism of mind and body; Frederick Winslow Taylor's theories of scientific management; the deterministic philosophy of behaviorism; and countless other economic, social, political, and psychological models and theories, including the factory model of schooling and the curriculum of disconnected disciplines.

From such a rational world-view it was easy for people to have faith in now-and-forever causation. Science had coalesced with the more established traditions of religion to support a world-view defined by absolute certainties. Despite the upheavals initiated by Darwin, most intellectuals, and certainly the masses, accepted the premise that the workings of God could be understood through math and science.

There was a general optimism that human life, despite short-term political and social conflicts, could only get better and better. The early 20th century was rife with World Fairs celebrating the technological marvels of the day. The subtext to their celebration was a belief that mankind was on an irreversible path towards neverending progress. If followed faithfully, the truths garnered from the physical and social sciences would lead to unlimited material bounty and progress. People of goodwill in 1900 believed in the inevitability of democracy, the invincibility of progress, the decency of human nature, and the coming reign of reason and peace.[20]

In 1910, four years before World War I and the automated death of 9 million soldiers, Norman Angell wrote *The Great Illusion*, which "proved that war had become vain." Angell showed that in "the present financial and economic interdependence of nations, the victor would suffer equally with the vanquished; therefore war had become unprofitable; therefore no nation would be so foolish as to start one."[21] *The Great Illusion* became a cult sensation that was published in 11 languages.

Yet, with the publication of Darwin's *On the Origin of Species* in 1859, parts of Newtonian physics, and the certainty it helped to instill, were beginning to be questioned. Powerful and contradictory ideas were starting to confuse people's basic beliefs. In contrast to the Newtonian approach that showed any system or object starting from some given state or position and acted upon by some given force would always behave in exactly the same way, Darwin proposed another world view. He demonstrated that "almost all evolutionary challenges have multiple solutions. . . . The lesson one must learn from this pluralism is that in evolutionary biology sweeping generalizations are rarely correct. Even when something occurs 'usually,' this does not mean that it must occur always."[22]

Darwin argued that evolution does not lead to perfection, nor does it necessarily even produce progress. It was just these sorts of pluralistic, nonlinear arguments that made Nietzsche exclaim "God is dead," for from the perspective of Darwin there was no master plan waiting for man to decipher.

Applying Science to Social Affairs

Darwin established five major themes relating to different aspects of variational evolution:

1. Organisms steadily evolve over time.
2. Different kinds of organisms descended from a common ancestor.
3. Species multiply over time.
4. Evolution takes place through the gradual change of populations.
5. The mechanism of evolution is the competition among vast numbers of unique individuals for limited resources, which leads to differences in survival and reproduction.[23]

Darwin's principle of uncertainty took awhile to enter the public consciousness because 19th century thinkers were most concerned with "the survival of the fittest," a phrase first coined by Herbert Spencer. For Spencer, it provided a rationale for the "expansionist and imperialist political economy of massive proportions; one on which the sun never fully set. . . . Spencer's version of [Darwin's] theory is a justification, a kind of moral gloss on the policies and practices of the developed nations in their dealings with those who had no choice but to cooperate."[24] This was the time of great empires and great empire "wannabees."

While Norman Angell was writing about the end of war, the German General von Bernhard advocated a different argument in *Germany and the Next War* when he applied the maxim of the survival of the fittest to the nation state and war. Von Bernhard said, "War is a biological necessity; it is the carrying out among humankind of 'the natural law, upon which all the laws of Nature rest, the law of the struggle for existence.' Nations, von Bernhard said, must progress or decay; 'there can be no standing still,' and Germany must choose 'world power or downfall'.... Conquest thus becomes a law of necessity."[25] The swirl of big scientific ideas that were part of the social milieu of Europe and North America at the turn of the century greatly impacted on national policies, including those for education.

Using Science Selectively

It is important to note that these scientific ideas were not accepted or applied in toto across all western countries and were first translated by the elites of individual nations to support their cultures and interests. For the British, science provided a defense for maintaining the global economic system and their colonial empire; for the Germans, science provided evidence to why it was necessary to overturn British hegemony.

The point here is that political activists seeking to promote a particular agenda have often used scientific theories, and these ideas often collide with one another at particular times in history. As the U.S. professor of physics Lee Smolin quipped in 1997, "In science, as in politics or love, one can have all the good arguments and still be in the wrong. When it comes down to it, what matters is not whose story is more logical or beautiful, but which leads to the greatest effect."[26] And in the case of the 19th, and for most of the 20th, century, the greatest effect referred to what supported the political and economic interest of the governing elite within individual nations.

As a general statement, it is fair to say that across North America and Europe the scientific ideas that informed the political and social mind-set of the time concentrated on observable data that could be analyzed and reduced to laws and principles. The reductionist method viewed systems in isolation from their environments, and broke them down into their simplest component parts in order to use the behavior of these parts to predict the unfolding future of the system. This scientific process had a profound impact on psychology and the study of human behavior, which in turn would greatly influence thinking about schools and how students should learn.

The school of psychological thought that emerged around the turn of the century, and which would dominate thinking about learning for most of the 20th century, focused on those behaviors that could be observed rather than those that were the result of internal biological processes. The behaviorist movement was launched by John Broadus Watson (1878–1958) in 1913, and "intentionally modeled closely on the physical sciences. Since the interpretation of subjective experience and the results of introspection are unclear and unrepeatable Watson . . . wanted to concentrate only on what a hard scientist could see and measure—the relation between a stimulus and the organism's response to it. The proper subject matter of psychology was therefore deemed to be observable behavior, the laws connecting stimuli to responses and conditioned responses. Both mind and brain were ignored."[27]

Behaviorism precluded causal explanations if they did not lie within the limits of ordinary everyday experience. If something could not be seen, tested, and confirmed in a controlled environment, then it simply did not exist. Unfortunately this excluded some central aspects of human behavior. These limitations, however, did not prevent Watson from claiming that behaviorism could create a better world by scientifically engineering the development of personality. The impact of behaviorism on education over the 20th century would be profound. The teacher-centered, input-output model of learning driven by standardized exam results and credentialling received its theoretical support from the "hard science" of behaviorism. Despite a massive amount of research from various fields of study showing the limitations of behaviorism, it has kept its hold on much of education because it offers the false promise of shaping children to the needs and desires of the larger society.

5 Scientific Schooling for an Industrial Age

Using psychological terms, the art of teaching may be defined as the art of giving and withholding stimuli with the result of producing and preventing certain responses.

EDWARD THORNDIKE

How the behaviorists applied science to education—and their excessive emphasis on nurture—was in stark contrast to the ideas about nature that had been developed earlier by Johann Pestalozzi in Italy and Friedrich Froebel in Germany. These early 19th century pedagogues built on the ideas of Socrates, Saint Thomas Aquinas, Kant, and Rousseau to suggest that successful education must start with a child's ability to understand his own learning and find his own place in the world. Their writings reflect an appreciation of apprenticeship systems that unite living, working, and learning in a single process.

Froebel, who opened his first kindergarten in 1836, stressed the concept of play. He asserted play was children's work and the way they discovered relationships, consequences, and solutions. He defined teachers as central in helping the child's mind to grow naturally and spontaneously, and he stipulated a well-trained professionalism to coax intellectual development. His ideas of experiential learning were much misinterpreted, and even his followers often trivialized his approach. The middle-classes-in-a-hurry misconstrued kindergartens as child minding and found an attractive alternative to being active parents. Toy manufacturers jumped on the bandwagon and exploited a market for complex toys that did little to stretch a child's imagination.

By the late 1800s the rigor of kindergarten had been replaced by the softer child-study movement that lacked the depth and perceptiveness of

Froebel's methods but provided a kind of justification for putting very young children into a nursery school. Such schools were rich in goodwill but difficult to evaluate in any scientific way. Consequently, as a new generation of educational innovators consumed with the idea of scientific study emerged in the early 20th century, they were quick to dismiss child-study as being unquantifiable and therefore irrelevant. They assumed it was a further development of Froebel's ideas, rather than a degenerate form of an earlier ideal. In particular they were critical of the concept of play, as indeed Froebel himself would have been if he had seen the lackluster application of his ideas. To this day critics of experiential education dismiss Froebel's work as little more than "play and sandcastles."

Edward Lee Thorndike (1874–1947) of Teacher's College, Columbia University, caricatured Froebel by suggesting a toothbrush should become the child's first artifact and sleep should become the child's first activity.[1] The behaviorists wanted their learning to be strictly quantifiable and promised extraordinary results. They held that if a child was physically healthy, they could persuade that child to do whatever they wanted. In 1925, John Watson made one of behaviorism's defining boasts: "Give me a dozen healthy infants, well-formed, and my own specified world to bring them up in, and I'll guarantee to take any one at random and train him to become any type of specialist I might select—doctor, lawyer, artist, merchant-chief, and yes, even beggarman and thief, regardless of his talents, penchants, tendencies, abilities, vocations, and race of his ancestors."[2]

At the core of behaviorism was the study of learning, and in particular the learning of animals. This was largely based on Thorndike's observations on trial-and-error learning in cats and the experiments of the Russian physiologist Ivan Pavlov on conditioning in dogs. For behaviorists the brain reflected Locke's notion of a blank slate waiting for external inputs to shape it. External motivation, argued the behaviorists, was the primary driver of behavior, and in particular of learning. In asking the question of how children become productive and satisfied adults, the behaviorists would give overwhelming primacy to environmental influences (the role of nurture) including the teacher, the school, and the curriculum.

Evolution in Mind

The behaviorists basically ignored Darwin's theory of evolution and nature's impact on the behavior and development of young people. "What behaviorism did was forbid causal explanations if they did not lie within the limits of ordinary everyday experience. Scientifically this was an extraordinary bankrupting stance."[3] This omission of evolution was essential for the behaviorist theories because "Darwin's theory gave scientific legitimacy to the idea that human behavior is to some extent determined by inbuilt or innate instincts."[4]

Such human predispositions could not be observed by conditioning and response experiments in laboratory animals, so they were effectively ignored. While behaviorism was emerging as the dominant school of thought within psychology, the most prolific advocates of Darwin's work on evolution were taking his ideas and working to use them as a scientific explanation for why certain races of people were superior to others. Unfortunately for students of human behavior, these "early attempts to apply Darwinian ideas to humans—and to social processes in particular—by thinkers such as Herbert Spencer were both wrong-headed and scientifically inept, and the political agenda derived from evolution rapidly became the politically unacceptable face of science."[5] This Nazi's misapplication of evolutionary ideas through the bogus science of eugenics in the 1930s was a huge setback for those wanting to better understand human behavior and, in particular, human learning.

During much of the 20th century there was little attempt at a synthesis between psychology and evolution. This is unfortunate for such a synthesis could have helped temper behaviorism's overemphasis on learning being nothing more than conditioned responses to stimulus. At the same time a better appreciation of the importance of nurture could have tempered the excessive emphasis on the role of genetics that many students of human behavior placed on human development. Two distinct, and separate, paths were followed. Unfortunately there was no meeting of minds between these two different approaches until evolutionary psychology emerged in the early 1990s, which was, not surprisingly, attacked by the established schools of psychology and evolutionary biology.

Science Reaches Industry and Changes the Way People Function

Despite the various conflicts between the different branches of science, many within manufacturing were starting to apply selectively the insights and methods of science to systems organizing the behavior of workers in factories. It was the U.S. efficiency expert Frederick Winslow Taylor who epitomized the convergence of industry and science more than anyone else. He melded his experience as an apprentice factory worker with his understandings of math and science from his university studies to develop a technique that would later be known as "time and motion studies." Starting at the Midvale Steel Works in Pennsylvania in the 1880s, Taylor sought to apply objective scientific data and models to human labor. He treated manual work as something deserving study and analysis, and by doing so he showed that the real potential for increased output was by "working smarter."

Taylor was right. According to Peter Drucker: "The application of knowledge to work explosively increased productivity. For hundreds of years there had been no increase in the ability of workers to turn out goods or to move goods. Machines created greater capacity. But workers themselves were no more productive than they had been in the workshops of Ancient Greece, in building the roads of Imperial Rome, or in producing the highly prized woolen cloth which gave Renaissance Florence its wealth. Within a few years after Taylor began to apply knowledge to work, productivity began to rise at a rate of 3.5 to 4 percent compound a year— which means doubling every 18 years or so. Since Taylor began, productivity has increased some fifty-fold in all advanced countries. On this unprecedented expansion rest all the increases in both standard of living and quality of life in the developed countries."[6]

There was a catch though. When Taylor spoke of "working smarter" he meant that a small team of engineering experts would work smarter and then use their "scientifically based" insights to tell everyone else what to do, how to do it, and when. For most people, scientific management meant following orders and being paid good money for not asking questions. The fantastic increase in productivity through the introduction of science to the industrial process came at a cost to the average person's initiative and learning. Working people no longer had any say in how to do their jobs; consequently, for nonmanagement workers, the workplace became highly repetitive, pressurized, and strictly unthinking.

Taylor's *The Principles of Scientific Management*, published in 1911, said: "The primary, if not the only, goal of human labor and thought is efficiency; that technical calculation is in all respects superior to human judgement; that in fact human judgement can not be trusted, because it is plagued by laxity, ambiguity, and unnecessary complexity; that subjectivity is an obstacle to clear thinking; that what cannot be measured either does not exist or is of no value; and that the affairs of citizens are best guided and conducted by experts."[7] The deification of efficiency and of the specialist had begun.

Taylor began the cult of the specialist, and there is a distinction to be made here between specialization and expertise. This is vital to educational policymakers for expertise enables transferable skills[8] to move from one set of problems to another. By working within the well-defined parameters of a specialism, a specialist knows a subject from top to bottom. A specialist is the ultimate analyst who knows all the rules, all the tests, and all the possible combinations and formulas. Authority rests on the depth of knowledge and is uncluttered by the need to assess extraneous influences. Specialists exude a confidence in their competence, and in some this comes through as arrogance. Discussion with such people is often difficult for they know all the answers "in their box," and if you come from a different box, they are not interested. Just where their specialties fit in a bigger synthesis does not trouble them, for that is essentially unquantifiable, imprecise, and highly uncertain. There are no rules for that kind of thing, they say, and so these questions are best left unanswered.

This is a caricature perhaps, but the world has come to be fearful of specialists for, in some hard-to-define way, we sense they are just not real. They break the work down into bits, and that gets us, both individually and collectively, into trouble and makes us schizophrenic. Such thinking is well-exemplified by the comments of a senior researcher at a leading U.S. research organization who asked, "Why do you want to use an evolutionary framework to understand the science of learning? We have a science of learning and it is not necessary to get into the nasty conflicts revolving around evolution. What you're doing," he continued, "only makes the issue more difficult for people to accept." Contrast this comment with those of the cognitive neuroscientist Michael Gazzaniga who observed, "If the evolutionary perspective is simply set aside, the data collected by psychologists and neuroscientists are likely to be grossly misinterpreted."[9]

Neurobiology gives us powerful snapshots of the brain as it operates in the current generation, but it does not tell us how we got here. Cognitive science delves into matters of learning that, so far, neurobiology can not explain. But both are about how the brain works now. Neither says anything about why our present brains are structured as they are, and neither deals very well with the issue of predispositions. For example, children do not learn the complexities of language from scratch; they have a "language instinct." We argue an evolutionary perspective provides a critical framework in the effort to understand the workings of the brain and the complexities of learning.

Canadian cognitive scientists Bereiter and Scardamalia argue that experts possess certain additional qualities that make them very special people. Experts start off as specialists. They know an awful lot about their own subjects; you can't fault them on detail, any more than you can fault a specialist. But experts have one vital attribute: They are able to "get outside themselves and their subjects" and look at their specialism from a distance. They are essentially quizzical. They ask themselves uncomfortable questions about their specialization's significance and its possible relevance. In a sense they know so much about their subject that their natural curiosity makes them inquisitive about many other things. They are quick to grasp the overall situation, rather than just deal with single parts. Big issues fascinate them.

The Italian geneticist Luigi Luca Cavalli-Sforza captured the essence of how an expert thinks in the introduction to his book *Genes, Peoples, and Languages* when he wrote: "This book surveys the research on human evolution from the many different fields of study that contribute to our knowledge. It is a history of the last hundred thousand years, relying on archeology, genetics, and linguistics. Happily, these three disciplines are now generating many new data and insights. All of them can be expected to converge toward a common story, and behind them must lie a single history. Singly, each approach has many lacunae, but hopefully their synthesis can help fill the gaps. Other sciences—cultural anthropology, demography, economy, ecology, sociology—are joining in the effort, and are justly becoming pillars of interpretation."[10]

Cavalli-Sforza described the problems the synthetic approach of the expert encounters when he noted: "It would be impossible to communicate the conclusions about human history and the causes of human evolution if one had to rely on the jargons of such diverse disciplines. Scientific terminology insures precision and increases the speed of communication among specialists, but it creates a barrier between them and the general public." He continues, "To some, history (including evolution) is not a science, because its results cannot be replicated and thus cannot be tested by the experimental method. But studying the same phenomenon from many different angles, from many disciplines, each of which supplies independent facts, has the value of largely independent repetition. This makes the multidisciplinary approach indispensable.[11] Bereiter and Scardamalia explained this in their own way: "Experts, we propose, tackle problems that increase their expertise, whereas [specialists] tend to tackle problems for which they do not have to extend themselves [by going beyond the rules and formulae they accept]. Experts indulge in progressive problem solving, that is they continually reformulate a problem at an ever-higher level as they achieve at lower levels, and uncover more of the nature of the issue. They become totally immersed in their work, and increase the complexity of the activity by developing new skills and taking on new challenges."[12]

The evolutionary biologist Ernst Mayr puts it even more succinctly when talking about the biologist's search for synthesis: "Being a biologist does not mean having a job; it means choosing a way of life. . . . They never lose the excitement of scientific discovery, nor the love of chasing after new ideas, new insights, new organisms. And so much in biology has a direct bearing on one's own circumstances and personal values."[13]

Experts with such high level "open thinking" are vastly important people in a culture that is changing so rapidly that it is hard to see where we are headed. Unlike the specialist's supreme confidence within a specialism (not much use when the walls of the specialism are falling apart!), the expert is essentially humble and questioning, more aware of what he doesn't yet know rather than what is already known. Experts, of course, know the rules, but they also know how to reformulate them, even when to break them so as to fit new circumstances. They are persistent, industrious, and always curious. They are always searching for the perfection that is always just out of their reach: "Let's back up on this problem. Think this one through again. See it from another perspective and imagine it in another way. Give ourselves a breather, and ask somebody else what they think." These are the words of the true expert.

The creation of conditions in which expertise can develop needs both the practices of constructivist learning and the rigors of subject-specific disciplines. It is in the study of expertise that we find the clues we need for developing models of learning that actively promote creativity, metacognition, and transferability. Expertise is a frame of mind that starts forming in the nursery and begins to mature in the primary school. While specialization has become a feature of modern society, it is not, however, particularly natural to the human brain that has evolved over the millennia to be a multifaceted, multitasked organism that is predisposed to think about any data, or ideas, from very many perspectives. It works in terms of wholes and parts simultaneously. The glory of human learning is that it is essentially a complex, messy, nonlinear process, and this fact collides with the central premises of behaviorism where the system must be first.

Taylor, of course, would have nothing to do with messiness, and in his scheme of things, craftsmanship was out and sense-making skills were deemed of no value. Productive work for the majority was no longer directly related to individual innovation and personal motivation. People were to be dumbed down, and Taylor understood this with brutal clarity. "In the past man has been first," he said. "In the future the system must be first."[14]

Taylor was only able to take control of the manufacturing process from the majority of workers by buying them out in a contract that precluded their individual thinking. Not surprisingly he initially faced much opposition from workers and their unions. A machinist gained prominence when he debated with Taylor in 1914 and remarked: "We don't want to work as fast as we are able to. We want to work as fast as we think it's comfortable for us to work. We haven't come into existence for the purpose of seeing how great a task we can perform through a lifetime. We are trying to regulate our work so as to make it auxiliary to our lives."[15] It was to placate this resistance that Taylor refused to take a factory as a client unless the owners first substantially raised wages, sometimes tripling them. Taylor's principle for increased productivity was simple: "You do it my way, by my standards, at the speed I mandate, and in so doing achieve a level of output I ordain, and I'll pay you handsomely for it, beyond anything you might have imagined. All you have to do is take orders, and give up your way of doing the job for mine."[16]

In defense of Taylor, the principles of scientific management would help alleviate the great social problem of his day: the schism between capital and workers. Taylor expressed before the U.S. Congress, and elsewhere, that by making manufacturing more efficient it would become more productive. In the end, workers would benefit most through higher wages, shorter work hours, better working conditions, and increasing access to the technological wonders of the time. Peter Drucker observed in the 1980s that, "It is Taylor who defeated Marx and Marxism. Taylor's scientific management not only tremendously increased output. It also made possible increasing workers' wages while at the same time cutting the product's prices and thereby increasing the demand for it."[17]

What role Taylor played in making the world safe for capitalism is open to debate, but what is beyond dispute is that his scientific management changed the relationship of workers to their workplace in a dramatic way. Edward Mott Woolley described a shop before and after scientific management: "Formerly, as in most shops, the mechanics did a large part of the planning how work was to be done. They studied their blueprints and what operations were necessary, which should come first and how they should be accomplished. They hunted up the . . . tools they needed, borrowing them with or without permission. They drove their planers or lathes at whatever feed and speed they thought right."

In the scientifically managed shop, the author went on, such archaic practices vanished: "Today the workmen do no planning. Every detail of work on every job is thought out for them and put down in unmistakable black and white. Not merely general directions but the specific instructions indicating operations necessary on each part and the factors bearing on these operations—the character and number of cuts, the depth of each, the tool to be used, the speed, the feed, the time allowed if a bonus or premium is to be earned, the hourly rate if the bonus is not attained."[18]

From the perspective of individual workers, accepting Taylor's scientific management was a Faustian bargain. They traded their own way of working things out for methods authorized by experts managing the industrial process from above the system, and in turn they received higher wages. The scientific management of work meant that most people would no longer need to "continue learning on the job" once they "found their proper role in the factory." This is an important point because Taylor, and his many disciples, felt a successful production system would help all men find their "natural place" in the work hierarchy. Such scientifically determined job placement would increase productivity because each man, based on an expert opinion from departments of personnel, would use his "natural talents" to improve the whole manufacturing process. However, "dumbed down" fathers no longer worked in an environment in which their children could learn experientially with them. The eons-old learning partnership between parents and children was severed within a generation. Children were probably the greatest of all losers within this bargain for parents who are not proud of their work often have little of practical experience to pass along to their children.

After World War I, and the obvious success of U.S. industrial production to provide the arsenal for the democracies, scientific management became influential outside of the United States as well as inside. The British were attracted to it due to their officer class mentality and their need to administer a vast empire. By 1920, a booklet by Taylor disciple Gustav Winter, *How to Introduce the Taylor System in Germany*, had sold 100,000 copies in that country. And Taylor's influence was not limited simply to the West. Lenin was one of his greatest advocates, stating that, "We must introduce into Russia the study and teaching of the new Taylor System and its systemic trial and adaptations."[19] Lenin, it should be noted, was also a follower of the psychologist Pavlov, and this gave a second scientific explanation for why communism could manipulate the human spirit.

So persuasive were the successes of scientific management that it spread in many countries across all aspects of social organizations. Taylor suggested that the lessons of improved factory production "can be applied to all social activities: to the management of our homes, the management of our farms, the management of the business of our tradesmen, large and small; of our churches, or philanthropic institutions, our universities and our government departments."[20]

Science Reaches the Schools

The overwhelming success of scientific management quickly spread into public schooling, and by 1910 Taylor's influence "extended to all American education from the elementary schools to the universities."[21] Primary players in taking the lessons of scientific management from the factory floor and applying them to social institutions, and in particular public schools, were the Carnegie Foundation for the Advancement of Teaching and the Carnegie Corporation of New York. Henry Pritchett was the first president of the foundation and remained in charge until 1930. During this time he managed to put an enduring stamp on the shape of its educational efforts. "Pritchett turned the foundation into a proponent of systematization in American education, and through education, American life. . . . His signal contribution . . . was to direct some of Carnegie's wealth and power that came with it to the organization of American education along more modern, national, scientific, and bureaucratic lines."[22] The factory school was delivered, ironically, through the wealth generated by the man who had such a strong affection for providing study in libraries.

Taylor's success at merging the understandings of science with the processes of industrialization had a profound effect on the relationship of learning to education, the goals of education, theories of education, and how it would be delivered. For starters, a primary aim of education became preparing workers for their place in rationally planned manufacturing. In the United States, the rhetoric of educational reformers and policy makers shifted from the emphasis on preparing citizens for a democracy toward how social capital could be developed most efficiently. Pritchett captured the spirit of the times when he argued in a 1907 speech that it is "more and more necessary that every human being should become an effective, economic unit. To accomplish this goal, what is needed is an educational system that is carefully adapted to the needs of the economy. Such a system must seek to produce economically useful knowledge and to sort people efficiently into the various positions that need to be filled in the stratified occupational structure,"[23] he argued.

Key to being able to function in a scientifically managed factory was the ability to read basic instruction manuals, fill out order forms and worksheets, and do basic mathematical calculations: in other words, to become an efficient economic unit. In short, all workers needed to be equipped with the three R's in order to navigate their way through the modern industrial workplace. The pedagogy that emerged in schools only took several decades for most countries to move literacy rates from the single digits into the 80 and 90 percentiles. Schools also became central in sorting individuals out to meet the various needs of the increasingly specialized labor market.

Education would identify, through a scientific merit-based process of sorting, those who should receive advanced education in order to move into managerial and leadership positions and those who should simply receive a basic education and then move directly out onto the factory floor. It was a system that operated under the premise that 10 percent would lead and 90 percent would follow. In 1897, Charles Eliot the president of Harvard, said: "The duty of democratic education, in addition to preparing a whole literate populace, was to cultivate the natural aristocracy, so that the whole community could benefit from the fulfillment of its ablest citizens . . . and so that educational resources would not be wasted on those unable to employ them profitably."[24]

This process of educational sorting may appear at first glance to us in the early 21st century as undemocratic, but in the United States 100 years ago it was accepted because it was seen by most as being a fair system. It was the same for everyone. If you had natural "smarts" you'd be very successful, and if you didn't the system would sort you out and give you the basic skills you needed to make a living on the factory floor. It was designed to offer rewards based on merit rather than on such ascribed characteristics as class, race, and gender. Additionally, such meritocratic systems were seen "as an antidote to corruption[;] good-government advocates sought to centralize decision making in the hands of professional administrators. They became infatuated with the creed of scientific management, which promised to improve organizational performance and promote new levels of efficiency."[25]

The factory system of education that emerged in the United States was not unique to that country. The English educational historian David Wardle noted the following about the English system: "It was the factory put into the educational setting. . . . Every characteristic was there, minute division of labor[,] . . . a complicated system of incentives to do good work, an impressive system of inspection, and finally an attention to cost efficiency and the economic use of plant."[26]

Compromise and Mixed Motives

Historically, schooling emerged through a series of compromises to serve diverse interests and needs. In the center of these compromises were the interests of the nation state, which was itself a new mass phenomenon in the middle to late 1800s. The learning needs of the child were never central or even really understood, and that was what people like Pestalozzi, Froebel, Dewey, and Montessori were up against. From this historical perspective it is fair to say that if schooling helped some children take responsibility for their own learning, it was more by accident than design, and it probably reflected the home influence more than the school.

Of the many factors that went into the creation and growth of state sponsored educational systems, few had anything to do with a serious attempt to understand children's learning. The sort of basic training that schools provided was effective for the time because what unlocked the door for success in a manufacturing workplace was literacy in reading and math. With the passing of compulsory education laws, if children complained at this simplistic curriculum as just not appealing to their interest then, to the purist, this simply meant they needed correction—originally with the whip and then psychological analysis.

Education systems emerged through a complex series of compromises to help national governments expand and maintain their credibility by dealing with the traumatic shift from agrarian societies of small communities to factory-based societies of large and impersonal cities and workplaces. The compromises were between political leaders and those they led in the form of educational opportunity and improving standards of living for trading in their earlier loyalties to small farms and small towns. They were also between workers and owners in the exchange of personal responsibility for bigger paychecks; they were between scientific ideas, technological change, and traditional values; they were between different ethnic groups; they were between families, communities, and economies of scale; and they were between children and adults.

Schools were designed to keep children out of the way of working adults while at the same time providing them with the skills, values, and attitudes necessary to survive in a mass-industrial society in as cost-efficient a way as possible. Mass systems of education carried out this mission admirably, and much of the world's economic growth over the past 100 years is largely related to this success.

Schools facilitated children's ability to make the transition from the old way (their parent's, grandparent's, and local community's way) of doing things to the new way defined by specialists and the technologies spawned by impersonal economic forces. "The world did not double or treble its movement between 1800 and 1900," the U.S. historian Henry Adams wrote in 1909, "but, measured by any standard. . . [,] the tension and vibration and volume and so-called progression of society were fully a thousand times greater in 1900 than in 1800; the force had doubled ten times over, and the speed, when measured by electrical standards as in telegraphy, approached infinity, and had annihilated both space and time."[27] The period of rapid change that propelled the emergence of the modern system of schooling led, after World War II, to a period of massive expansion and consolidation for education systems. In 1997 in the United States, education was a $564 billion enterprise.[28] The OECD observed, "This expenditure is difficult for governments to contain, since most comes from public sources and pays for schools, whose resourcing structures are well entrenched."[29]

The growth in education systems since the 1980s has exceeded that of the growth in gross domestic product for most western countries. It is doubtful, over the long-run, that these systems will be able to expand upwards and downwards indefinitely. This is especially true when one considers the approaching retirement of the babyboom generation that will undoubtedly stretch government coffers on both sides of the Atlantic. Also, it is important to consider the fact that "between 1987 and 1996, the average tuition price jumped 132 percent for public, four-year colleges and universities and 99 percent for private ones in the United States."[30] Tuition increases have dramatically outpaced inflation and wage increases for all but the richest.

The point here is this: If we are serious about giving all children a chance to enjoy the fruits of success in the 21st century, then it is necessary to be more creative than just seeking more schooling in the same way we have always pretty much gone about providing it. This is a central reason we argue for "turning systems of education upside down." For example, if young people have taken responsibility for their own lifelong learning by the age of 18, then they do not necessarily need four or five years of classroom based higher education. They could be just as successful studying two or three years on campus and two years studying on-line while taking an internship. This would lessen the cost of higher education and, managed correctly, could make receiving a college degree far more commonplace.

●　　　●　　　●

The problem facing education systems at the close of the 20th century is that while the economies, societies, and cultures of which they are a part are changing radically, schools continue to do what they have done for a better part of a century in pretty much the same way the early behaviorists suggested they should. The conflict emerging at the beginning of the 21st century is between massive and entrenched systems of education designed for a very different time and the needs of post-industrial societies being transformed in ways possibly even more radical than that of 100 years ago.

6 The Struggle of Ideas

*Reforms that deal with the fundamental stuff of education—
teaching and learning—seem to have weak, transitory, and
ephemeral effects; while those that expand, solidify and
entrench school bureaucracy seem to have strong, enduring
and concrete effects.*

THE RAND CORPORATION

For most of the 20th century, there were two dominant, and competing, schools of thought about learning and curriculum development. These dueling philosophies had their roots deep in western thought, and are in many ways diametrically opposed. The first had its origins in Plato's Republic while the other emerged from the thinking of the Naturalists, of whom the French philosopher Rousseau was the first of a number of influential 18th and 19th century thinkers.

Plato and Rosseau: The Teacher-Based Approach, or the Child as Instinctive Learner?

Plato saw the role of education as providing students with the knowledge necessary to achieve a foundation of truth and certainty. Education, to a large extent, was about refining the human spirit and honing it to the higher ideals of the state.[1] For it was learning and appreciating the reality defined by the polis (through government, preferably a just one) that provided the raison d'être for education. The University of Chicago scholar Kieran Egan has observed that for Plato, "Education was to be a process of learning those forms of knowledge that would give students a privileged, rational view of reality. Only by disciplined study of increasingly abstract forms of knowledge, guided by a kind of spiritual commitment, could the mind transcend the conventional beliefs, prejudices, and stereotypes of the time and come to see reality clearly."[2]

Ever since, all forms of Western education have resonated to varying degrees with Plato's view of education, and in particular his emphasis on an academic curriculum being central to the development of a strong and rational mind. In this view of education and learning, the teacher played the central role because he was the expert who provided students with the knowledge-base necessary to understand reality. In this teacher-centered form of education, it was assumed that the student would simply absorb all the knowledge and wisdom of the instructor through active participation and dialogue. This model of learning worked well for an elite minority with little access to books because they had plenty of time to talk and question their teachers who were the top thinkers of their day. Additionally, what they taught mattered because it was connected to the political gestalt of the city-state.

This didactic form of education for the elite would be the dominant model of learning until well into the 19th century.[3] It assumed that a child was a still-to-be-formed creature whose instinctual impulses need less to be encouraged than to be molded to the ways of society. From this unambiguous perspective the only issues really worth fighting about would be over access (who would get to be educated) and content (what would inform "an academic curriculum"). To achieve cultural literacy, should the curriculum be religiously based, scientifically based, classical, or a mixture of all three and more? Early in the 20th century on continental Europe, the discussion on the curriculum often dealt with issues of what to teach in history and languages. For example, should the Polish language and history be taught to those students from the Polish minority in German schools?

The Enlightenment thinker Jean-Jacques Rousseau in his book *Emile*, published in 1762, challenged this singular focus on specific teacher-based knowledge driving the learning process. Rousseau argued that, "Education results from an internal, developmental process unfolding within a supportive environment; development drives knowledge, determining what knowledge is learnable, meaningful, and relevant."[4] In contrast to Judeo-Christian thinking about education that had built on Plato's views, Rousseau believed children are born in a natural state of goodness and need to be protected from the sins of the world and allowed to develop their basic good nature. In his perspective, childhood meant more freedom for the child and a more open form of teaching. The child should have an influence over what was taught and how it was taught. Rousseau moved the debate about education well beyond just issues of content to issues of methods and form.

For Rousseau, the role of the good teacher was vastly different from that of Plato. The teacher was to help allow the natural inclinations of the human individual to unfold and endure through personal discovery and experience. Process was more important than content. Inherent to such thinking about the nature of human uniqueness was the acceptance of children being born with differing traits and predispositions, and as such this was fertile ground for the idea of child-centered learning.

The brain of the child, according to Rousseau's thinking about learning, was far more than just a blank slate waiting for the environment to mold it. There was a political aspect to all this as well. Rousseau believed strongly in individual responsibility and the rights of all citizens to be free. He also pleaded for a utopian system of world peace and world citizenship. For these reasons, the ideas of Rousseau would be attacked by those who argued, in the spirit of Plato, that self-realization meant obedience to authority because the individual will, the true rational will, was part of, and expressed in, the will of the state. Rousseau's ideas therefore collided head-on with the 19th century struggle between the rights of individuals and the controlling interests of the nation-state.

Teacher-Centered Instruction vs. Student-Centered Instruction: John Dewey

These competing philosophies of learning and education endured to inform the work of John Dewey and Edward Thorndike. Dewey, whose philosophic writings spanned more than half a century before his death in 1952, built on many of these ideas about natural learning when he advocated an experiential form of learning that focused on the particular strengths and weaknesses of individual children. His thinking about how children learn, the nature of the schools that would support this, and the relationship between schooling and the kind of community that this would create led Dewey in his later years into many contentious areas, including a visit to the Soviet Union in 1928.

These controversies, however, should not minimize the extraordinary insights he developed on the nature of human creativity. He was one of the first to comprehend the radical significance of Darwinian theory on the operation of the human brain, and he opened up questions about the relationship of human nature to the kinds of experience that would, or would not, nurture powerful learning. Inevitably, his energy and idealism led him to articulate concepts that slower and more traditional thinkers found hard to accept. Yet, in his understanding of the relationship of the young learner to the life of the community, Dewey set an agenda that has still to be fully realized.

Dewey held that the individual learning process was as unique as the human fingerprint. This meant each child needed the freedom, challenge, and responsibility to develop his or her own powers to some ultimate purpose through the guidance of one whose own experience was richer. His theory of effective learning reflected more of a mentor/apprentice group relationship than a formal instructor working in the closed environment of a structured classroom with pupils. It was as if Dewey looked backwards to a pre-industrial age to see what life could be like in a modern democracy.

Dewey appreciated the fact that in apprenticeship, learners saw the processes of work unfold in its totality. Young people understood how what they learned was connected to a greater whole. It was just this sort of learning environment that had influenced Dewey himself as a child growing up in Burlington, Vermont, in the 1860s. In his youth, all children were brought into the intimate contact of a whole range of simple industrial and agricultural occupations. Young people at this time, wrote Dewey's daughter years later, were responsible for "assuming a share in household activities and responsibilities. . . . On the other hand, school was a bore, not only to his companions, but to himself, who were interested in reading almost anything except their school books, and its tiresomeness was mitigated only by the occasional teacher who encouraged conversation on outside topics. . . . The realization that the most important parts of his own education until he entered college were obtained outside the school-room played a large role in his [adult] educational work, in which such importance is attached, both in theory and in practice, to occupational activities as the most effective approaches to genuine learning and to personal intellectual discipline."[5]

This more inclusive form of learning set Dewey apart from most educators of his time, and it sets him apart from many today. He was convinced that learning and education were far more than schooling. For him, "education includes schooling, but is by no means restricted to it. In its most inclusive meaning education denotes any change wrought in an individual as a result of experience. In its narrower, deliberate form education signifies conscious effort by some organized group to shape the conduct and the emotional and intellectual predispositions of its young."[6] In his view this more inclusive and open form of education was liberating, while the more closed method of formal instruction was potentially deadening.

The work of Dewey reflected his deep appreciation of Darwin's work on evolution. He, however, went much further in his thinking about evolution than just focusing on the survival of the fittest. This set him apart from many of his peers who were preoccupied simply with cultural concerns. He accepted that humans entered the world with traits, capacities, and interests inherited from a long evolutionary history, but he also believed upbringing and experience greatly influenced what a child would become. It is important to remember that for the first half of the 20th century, Western philosophers, despite the uncertainty created by Darwin's theory of evolution and even Einstein's 1915 theory of relativity, sought certainty in the social sciences. They looked to the physical sciences and the mathematics of Newton for compelling models of rigorous inquiry that led to firm results. "Students of society and politics, unhappy with merely descriptive accounts, struggled to construct a social science that would produce quantifiable, verifiable, and, above all, value-free knowledge useful to social engineers as well as scholars."[7] Behaviorist psychology epitomized this model of scientific inquiry. This did not satisfy Dewey, whose whole career was largely dedicated to finding an appropriate balance between nature and nurture.

Dewey was unusual in that he accepted uncertainty and the open and dynamic nature of life. In their quest to understand what this meant, many of his followers later trivialized his thinking to suggest that he was no more than a moral relativist. This is to oversimplify a man who was one of the first to struggle with the complexity and messiness of human learning and development. He argued that "our world is not one, but many; that it is a dynamic, changing world, not static and finished; that in this plural world from which individuality is not to be eliminated, the course of events is contingent, not predetermined by antecedent forces, either material or spiritual . . . although existence is characterized by recurring sequences and many relatively constant correlations between events, nature as a whole is 'an affair of affairs' with no once and for all beginning of everything, and without any final, all-embracing end toward which it trends . . . although our world is such as to permit the emergence and continued existence of living forms, including human beings with all their distinctive intellectual and moral traits, 'nature has no preference for good things over bad things, its mills turn out any kind of grist indifferently'."[8] To those already struggling with the spiritual implications of Darwinism, the proposition that nature might well be indifferent to moral virtue was hard for his contemporaries to take. Many traditionalists feared his message.

For Dewey, unlike Rousseau, there was no certainty that all children were born good or that knowledge was absolute, immutable, or eternal; rather, knowledge was relative to the developmental interaction of man with his world. Not surprisingly, because Dewey accepted the evolutionary argument that nature is incredibly diverse, and changes over time, he held that human societies, values, and belief systems should evolve over time. Dewey was not alone in raising difficult issues. Maria Montessori spoke for many thoughtful educational reformers in Europe and the United States in the early 20th century when she asked, "How will we solve the many wide-spread detrimental conditions of crime, violence, poverty and environmental devastation that threaten to destroy our civilized way of life? I believe that these imposing man-made problems have their origins in the formation of the human personality, and that we should therefore look to the child's formative development for an ultimate solution."[9]

Such progressive educationalists challenged society to understand that the way in which it treated children would directly condition the kind of society it would eventually create. School and community were not isolated institutions but were interconnected at every level. Again this was hard for social commentators of the day to stomach. Critics were bent on scientific descriptions of development that sought to reduce everything to quantifiable and individual subcomponents. In an England where Queen Victoria's view was that "little children should be seen and not heard," and in the United States where the 1920s Scope's trial pitted the forces of science against religious tradition, such a well-articulated case that nature and nurture were finely and dynamically balanced in every child was too strong a prescription for many to accept.

Learning, such radical educational philosophers argued, was significantly more than just schooling. Therefore, they sought to develop forms of education that were concerned to develop the child as a responsible thinker. They were not simply concerned with the functional skills of schooling, but they were deeply interested in the development of young minds that could play a responsible part in democratic discussion. Again, this antagonized conventional thinking, which, not without reason, was terrified at the implications of the masses becoming too thoughtful for fear it would upset the status quo.

The Swiss developmental psychologist Jean Piaget suggested as a young man in the 1920s the presence of well-defined "developmental stages" that argued the child was constantly creating and then refining his own model of reality. Mental growth was achieved by integrating simpler concepts into higher-level concepts at definite stages of the child's life. Piaget identified four stages within his "genetic epistemology," which he tied, perhaps too tightly, to chronological age. The theory of distinct developmental stages strengthened the appreciation of genetic (nature) predispositions linked to overall mental development. Critically, Piaget saw the teacher not as just the transmitter of knowledge but as a guide to the child's own discovery of the world.

This more inclusive view of learning was echoed by the CEO of the Boeing Corporation in 1991 when he told the National Association of Secondary School Principals, "Give me guides on the side, not sages on the stage."[10] This is a fascinating example of the way in which leading late

20th century employers who are so frequently quoted by politicians as demanding only basic skills are actually far closer to the realities expressed by the early 20th century "progressive educators " than are the policymakers themselves.

Dewey and the Tension Between Economics and Education

Dewey was consciously reacting against the deadening effects of scientific management when he argued "a society is a number of people held together because they are working along common lines, in a common spirit, and with references to common ends."[11] At the time he was writing, communities were being pulled apart by economic forces that were of an impersonal scale, yet few other than Dewey saw the direct connection between the new dynamic industrial structures, the destruction of community, and the impact it would inevitably have on children's learning. Dewey was an inclusive thinker at a time when most of his contemporaries were content to look at aspects of the whole—but not at the whole itself.

Dewey saw that the mass industrialization of work and consumption led to a disconnected world of individual bits that made little sense to the average person. In 1929 he wrote: "If few workers know what they are making or the meaning of what they do, and still fewer know what becomes of the work of their hands—in the largest industry of Middletown perhaps one-tenth of one percent of the product is consumed locally—this is doubtless because we have so perfected our system of distribution that the whole country is one. And if the mass of workers live in constant fear of loss of their jobs, this is doubtless because our spirit of progress, manifest in change of fashions, invention of new machines and power of overproduction, keeps everything on the move. . . . We live as if economic forces determine the growth and decay of institutions and settled the fate of individuals. Liberty becomes a well-nigh obsolete term; we start, go, and stop at the signal of a vast industrial machine. . . . The philosophy appropriate to such a situation is that of struggle for existence and survival of the economically fit."[12] Dewey, the philosopher deeply committed to helping young people develop their full potential, was much troubled by the schism between our natures as human beings and the societies that mass industrialization was creating.

This singular emphasis on economic efficiency, to Dewey's mind, was a public philosophy degrading to humanity. Economics for Dewey was not an end in itself but a means to an end: the creation of a just and equitable democratic society. Dewey saw mass industrialization as curtailing democratic freedom and the sort of community cohesiveness he saw as central to successful induction of young people into a thoughtful world. As a philosopher, Dewey floundered in his search for an economic theory which would sustain his participatory democratic ideals. His faith in the benign power of the state to provide stability and intellectual and social openness was, in hindsight, misplaced. State-dominated economic stability, the second half of the 20th century has taught us, came at the cost of restricting personal initiative, personal responsibility, and critical independent thinking.

The paradox that Dewey didn't appreciate was that state domination of economics, which he advocated in the name of open democratic thinking, did not free the individual to take on more thoughtful pursuits than the grubbiness of making money. Instead, state domination of the economy actually facilitated the mediocre standard of group consensus.

Teacher-Centered Instruction vs. Student-Centered Instruction: From Plato to Thorndike

As much of Dewey's philosophy about learning, education and community reflected Darwin's ideas about dynamic living systems, so Edward Thorndike's *Educational Psychology,* published in 1913, followed Newton's methodology of using measured observations and predictions to come up with once and for all answers to complex issues, such as how it is people actually learn. To the United States in the early 20th century, this was a critical issue. It was a time of massive immigration. Fully 72 percent of children in New York had parents who were born outside of America, while a massive one in seven of the total population had themselves been born outside the United States.

The rapid assimilation of millions of immigrants into the mainstream culture of the United States became a task that came to dominate educational thought. Attractive as were Dewey's ideas to thoughtful people in a stable society, they seemed far too idealistic to policymakers working a short-term agenda to radically transform people and their attitudes. Within this cultural milieu a common view of U.S. community was an almost nonexistent concept, other than at the school. Schools had to function quickly, efficiently, and cheaply, and Edward Thorndike stepped into this with arguments that it was possible to develop a reductionist basis for classroom instruction that would build on the work of behaviorist psychology.

As we have already seen, behaviorism emphasized the precise quantification of the conditions of learning (the input) and the learner's response (the output). Thorndike claimed that "items to be learned—such as vocabulary words or arithmetic facts—could be quantified, as could the speed and accuracy of a pupil's response. With a theory of the relationship between what goes into a student in the classroom and what comes out, Thorndike had a science of education."[13] The problem with this approach, we can now see at the beginning of the 21st century, was behaviorism's highly simplistic view of the relationship between learning and the brain. The brain makes sense of the world by making its own connections, not simply by being fed information.

It is now fair to say that Thorndike's scientific model of education was no more scientific than Taylor's scientific management of factory workers, but both have had staying power because they provided results. Both shaped individuals to fit the needs of systems, and this led to increased efficiency. Thorndike's model of education created a classroom environment that successfully equipped most young people with the basic skills necessary for surviving in a manufacturing environment, and it prepared them for a life in a bureaucracy where they were largely told what to do and how to do it. It also worked to make Americans out of millions of immigrants, and in turn it has helped to create a relatively stable and prosperous democracy.

These are major accomplishments, but the success of such systems of education came at the cost of individual responsibility, in particular individual responsibility for students' own learning. Learning became something schools did to you. In a perversion of the learning process, teachers became more important to learning than did the students' responsibility for developing their own learning strategies.

It was this primacy given to teachers and teaching that informed Thorndike's dream "to turn all teaching into a scientific profession in which all educators would be guided by the scientific method and spirit. As scientific professionals, educators would be concerned with controlling the learning of students and with scientific measurement of results. In Thorndike's world, the scientifically constructed test was at the heart of the educational process: "Testing the results of teaching and study is for the teacher what verification of theories is to the scientist. . . . It is the chief means of fitting teaching to the previous experience and individual capacities of pupils."[14] The problem with Thorndike's theory of learning was that it assumed learning to be highly linear and completely driven by rational thinking and extrinsic motivation. The point to remember, in hindsight, is that Thorndike's theory of learning was incredibly limited.

Thorndike's theory that a standard form of testing was the only scientific way to measure learning was widely accepted. "A particular advantage of tests is that they make it possible to specify instructional goals in terms that are easily quantifiable. Instead of saying, 'The child is expected to learn . . . ,' a teacher can say, 'The child is expected to answer correctly eight out of ten questions on his test'."[15] Within such a model of learning, once the tests are constructed and agreed upon, then teachers can start working with children to develop expertise in solving problems based on the content of the tests. The curriculum can be designed for the testing regime, and a successful teacher is one who can adequately prepare all students to excel at answering correctly the questions on the tests. For the student, being able to recall information becomes central to the education process. Rote learning was now ready to come to the forefront.

Standardized tests utilizing multiple-choice questions now popular in many communities do measure how well someone has received information and how well they have retained it, at least in the short-term. But these tests do a poor job of identifying thinking and reasoning skills. This is a critical point, because if one accepts the premise that high test scores mean the same thing as actually developing understanding about a topic or field of study, then a successful system of education is one that annually produces increased numbers of young people who score higher on test scores than those of earlier years. Such systems are attractive to politicians and policymakers because they provide clear markers for success and failure. They offer the basis for accountability (their own accountability, at least, if not students'). In this view of education, learning is a straightforward proposition: tell 'em and test 'em.

The Middle Ground Between Basic Skills and Thinking Skills

Dewey didn't believe education was as simple as Thorndike's science of learning made it seem. "In school amassing information always tends to escape from the ideal of wisdom or good judgement. The aim often seems to be to make the pupil what has been called a 'cyclopedia of useless information.' 'Covering the ground' is the primary necessity; the nurture of mind a bad second. Thinking cannot, of course, go on in a vacuum; suggestions and inferences can occur only upon a basis of information and matters of fact. . . . But there is all the difference in the world whether the acquisition of information is treated as an end in itself, or is made an integral portion of the training of thought. The assumption that information which has been accumulated apart from use in the recognition and solution of a problem, may later on be freely employed at will by thought is quite false. . . . Because their knowledge has been achieved in connection with the needs of specific situations, men of little book-learning are often able to put to effective use every ounce of knowledge they possess; while men of vast erudition are often swamped by the mere bulk of their learning, because memory, rather than thinking, has been operative in obtaining it."[16]

Dewey maintained that humans actually achieve understanding when they can make connections among two or more apparently separate problems or disciplines. In other words simply understanding academic positions can often confuse people's thinking. Because of the sheer volume of what they have read, many that use strictly academic thinking become muddled in their understanding of the world. They have less understanding of the total picture than more practical people, people often decried by the academic as not being properly knowledgeable. This point has been made time and again by such thinkers as Jefferson, Rousseau, and, of course, the writer of Ecclesiastes who said "of the writing of books there is no end, and much study wearies the mind."[17] The problem of information overload is even more acute at the beginning of the 21st century when it seems that there are few people wise enough, or who even have the attention span, to distil valid generalizations out of such a surfeit of information.

In an appreciation of the paradoxes of much of modern life, when Dewey sought a middle ground he criticized both traditionalist advocates of a studies-centered curriculum based on rote memorization and those reformers given to a romantic, child-centered pedagogy. In his seminal work, *Democracy and Education*, Dewey called on educators to build upon the impulses that children brought with them to school, but he attacked those who would merely give those impulses free-rein. Rather than leave children to their own devices (as romantics recommended), or impose subject matter on pupils (as traditional pedagogues endorsed), Dewey proposed creating an environment in which the child, engaged in a familiar activity, would be confronted with a problem solvable only with the aid of the knowledge and skills supplied by traditional subjects. Dewey equated successful learning with the ability of children to make valid and useful connections between current knowledge and applying it to new information.

It may come as a surprise to many in our time that the balance that Dewey sought is now central to the work done on metacognition by cognitive scientists. Cognitive scientists argued in the 1990s that the development of basic skills and higher-order skills is not contradictory, but that these skills are actually developed in concert.[18] This balancing act between content and process, Dewey admitted, required excellent teachers to facilitate the learning needs of students.

Unfortunately, as with Froebel and others, many of Dewey's greatest advocates misapplied what he taught, and over time this has led to unsound, careless, and even extreme expressions of educational philosophy. It is just this sort of muddled educational thinking that has been so easily discredited as faddish innovations. The conflict between formal instruction and experiential learning that has characterized so much of educational debate in the late 20th century was first played out with Dewey's emphasis on a balance between good teaching and children's differing learning styles and Thorndike's vision of education that was highly analytical, uniform, clear, and measurable. Thorndike's model assumed that everything that matters can be counted, and that which can't be counted doesn't matter.

What Thorndike did for education was similar to what Frederick Winslow Taylor did for manufacturing. He selectively applied the scientific understandings of his day to study how people learned and then used this knowledge (which we now understand to be limited) to develop methods of delivery that would be highly efficient, highly replicable, easily measured, and politically acceptable. Thorndike helped to make teaching so well planned that the teachers operated as well-trained line managers delivering a standard product in the same way to all pupils. Just this sort of mechanistic reasoning allows educational policymakers, as a spokesperson for the British Prime Minister did in 1996, to feel confident in making the argument that, "We are not convinced that there are enough good teachers so we have emphasized a 'teacher proof' curriculum." Much of this book will show just how inappropriate Thorndike's and Taylor's ideas now are to the kind of world in which we live and in which children have to learn. If this is the case, then it is not difficult to understand why far greater attention needs to be given to the theory of metacognition as going well beyond the mechanistic thoughts of Edward Thorndike and his followers and giving a more secure neurological base to Dewey's theory.

Thoughtful teachers have always had to live with paradox. Not only do no two children learn the same way, but a single child learns different things in different ways. Not only does education involve the transmission of culture, but it also has to involve the development of those critical skills that challenge that culture to evolve.

Teachers understood quickly that Dewey's theories captured the essence of the learning they saw going on with their students every day, but they also recognized that a complex society sought systematization. The problem facing several generations of teachers "was that many of these approaches to instruction contradicted one another. It was difficult to reconcile the doctrines of John Dewey with those of Edward Thorndike, for example, or the demands of efficiency with those for child-centered education. . . . Teachers were beset with contradictory 'impulses to be efficient, scientific, child-centered, and authoritative,' and the result was that 'teachers constructed patchwork compromises to contain these competing, often contradictory, impulses but at a cost of leaving within many a vague uneasiness over the aims of classroom discipline, and relations with students that seldom [went] away'."[19]

The tensions remain obvious to everyone concerned with learning and education, and much government policy in the United Kingdom and the United States has been about trying to resolve the paradox by discrediting any ideas that hold learning to be both messy and complex. But, regardless of what the powerful might say, many teachers and parents see that learning cannot be easily packaged, delivered, and assessed. While we shouldn't minimize the importance of all children being able to read, write, and do mathematics, we should also recognize that learning the skills, attitudes, and values to be a productive citizen and worker in the 21st century requires more than excelling at academic tests. The basic skills are the foundations on which other learning is built, but it is simplistic to see these as the final terminus or even an intermediate point for any child.

Unfortunately, as we zoom into the 21st century, "the reforms that deal with the fundamental stuff of education—teaching and learning—seem to have weak, transitory, and ephemeral effects; while those that expand, solidify, and entrench school bureaucracy seem to have strong, enduring, and concrete effects."[20] So stated the RAND Corporation, a premier, nonpartisan research group, in a major study on education systems in 1988. The system reigns supreme at the expense of many young people who are not developing the skills necessary for success in a world defined by rapid change and adaptation.

Intelligence and Its Development

During the creation and consolidation of education systems in the first half of the 20th century, big ideas from biology, psychology, and philosophy profoundly influenced the thinking of teachers, administrators, and educational policymakers, yet the needs of the systems to be efficient largely channeled how these ideas were used. An excellent example is provided by the way new understandings about intelligence, and how it could be measured, were applied. The concept of intelligence was certainly not new. It had long been recognized that some people had got "it" while others did not, but the whole idea was so nebulous that it was comfortably left as something that could not be usefully quantified.

Consistent with the behaviorist principle that what matters can be counted, Francis Galton (1822–1911) believed not only that intelligence was determined by nature, but that it was static and could therefore be fully measured by IQ tests. (He went even further and suggested that future society would benefit if intelligent people were encouraged to procreate more frequently.) Galton was the first of many to form a narrow and "scientifically supported" interpretation where children's intelligence was seen strictly as inherited and static. This view was to be the overwhelming position of psychologists—and to many within education—until well into the later half of the 20th century, and arguments over the credibility of IQ testing echoed the behaviorist vs. child-centered, progressive vs. traditionalist debates. As Michael Gazzaniga says: "The entire history of intelligence testing spells out a story of how the personal beliefs of each investigator correlate with the side of the nature-nurture question each defends."

The name of the French psychologist Alfred Binet (1857–1911) is synonymous with the IQ test. Binet and his colleague Theodore Simon were commissioned by the French ministry of education "to devise a means to predict school performance[;] he cast around for test items. . . . He developed a test of intelligence, published in 1905, that measured things such as vocabulary ('what does misanthrope mean?'), comprehension, ('why do people sometimes borrow money?') and verbal relations ('what do an orange, an apple, and a pear have in common?'). Binet's tests of judgement were so successful at predicting school performance that a variant of them, called the Stanford-Binet Intelligence Scale (fourth edition), is still in use today."[21] An irony in all this is that Binet developed the IQ test to help identify children with specific learning problems. He felt that "intelligence, in any meaningful sense of the word, can be augmented by good education; it is not a fixed and inborn quantity."[22] He wrote: "It is in this practical sense, the only one accessible to us, that we say that the intelligence of these children has been increased. We have increased what constitutes the intelligence of a pupil: the capacity to learn and to assimilate instruction."[23]

Binet fully appreciated that the nature of intelligence was too complex to be defined entirely by a single test, no matter how clever the test itself might be. Even more radically for the time, Binet felt education and learning could actually improve a child's intelligence. Work over the past 20 years by researchers into the nature of human intelligence has revolutionized the way we understand such innate abilities. In 1984, Gardner postulated the concept of multiple intelligences. Initially he identified seven forms of intelligence, each one of which could be separately identified, and measurements suggested that none of them was directly correlated to any other. These different intelligences enable each person to find their way around the world in different ways: linguistically, numerically, spatially, kinesthetically, musically, and in terms of interpersonal skills and intra-personal skills.[24] With this analysis, researchers have become fascinated in trying to understand the mechanisms by which each child inherits a unique profile of these varying skills. (Why is it that one child is like a poet, another like a mechanic and another apparently nothing, even when their home culture appears identical?) Gardner's work argues that to reduce all forms of intelligence to a single quotient is largely meaningless.

David Perkins's work on the "learnability of intelligence" makes a distinction between the genetic base of intelligence and those forms of intelligence based on content specific skills (i.e. what makes a good car mechanic or a heart surgeon), as well as that form of intelligence that is based on reflection and a quizzical approach characterized by the nature of expertise.[25] Perkins argues that "most young people operate well below their natural level of intelligence, and if this could be raised by 20 percent the results would be a very different world indeed."[26] He has identified three components to intelligence: the fixed neurological intelligence linked to IQ tests; the specialized knowledge and experience that individuals acquire over time; and reflective intelligence, the ability to become aware of one's mental habits and transcend limited patterns of thinking.

Although all these forms of intelligence function simultaneously, it is reflective intelligence, Perkins says, that affords the best opportunity to amplify human intellect. This is the kind of intelligence that can be taught, and it helps people make wise personal decisions, solve challenging technical problems, find creative ideas, and learn complex topics in different areas. Perkins noted in 1992, however, that "Hardly anything in the conventional education practice promotes, in a direct and straightforward way, thoughtfulness and the use of strategies to guide thinking. Those students who acquire reflective intelligence build it on their own, by working at personal repertoires of strategies. Or they pick it up from the home environment, where some parents more than others model good reasoning in dinner table conversations, press their children to think out decisions, emphasize the importance of a systemic approach to school work and so on."[27]

Since the early 1990s, there has been pioneering work on emotional intelligence, which was first lucidly described by Joseph LeDoux, Antonio Demasio, and Daniel Goleman. The key point emerging from this work is that learning is driven as much, if not more, by emotions as it is by intellect. The link between the emotions and intrinsic motivation should surprise no one; consequently, the sterility of emotionally drained and aesthetically neutered learning environments has to be understood as contributing to low learning achievement.

Intelligence Is Far More Than Just IQ

Expanding on Gardner's ideas of multiple intelligence, Zohar and Marshall argued in their 2000 book *Spiritual Intelligence: The Ultimate Intelligence*[28] that to think in terms of humans as being shaped by "selfish genes" defined solely by intellectual powers was, at a philosophical level, to minimize the individual's perceived identity, self-worth, and uniqueness. Such reductionism left vast numbers of people numbed by a sense of isolation. Zohar and Marshall describe contemporary work, emerging out of the study of consciousness, that could begin to create a more hopeful set of scientific theories about how we view ourselves and our relationship to others.

As noted earlier in this book, the 30,000 year old bone with the inscriptions of the phases of the moon revealed humans to be an inquisitive species. Throughout our history we have been pondering eternal questions about the meaning of life, our place in the universe, the nature of God, and ultimate purpose. The search for a better understanding of such fundamental questions has led to some of the greatest works of art, literature, music, and architecture, and it is the essence of philosophy and the sciences. Every civilization has channeled the spiritual search for ultimate meaning into some form of religious observation, and not always with benign results.

Studying this phenomenon evolutionary psychologists have reached what to many is a most obvious conclusion: A developed sense of spiritual intelligence is an evolutionary advantage. Those who have it are better able to keep going in conditions when others might simply give up. This sense of purpose gives a heightened intrinsic motivation and a reason for living. Despite our technologically advanced societies, people in the early 21st century still seem to be aware that there is some form of spiritual dimension to life that is not accounted for by our current understandings of the mind or of intelligence. Human beings, it seems, are essentially spiritual creatures because we are driven by the need to ask fundamental, or ultimate, questions.

Zohar and Marshall seek to understand "spiritual intelligence" by addressing the possible significance of high frequency (40hz) neural oscillations in the brain. New brain imaging technologies have shown that these oscillations move as ripples right across all aspects of the cortex, the retina, and the thalamus. Thus, both localized and more generalized oscillations transcend the ability of any single neuron or groups of neurons to communicate and collate perceptual and intellectual processes across the whole brain. They give a form of mental cohesion that had earlier been seen as simply separate intellectual and emotional intelligences. Unlike all other forms of neural oscillations, which are directly related to some form of external stimuli, these high-level neural oscillations (most commonly associated with transcendental states of mind) do not originate in any known form of external stimulation. They just "are." From this, Zohar and Marshall have concluded that these oscillations are the neural basis of spiritual intelligence, a form of intelligence that places our actions and experiences in a larger context of meaning and value.

Zohar and Marshall's work in this field, and in unifying the sciences with theology, philosophy, and poetry, may well set a 21st century agenda to develop a mind-set that will enable us to deal with issues that so depressed morale in the late 20th century. It could, put simply, provide a transcendental reason for living. Such a view of consciousness and spirituality adds quite enormously to the arguments of this book that learning systems have to be developed that draw out children's full, spiritual intelligence, as well as our intellectual and emotional needs. There is plenty of evidence now available that tells us that human intelligence is even more complex than we previously thought, and that it goes beyond what standardized exams can ever hope to measure and quantify.

The Nobel Prize winning economist Robert Fogel puts an economic spin on the concept of spiritual intelligence when he argues that the battle over equality in the 21st century will not be over material issues, at least not in rich countries, but over spiritual issues. His comments are highly relevant to those concerned about equity in education. Fogel writes, "The quality of choices and the range of opportunity depend critically on how well endowed an individual is with spiritual resources. The quest for spiritual equity thus turns not so much on money as on access to spiritual assets, most of which are transferred and developed privately rather than through the market. Moreover, some of the most critical spiritual assets, such as a sense of purpose, self-esteem, a sense of discipline, a vision of opportunity, and a thirst for knowledge, are transferred at a very young age. The reforms required to achieve spiritual equity overlap with, but are not identical to, those required to achieve material equity. Shaping a new, broader program of equalitarian reforms, while continuing to pursue the unrealized objectives of the program for material equity will not be easy."[29]

Human Intelligence Goes Beyond the Limits Defined by Those Who Focus on the Agenda of Schools

While scientists in the early 21st century struggle to come to terms with a convincing set of definitions for intelligence, it is useful to note that policymakers and educators early in the 20th century acted as if there was an already agreed definition of intelligence. Psychologists and educators romped ahead with batteries of tests that they promulgated as being good predictors of millions of children's intellectual potential and life chances. This confidence in IQ testing came from the U.S. Army's success during World War I in using IQ tests to sort soldiers according to intellectual capabilities. Advocates of IQ testing argued they were easy to administer, cheap, and led to the efficient sorting of human potential.

In 1923, a bulletin prepared under the auspices of the American National Research Council heralded a confidence in the new science. "These tests are the direct result of the application of the army testing methods to school needs. They were devised in order to supply group tests for the examination of school children that would embody the greater benefits derived from the Binet and similar tests. The effectiveness of the army intelligence tests in problems of classification and diagnosis is a measure of the success that may be expected to attend the use of the National Intelligence Tests, which have been greatly improved in the light of army experiences. . . . They are simple in application, reliable, and immediately useful for classifying children in Grades 3 to 8 with respect to intellectual ability."[30]

The dream in the early 20th century that was offered by science was similar to the dream espoused by advocates of scientific management in business. It promised that "if all people could be tested, and then sorted into roles appropriate for their intelligence, then a just, and, above all, efficient society might be constructed for the first time in human history."[31] By the 1920s the intelligence test had become a fixture in educational practice in the United States and much of Western Europe.

The 1944 Education Act in Britain used IQ testing at the age of 11 to differentiate children into academic, technical, and nonacademic classes. It did this because of the faith expressed in 1935 that IQ testing was "scientific and an accurate prognostication" of children's future ability. Yet, even by the time it came to be implemented very serious flaws in this thinking were obvious. It was to be a further 21 years (1965) before public acknowledgment of the failure of such testing was to lead to the backlash of establishing the comprehensive secondary high school, which, maybe somewhat naively, sought to provide trilateral education for all kinds of pupils.

In the last half of the 20th century, the belief that children's innate natural abilities have emerged by the age of 10 or 11 and could be fully scientifically assessed led to the accepted view that secondary education was more important than primary. The education of the few at tertiary level, those who would then be responsible for directing the destinies of everybody else, justified still higher levels of expenditure. In both Britain and the United States, this set of assumptions reinforced the belief in Thorndike's commitment to instruction and left Dewey's concept of a community of learners as being somewhat woolly and imprecise, and not worthy of serious attention beyond the end of elementary education. There was a curious twist to this in North America where from the later years of the 19th century, wealthy benefactors started to invest heavily in the funding of numerous universities. So many universities sprang up, in fact, that there were initially too few students from secondary schools to support them.

The growth of secondary education in the United States was very different from that in Europe as a whole. In Europe, secondary education probably marked the conclusion of most people's formal education, and so this was ever more tightly prescribed along the lines that Thorndike would have recognized. But in the United States, it was accepted that young people should have a broad general education up to the end of high school, with all those who might need something more detailed and specific going on to some form of tertiary education. Contrary to what Dewey would have anticipated, by the 1950s a hierarchical funding regime emerged in the United States that saw tertiary education being given the highest priority and primary education the lowest.

The rationale for this funding ratio was that it would support a system of education that developed human capital that, in turn, would lead to an increasingly efficient and prosperous society. The logic supporting this hierarchy of education was rooted in:

1. Ideas about intelligence being static and easily measurable.
2. The behaviorist view that children were pretty much empty vessels waiting to be filled.
3. The faith in the ethic of the survival of the fittest.
4. The view that young children can't learn as well as older children.
5. The belief that learning is largely the result of teaching.
6. The assumption that learning occurs in a logical and linear way.

These assumptions, dating back to the end of World War II, had been arrived at through a struggle of ideas and a series of compromises (often those of the lowest common denominator), which informed thinking about education and learning in the United States, and indeed much of the world. The funding ratio that grew out of them, favoring tertiary education, is one that still predominates across the western world.[32] But, as we argued in Chapter 2, it is not necessarily a fair one, or one that supports what we now know about how children naturally learn.

7 Big Is Better

I drive my car to supermarket, The way I take is superhigh,
A superlot is where I park, and SuperSuds are what I buy.

JOHN UPDIKE

If there was ever a golden era of education in the
United States and England, it was the 25 years after
World War II, a time of phenomenal economic
growth when, for one example, the real wage of the
American worker more than doubled.[1] Similar economic growth in Europe
fuelled the expansion of their education systems, and in all cases schooling
was seen as the driver of economic success both at personal and societal
levels. Rapidly growing white middle-classes gained most from this expansion,[2] and, despite the dangers of the cold war, this was a period of optimism and positive feelings towards public education, and government in
general.

The best evidence for this faith in formal education lies in the fact that
taxpayers of the time were willing to put more and more money into public schools. In the United States, "recognizing that teachers generally had
low salaries and overcrowded classrooms, in the 1950s, two-thirds of citizens polled said they would be willing to pay more taxes if the extra
money went to higher pay for teachers."[3] Adults in general still believed
that they had personal responsibility for the children in their communities, and this was the heyday of support for extracurricular activities by numerous, if nameless, individuals who were driven by a belief in their personal responsibility to replenish the social capital[4] of their community.
Organizations such as the Boy Scouts, the Girl Scouts, 4-H, choirs, youth
clubs, and the Outward Bound Movement flourished, mainly staffed by

volunteers who felt this was a valuable use of their time. Volunteering was seen as synonymous with good citizenship.

For many in the United States, the 1950s reflected the idealistic values of civil society described in 1835 by the Frenchman Alexis de Tocqueville (1805–1859) in *Democracy and America*, this despite the largely hidden injustices of racism and the fear-mongering of McCarthyism. De Tocqueville described a United States that was moving inexorably towards the "gradual development of the principle of equality."[5] He wrote of a thriving, decentralized U.S. political society that was made up of independent churches, schools, scientific societies, and commercial organizations. For de Tocqueville, this civil society supplied "the independent eye that exercised surveillance over the state."[6] Through active participation in the affairs of the community, de Tocqueville believed, citizens saw the value of curbing the pursuit of their own private self-interests for the common good.

In post-war America, respect and support for mass public education, which expanded greatly to provide for the baby boom cohort, translated into a massive burst of growth in the construction of schools and universities. In the United States, "total expenditure for all public schools increased from $2,906,886,000 to $10,955,047,000 in the decade after 1945, far outpacing the growth in the population of students."[7] This growth was largely mirrored in other industrialized countries.

In the free world, education systems were given lofty (and very public) political goals to achieve. The first of these goals was to help keep the world safe from the scourge of communism, and in fact competition with Soviet expertise became a leitmotif of educational policy during the 1950s and 1960s. It was at Westminster College in Fulton, Missouri, in 1946 that Winston Churchill declared, "From Stettin in the Baltic to Triest in the Adriatic an Iron Curtain has descended across the continent." This political competition culminated in President Kennedy's challenge in 1961 to put a man on the moon before the close of the decade in order to display America's superiority in science and, by direct extension, the arms race. This international collaboration between the western powers against the Soviet bloc became a powerful incentive for industry and business to excel. There was no doubt about the purpose of education: It was to ensure the survival of the democratic way of life and, even more, to show its superiority in providing for its citizens.

The Supreme Court's 1954 desegregation decision, Brown vs. the Board of Education, was a defining moment for domestic politics and education in the United States. With this seminal decision to integrate public schools, they became central to the Civil Rights Movement and later to President Johnson's efforts to build a Great Society. The intervention of

Washington in the affairs of states demonstrated how educational issues were to become increasingly a national concern rather than the concern of just local and state governments. The post-war years were times of great national challenges articulated by respected national leaders on both sides of the Atlantic. President Johnson captured the spirit of the times when he told a gathering in 1964: "Hell, we're the richest country in the world, the most powerful. We can do it all. . . . We can do it if we believe it."[8] This confidence in the power of government to eradicate poverty, institutionalized racism, and suffering in the United States; to put a man on the moon; and to achieve grand designs abroad epitomized the optimism of the early 1960s.

A whole generation of young Americans believed their President and dedicated their lives to public service only to have their idealism progressively shattered in Vietnam, by Watergate, and in the tawdriness of domestic politics in the 1980s and 1990s. A similar shattering of idealism played out in Europe as the difficulties of rebuilding an economy across established nation states made the contribution of individuals seem insignificant.

The Cult of "Bigism"

During the quarter century after World War II, education was at the center of an intense climate of national purpose and faith in "big ideas": big science, big corporations, and big government. This faith that big was better was expressed by national politicians and delivered most effectively to citizens through the expanding and ever more centralized media. These big ideas resonated throughout the land because this was also a period dominated economically and socially by the same faith in bigness. In 1950, "500 major corporations produced about half of the nation's industrial output (about a quarter of the industrial output of the free world)."[9]

Big business was balanced by big labor, which helped fuel the economic expansion by supporting big consumers who were multiplying, literally, in leaps and bounds, as U.S. families spawned the baby boom (1946–1960). By 1950, 15 million Americans belonged to unions: "[F]ully 70 percent of America's factory workers, miners and railway workers belonged to trade unions."[10] The rate was even higher in the United Kingdom and across much of Europe. U.S. families, with the material deprivations of the 1930s still etched deeply in their minds, went on a buying binge unparalleled in human history up to that time. "Spending on personal consumption, measured in constant 1954 dollars, increased from $128.1 billion in 1929 to $195.6 billion in 1947, and to $298.1 billion in 1960."[11]

Coordinating the productive energies of big business, big labor, and big consumers in the United States was a large regulatory apparatus under the banner of the federal government in Washington. To put this into proper perspective it is important to remember that immediately following World War II, the central concern among policy makers in the United States and England was that the pre-war unemployment rolls would return as millions of troops demobilized. The best way to prevent this calamity from happening, government officials on both sides of the Atlantic agreed in almost complete unanimity, was to continue the Keynesian economic policy of "the vast intervention of government and the expenditure and investment that produced the full wartime employment."[12] But rather than producing just military goods, the post-war economies would focus on producing consumer goods. This form of state-dominated economics lasted well into the late 1970s, and even the Republican President Richard Nixon was able to publicly acknowledge, after signing a series of regulatory acts in 1971, that "We are all Keynesian now." It was in 1968 that Americans first bit into the Big Mac.

This public confidence in bigness, and in particular big government, to coordinate economic growth with big business and big labor was a transnational phenomenon. The pre-eminence of big government in the economic sphere across the world in one form or another was "propelled by revolution and two world wars, by the Great Depression, by the ambitions of politicians and governments. It was also powered by the demands of the public in the industrial democracies for greater security, by the drive for progress and improved living conditions in developing countries—and by the quest for justice and fairness."[13] From the late 1940s until well into the 1970s, this system of cooperative bigness supporting mass production really did deliver the goods. "For almost a quarter of a century, America's middle class expanded and prospered. Europe and Japan participated in the boom. Their own national bargains—more explicit than America's—were premised on the same logic of high-volume, standardized production."[14] Make more, earn more, buy more: The consumer society took off in the 1950s, and more and more people worked harder to buy more and more goods. Paradoxically, they found themselves with less time to enjoy them.

It was faith in "bigism" and the assumed ability of the power of government to make life better for all citizens that was behind the British government's 1942 Beveridge Report. "Implementing the recommendations of the report, the Labor Government (1945–51) established free medical care under a newly constituted National Health Service, created new systems of pensions, promoted better education and housing, and sought to deliver on the explicit commitment to 'full employment.' All of this added up to what the Laborites were to call the welfare state—and they were very proud to do so."[15]

107

Key to big business and big government working effectively was the support of big science, massive bureaucracy, and central planning. Planners in business and government built on the certainties and experiences of scientific managers such as Taylor to scale-up the lessons of factories and the military in developing elaborate hierarchical systems of management. The ethos of an unlimited faith in the science of management extended far beyond the factory to an oligopolistic industrial state where the future was carefully planned in advance, through either government or private bureaucracy. Technology and capital markets had made entrepreneurship, and unpredictable economic evolution, obsolete. At least that's what the technocrats of the era believed.

The Organization Man

For critics of the systemization of humanity in the 1950s, the danger of such a scientifically based, centrally planned society was conformity and eventual social stagnation. The social critic William H. Whyte warned in his 1956 bestseller *The Organization Man* that through "a worship of organization" there was a real danger that society would accept the premise that institutionalized "man exists as a unit of society. Of himself, he is isolated, meaningless; only as he collaborates with others does he become worth while, for by sublimating himself in the group, he helps produce a whole that is greater than the sum of its parts. There should be, then, no conflict between man and society. What we think are conflicts are misunderstandings, breakdowns in communication." The organization man was born: "[B]y applying the methods of science to human relations we can eliminate these obstacles to consensus and create an equilibrium in which society's needs and the needs of the individual are one and the same."[16]

Like other believers of individual genius and creativity, Whyte was rigorous in his criticism of allowing economic efficiency—based on economies of scale within large corporations, big government, and big science—to reign at the expense of the individual. He cautioned his readers that there had to be space in organizations, and by extension society, for uniqueness and creativity. These qualities needed to be nurtured, even if at the expense of short-term efficiency, because they spawned leaps in both economic and social progress.

Whyte warned that the dominant cultural influences (big government, big unions, large foundations, big business, big media, and factory schooling) bred conformity and mediocrity. He attacked big science in particular for, by the 1950s, it was held in an esteemed position above all other cultural influences, even religion. It was the Manhattan Project and the development of the atomic bomb that had inaugurated the age of colossal science. This dramatic effort led by a team of internationally renowned physicists completely changed the way applied scientific research was done. From that point onwards, "science involved vast establishments, usually but not exclusively on or contiguous to university campuses, and billions of dollars of annual government expenditure. It was to involve so-called peer review, which meant in practice that a handful of established scientists decided how the government support for research should be distributed."[17]

Whyte criticized how bigness dominated, even in the one place where innovation and individual creativity should have been most nurtured, and that was in scientific committees sponsored by foundations such as the Ford Foundation in the United States, whose job it was to decide what new research should be supported. This example of the pre-eminence given to the big scientific committees at the major universities at the expense of ignoring individual noninstitutional creativity is highly relevant, and sadly familiar, to anyone who has worked within such an environment in the late 1990s. Therefore, it deserves an extended treatment here. Whyte wrote in 1956: "In applied as well as basic science, many advances have succeeded because they bypassed the problems the majority thought were most pressing. When Frank Whittle first presented his idea for a jet engine, he was met with massive indifference from the scientific bureaucracy; they were interested in new problems, but the kind of new problems they were interested in were better pistons, improved propellers and the like. For the very reason that his idea was brilliant, it failed to mesh with the ideas of the fund-givers of the time, and it got support only because a few men, like Launcelot Law Whyte, decided to back the man.

"There is a clue here of wide significance," continues Whyte. 'The most fertile new ideas are those which transcend established, specialized methods and treat some new problem as a single task. . . . Co-operative groups, from great industrial concerns to small research teams, inevitably tend to rely on what is already acceptable as common ground, and that means established, specialized techniques."[18]

This is as good an illustration as any of the stultifying impact of establishment thinking on the development of innovation; entrepreneurs are too often killed off by the very institutions originally set up for their support. In the 1990s, the entrepreneurs who created the digital economy succeeded by bypassing the incrementalism and ideas of slow steady progress favored by administrators and managers steeped in the thinking of Taylor and other industrial age management experts.

What Whyte had to say about the implications of bigness applies very directly to what is now understood about the need for cross-sector thinking to support the brain's natural pattern seeking processes. Here is the key not only to creativity but also to adaptability and the realization of intrinsic motivation. Bigness has the unintended consequence of so distancing the individual from such integrated thinking that large, centralized organizations wither through lack of individual creativity. It is for this reason that large corporations in the early 21st century increasingly subdivide themselves into smaller cohesive teams. In business this process is known as modularity: building a complex product or process from smaller subsystems that can be designed independently yet function together as a whole.[19]

True innovation, as noted above, rarely occurs within pre-existing paradigms, and therefore this tendency to support programs that fit pre-existing criteria, each administered by a specialist program officer, does not support truly original thinking and is hostile to innovators attempting to synthesize across pre-existing academic subdivisions. The issue is made worse by the convention of peer-group review, which overemphasizes the significance of the already established positions by people who are well-versed in earlier solutions and are themselves not quick to take up new and innovative ideas. Political correctness is the result, and this too often leads to mediocrity and the lowest common denominator. From this perspective it is not surprising that the economic expansion of the late 20th century was driven by young entrepreneurs who constructed knowledge-based industries that operated under premises vastly different from the big business ethic of earlier times.

Education and the Cult of Bigism

Of course education systems, political constructs that they are, reflected the same ethos of bigness in structure and goals that government, business, and foundations had after World War II. A telling statistic is the fact that "early in the 20th century the model American high school had perhaps 100 students, but by 1986 over half enrolled more than 1,000 students. The total number of high schools remained fairly constant at about 24,000 between 1930 and 1980, but the number of high school graduates jumped in those years from 592,000 to 2,748,000."[20]

In the year 2000, "71 percent of all high school students in the US attended facilities with an enrollment higher than 1,000."[21] In the case of public schools, big was better because it led to an economy of scale and was simply cheaper. At its most absurd level, at least to those who believe that place matters, this meant that two students could attend different high schools in entirely different parts of a city, but the building housing each would be exactly identical in design. Why pay to have two sets of architecture plans?

Big high schools also made the differentiation of the curriculum possible, so the enthusiasts argued. This meant that in a high school of 1,000 students the system could track groups of students in very different programs. One group could take strictly academic courses while another took primarily vocational ones and a third took a watered-down general one. Even though students were on vastly different life trajectories, this was seen, particularly by those in the United States, as being democratic because all students were at least in the same physical structure. This had the added benefit, proponents argued, of preparing students for life in highly stratified workplace and centrally administered social environments. Yet, at this point it's important to remember the human aspect of all this.

In the case of large high schools, hundreds, and even thousands, of emotionally and hormonally charged teenagers were all seeking to understand themselves and their place in the larger scheme of things, but they were doing this within institutions infinitely larger and more confusing than anything they or their parents had previously experienced. To keep such a vast and impersonal system of education from being overwhelmed by pent-up adolescent energy, ambition, and cynicism required a strong emphasis on discipline, order, and standardization. A new career as "school counselor" emerged, far removed from the inclusive craft of classroom instruction. More significantly, however, such schools also required a system of external rewards to keep students motivated and on the right track. As early as the 1940s, the credentialing system that emerged to support education and the successful sorting of "human capital" became the driving force behind student motivation. All those who wanted to enter the "white collar" world of management would in the future need at least a college diploma; the person with practical, hands-on, apprenticeship-type skills ceased to be qualified for advancement.

The Rapid Rise of Experiential Education

In England, the 1965 Education Act, in removing the 11-plus examinations, stimulated some very real and meaningful innovations within primary education, and these were reported on by the Plowden Report. The methods that emerged out of the report sought to balance the needs of large schools and education systems to be efficient with the personal learning needs of children. These efforts were the result of a significant number of thoughtful, well-motivated, primary school teachers, mainly women who, at that time in England, had relatively few quality career opportunities outside of schools. Drawing on their daily experience of teaching in the classroom, and their own experience of having been mothers in the tough immediate post-war years, many of these women were attracted to the earlier writings of Pestalozzi, Froebel, and Dewey and the contemporary thinking of Piaget and Montessori.

Essentially these were practical, hands-on teachers simply looking for what actually "worked" with "their children" in the classroom. They were not seeking to make dogmatic points, and they would have been surprised that history would cast them as latter day child-centered progressives. These teachers were fortunate to have been practicing at a period in time when there was actually space for such innovative activities. Britain was experiencing a period of economic boom; optimism was in the air; society was still relatively stable; and there was bipartisan support for education encompassing a support and respect for the craft of teaching and a deep-rooted concern to do something better for the youngest children.

With the active support of several leading chief education officers (Clegg of Leicestershire was pre-eminent), some authorities began to support educational practices that focused on the individual learning styles and needs of youngsters with a radical redesign of classrooms. "Open classrooms," as they quickly came to be known, would have immediately been recognized by Froebel. The teaching methods had great similarities with many of the earlier innovations. Such flexible spaces allowed for a great variety of pedagogy. With well-prepared and thoughtful teachers and stable families, these progressive and child-centered methods met with considerable and very obvious success. A key point here is that the progressive style of education that the Plowden Report was referring to emerged out of the work of excellent classroom teachers. It was not, initially, something that came from the outside and was imposed on teachers. It was pragmatic and grew from the bottom-up. It was not ideological.

The Labor Party quickly heralded progressive education as a way to help the children of blue-collar workers escape the drudgeries of manual employment. Government actively encouraged educational authorities to adopt such techniques, though without providing any of the necessary training for teachers. All too often such rapid expansion, unaccompanied by properly prepared teachers, led to extremely disappointing results. Classroom discipline in too many instances suffered, and many parents felt maneuvered by a theory that had never been properly explained to them.

Even with these difficulties, the English model of progressive education came to be so well regarded internationally that many teachers from overseas trained at the London Institute of Education, particularly educators from the United States. In 1961, "William Hull, a Cambridge, Massachusetts, private school teacher, went to England to observe and report on the work of primary schools. His enthusiastic words led a growing number of American educators to travel to England to see firsthand the 'Leicestershire plan,' the 'integrated day,' and the 'developmental classroom.' The Educational Development Center in Newton, Massachusetts, where Hull worked became a clearinghouse for information and materials about English primary schools."[22] By the early 1960s, the English version of progressive education had swept into the United States. But, as "Labor" and "Liberal" politicians fuelled the too rapid expansion of experiential education, the seeds of its political rejection on both sides of the Atlantic were planted from almost the very beginning.

Schools Are Limited in What They Can Do

Thoughtful teachers believed that progressive open education could only work if it took place in partnership with parents and the larger community. Educators who sought to build on the learning needs of individual children never accepted the notion that schools could largely take over the process of raising children while at the same time providing them with a quality education.

The seminal report on progressive education, the 1967 Plowden Report in England, made this fact clear when it "examined primary education in England 'in all its aspects.' Based on extensive research, it concluded that parents' attitudes to education were of *supreme importance* in influencing children's educational success—more so than the parents' educational or occupational status, than material circumstances at home, and than schools themselves. It approved of 'progressive' child-centered teaching methods, a broader curriculum and increased parental involvement; it recommended that schools should become involved in their communities."[23] It sought a balance between the formal sector of schooling and the informal factors that influence so greatly children's learning.

The conviction of progressive educators—that successful learning required a partnership between schools, families, and the community—was strengthened by two large U.S. government-funded studies published in the mid-1960s: "Daniel Patrick Moynihan's report, The Negro Family: The Case for National Action (1965), and James Coleman's Equality of Educational Opportunity (1966). Moynihan, then working for the US Department of Labor, argued that family structure, and in particular absence of fathers in many African American homes, was directly related to the incidence of crime, teenage pregnancy, low educational achievement, and other social pathologies. Coleman's study showed that student educational achievement was most strongly affected not by tools of public policy, such as teacher salaries and classroom size, but by the environment a child's family and peers create. In the absence of a culture that emphasizes self-discipline, work, education, and other middle class values, Coleman showed, public policy can achieve relatively little."[24] What these reports argued was that education could really only be successful in partnership with families and the community.

Coleman, clarifying his position in 1987, wrote schools could make a difference, but that they are greatly limited in their potential impact by factors relating to the family and the community. Coleman wrote, "As the Equality of Educational Opportunity report of 21 years ago first made clear, variations among family backgrounds make more difference in achievement than do variations among schools. This does not imply that 'schools don't make a difference.' There is evidence that in the absence of schooling, children from whatever background learn very little of certain things, such as mathematics. What it does imply is that schools, of whatever quality, are more effective for children from strong family backgrounds than for children from weak ones. The resources devoted by the family to the child's education interact with the resources provided by the school—and there is greater variation in the former resources than in the latter. The strategy of career-and-income oriented households in shifting burdens of child-rearing onto the state, or onto the schools, and supporting those activities through taxes or tuition, runs into this fact."[25]

A key point Coleman makes is that schools that are actually integrated within the values of a larger community (such as parochial schools in the United States) can counter the negative effects of disengaged parents if there is enough social capital within the school's community to make up for the deficit. What Coleman means by social capital in the raising of children "is the norms, the social networks, and the relationships between adults and children that are of value for the child's growing up. Social capital exists within the family, but also outside the family, in the community.[26]

Parochial schools are based on the values of religious organizations, and Coleman notes, "Religious organizations are among the few remaining organizations in society, beyond the family, that cross generations. Thus, they are among the few in which the social capital of an adult community is available to children and youth."[27] This means a good religious school may have enough left-over social capital (concerned and committed adults beyond just the professional teachers) to make up for the deficit faced by a few children in the school. Yet, at some point when the number of children in the school reaches a threshold where a large minority of children

114

come from homes with little or no parental influence, the effect of the school becomes increasingly marginalized.

What this means for children was described by the former head of an inner London comprehensive school, Margaret Maden, when she wrote, "If you have around 20 to 25 percent in a class or in a school who are well-motivated and come from homes where it's instilled in them from very early on that education and learning matter and are fun and make a difference to your life, then that makes the progress with less well-motivated children and families much, much easier." In contrast, she continued, "When you get a concentration of children—disturbed or disadvantaged—there is a critical mass of children who will wreck any school. I will defy any teacher to teach when you have got more than 30 percent of kids like that in the school. . . . Beyond a certain point, children will not succeed if they are concentrated in a school where the majority of children need to be persuaded that education matters."[28]

Harvard's Robert Putnam has written and spoken extensively about the concept of social capital, and why it matters for children's learning. Following is what he told a 2000 gathering discussing the new economy at the White House: "The basic idea of the concept of social capital is that networks have value. . . . What I've been doing in the last several years is studying the value of those social connections for communities. And it's quite clear that social capital is one of the most important assets that a community can have. I'm very impressed as an educator with the administration's efforts to make investments to decrease class size. *But the statistical evidence is that the best predictor of the performance of a community's schools, the best predictor of math scores and science scores, for example, is the social capital in that community, even better than the class size.*"[29]

For proponents of vouchers to help children transfer from public schools to private religious schools, these conclusions are evidence both to support the cause for vouchers as well as to provide a long-term warning. Vouchers can help some children, but at some point the social capital (committed adult involvement and motivated youngsters) that leads to improved standards in parochial and other private schools will break down as more and more young people come from homes with little or no parental involvement. Thus, private schools would eventually have exactly the same problems the state-sponsored schools face. This is a sobering realization, but it puts the proper role of the school into a better perspective: School and the community of which it is a part work in tandem. By itself, a good school can't compensate, over an extended period of time, for the negative influences of a collapsing community.

The Fall of Experiential Education

As it developed, the foundations on which experiential education was built were already starting to crumble at the very moment when the informing ideas and concepts started entering the system. If necessity is the mother of invention, then it made sense that schools were called on to increasingly provide the "care, discipline, and values" originally provided by the home and community. Yet, the ability of open experiential education to work with the community and parents to help all children become successful lifelong learners got sidelined by the need for schools to act as full service social agencies.

From the beginning, supporters warned against the inevitable backlash that such a diluted form of progressive experiential education would encourage. One U.S. educator warned that the confused practices of child-centered education "would do what drunks did to alcohol: give it a bad name."[30] A lesson from this period is that where teachers were insufficiently prepared to handle progressive concepts, such as open classrooms and child-centered learning, the results were often disastrous. This fact exactly paralleled what happened to Froebel and Dewey when their latter day followers totally misunderstood the nature of play and the role of the teacher.

The pattern of progressive education over the past century has been roughly like this: Thoughtful educators on the ground develop highly effective forms of education, based on their observations of how children actually learn, that help children become masters of their own learning. Excited, partially informed, advocates see how effective progressive education can be when facilitated by exceptional teachers, so they feel inspired to try and replicate what they have seen. They then respond to the needs of the system and develop mandated programs from the top down that are watered-down versions of what the original progressives were doing at the classroom level. But it just doesn't work because the programs are mandated from the top down and are rarely supported with appropriate teacher development and input. The key to building a successful learning organization lies in managers at all levels learning within the organization and sharing this experience throughout the system. Ideas and experience must be able to flow smoothly in both directions, not just from the top down. Every person, from parents and teachers to ministers and administrators, must feel that he or she shares equal responsibility for the development of children's learning.

Added to the difficulties of "managing learning," because of the complexity of children's learning, advocates of progressive education too often took an "anything goes" attitude towards schooling and teaching. There were no agreed to values and purpose behind the activity of teaching. For example, did the following comment come from the early 1900s or the late 1960s? "The principal business of the child is to play and to grow—not to read, write, spell and cipher. These are incidental in importance. If they can be made part of the play, it is well to use them; if not, they should be handled sparingly."[31]

In fact, this quote is the comment of the Los Angeles superintendent of schools way back in 1913. Such ill-informed and simplistic views of progressive child-centered education trivialized the powerful ideas of Dewey, Montessori, and Frobel. The progressive educators who informed the Plowden Report would have also seen such a flawed view of child-centered education as abhorrent. It is interesting to note that three years before the L.A. superintendent's comment, Dewey, in criticizing education based on simple rote learning, warned against the "other extreme."

Dewey wrote, "The other extreme is an enthusiastic belief in the almost magical educative efficacy of any kind of activity, granted it is an activity and not a passive absorption of academic and theoretical material. The conceptions of play, of self-expression, of natural growth, are appealed to almost as if they meant that opportunity of any kind of spontaneous activity inevitably secures the due training of mental power; or a mythological brain physiology is appealed to as proof that any exercise of the muscles trains power of thought."[32] A key to successful experiential learning is that the learner has to be continuously reflective and analytical of the processes he or she is using. The implications for the teachers were immense, and it was when teachers were not prepared to handle this that experiential learning fell to pieces and deserved the hostile criticism that it attracted.

"Bigism" Under Assault

The final reason for the political demise of progressive education relates directly to the social and political passions of the late 1960s and early 1970s. In both the United States and the United Kingdom, the schools had become battlegrounds for competing political philosophies and interests. As far as the media was concerned, it was easy to classify discontented teachers, alongside a tiny minority of almost anarchic teachers, as left-wing loonies. Relatively quickly this criticism was applied to any teacher who advocated theories of education that were seen as counter to the traditional methods. This was the beginning of a political reaction against big government systems that seemed infected by radicals seeking to use the state to engineer a socialist society. Those on the Right attacked big government as a threat to individual freedom and personal enterprise.

The intellectual source for much of the criticism of big government being dominated by central planners came from the economist F.A. Hayek (1899–1992).

Hayek, who inspired economic thinkers at the London School of Economics and the University of Chicago, warned in his 1944 book *The Road to Serfdom*: "The most important change which extensive government control produces is a psychological change, an alteration in the character of the people. This is necessarily a slow affair, a process that extends not over a few years but perhaps over one or two generations. The important point is that the political ideals of a people and its attitudes toward authority are as much the effect as the cause of the political institutions under which it lives."[33]

It wouldn't be until the 1970s and 1980s that the ideas and values of the political Right would take firm root again in England and the United States, but the seeds of their successes were planted in the failures of big government in the 1960s and early 1970s. The seeds of failure were planted by the U.S. involvement in Vietnam and the distortions this massive undertaking had on the U.S. economy and on the world economy. The high inflation of the 1970s and the government debt of the 1980s and 1990s were directly tied to President Johnson's decision to fight the war in Vietnam on credit rather than to raise taxes.

The attack on the centralized, expert-oriented, and bureaucratized kind of society initiated by Whyte and other social critics in the 1950s was picked up by E.F. Schumacher, who had been the chief scientist responsible for the technical arrangements for setting up the European Coal and Steel Community (the archetypal big international combine which eventually gave birth to the European Union). Schumacher gave voice to those on the Left when he published *Small Is Beautiful: Economics as If People Mattered* in 1973. He said big business and big consumption were "soul destroying, meaningless, mechanical, monotonous, moronic work, [that was] an insult to human nature which must necessarily and inevitably produce either escapism or aggression, and that no amount of 'bread and circuses' can compensate for the damage done—these are facts which are neither denied nor acknowledged, but are met with an unbreakable conspiracy of silence—because to deny them would be too obviously absurd, and to acknowledge them would condemn the central preoccupation of modern society as a crime against humanity."[34]

These criticisms of the status quo from both the right and the left set the ground for a reaction, and, as Schumacher noted, the reaction to bigism in the late 1960s and 1970s was "escapism and aggression." It was extreme. Counter-cultural advocates "argued for the liberation of the self.

118

In the name of personal freedom they attacked the restraints and compromises of civil society. In a phrase introduced to American life by 60s' young people, they were dedicated to 'doing their own thing.' "[35] What had started off as a thoughtful reaction to the extremity of bigness became overtaken by an array of radical discontent partly made possible by the easy availability of drugs, contraception, and the popularity of anarchism.

All aspects of established behavior became subject to outrageous and often ill-informed criticism acceptable within a society that, consciously or unconsciously, felt totally dehumanized by bigism. As the U.S. scholar Francis Fukuyama wrote in his 1999 book *The Great Disruption*, "No one who has lived through the last several decades can deny that there has been a huge shift in social values, a shift whose major theme has been the rise of individualism at the expense of communal sources of authority from the family and neighborhood to churches, labor unions, companies and the government."[36] The English journalist Libby Purves, picking up on the paradox of economic change, individual insecurity, and community breakdown noted by progressives throughout the 20th century, wrote in early 2000 that, "Unfettered, me-first capitalism and the loss of community are a strain on the family. So is an ever more hopeless sense that 'they' are in control and make a new rule every week. If you create an edgy, uneasy, tired and hypochondrical society, its members get more prone to give up the struggle and fall for irresponsible moonshine about nothing being anyone's fault."[37]

So, at the beginning of the 21st century, by what authority do schools teach; what do they teach; how should they teach; and what, or whose, values are they assumed to be inculcating? In the absence of clear answers, schools struggle and seek refuge in relatively safe initiatives that give the impression of activity but in reality compound the problems. This has been the case within educational reform movements since the 1970s, and it is directly related to the uncertainty facing politics generally. What is the purpose of being a wealthy country, and towards what common good should such wealth be used? These are the big questions political leaders leave largely unasked, and the void is felt by those working to bring young people up as responsible adults who value where they come from and who they are.

8 The Case for Working Smarter, Not Just Harder

The emerging shift in the workplace from "command and control" hierarchies to empowered high-performance teams has powerful implications for schools, if schools were ever allowed to truly experiment.

The Institute for Research on Learning

B y the mid-1970s, the liberal consensus of a Keynesian bargain between big capital, big government, and big labor had begun to fall apart on both sides of the Atlantic. The social and political turmoil of the 1960s and early 1970s that, in large part, had been a revolt against everything big, bureaucratic, and centralized had led to an increasingly fragmented society. Because of increased political and social tensions, the United States seemed in danger of falling into a balkanized collection of competing ethnic, racial, and even demographic self-interest groups. Confrontational tactics that stirred up group animosity, and fostered dissent rather than unity, often typified social relations.[1] Of course these tensions spilled over into education where schools played a central part in the politics of the time. In this fragmented social environment, anything that required long-term collaboration across groups was out, and talk about how children learn seemed inconsequential in comparison to the sometimes violent rhetoric of ethnic identity and cultural nationalism.

In New York City, for example, African American community leaders argued it was necessary to change the educational environment so that it no longer kept their children from learning about their African American heritage and forced them to conform to white, Euro-centered norms. Central to this effort, African Americans and other urban "outcast groups demanded community control by their own people in place of the traditional corporate model of governance which sought to rise above 'interest groups.' Such groups substituted self-determination as a goal instead of assimilation; they rejected 'equality' if that meant Anglo-conformity, sameness, and familiar failure in the 'one best system'."[2] The efforts by minority groups to take local control of New York City schools put them into direct conflict with the traditional Anglo-Saxon raison d'être of education, community interdependence, and with the interests of the 300,000 teachers of the United Federation of Teachers (UFT).

This struggle between interest groups was described by the American professor of education David Tyack in 1974 when he wrote: "Pressing for ever larger scope for negotiations, the UFT bitterly fought for the movement in the mid-1960s to vest control of schools in decentralized boards of education; indeed, the long and bitter strike of 1968 in New York—which polarized black and white to an unprecedented degree there—focused on the powers of the local boards with respect to teachers. Because of their common opposition to community control, the union and the supervisors—former adversaries—joined forces. The UFT managed to persuade the New York legislature to grant only minimal influence to the 31 local boards in its decentralization law of 1969.... Although the UFT and leaders like Shanker had been active in the campaign for civil rights and against racism, many ghetto residents perceived the quest for teacher power as an assault on their own legitimate aspirations and prerogatives."[3]

The traditional interests of the members of the New York boards of education had coalesced, at least in the short-term, with the interests of the emerging power in the world of education: the teachers' unions. From the perspective of the New York Teacher's Union, large centralized systems of education were worth fighting for because they were more open to collective bargaining than were numerous smaller, community-controlled systems. Critics saw in such conflicts a turning upside down of the traditional role of the school and education. The economist Milton Friedman observed in 1979: "Instead of fostering assimilation and harmony, our schools are increasingly a source of the very fragmentation that they earlier did so much to prevent."[4]

Though the late 1960s and early 1970s were riddled with strife, the United States was held together by the glue of a large middle-class united by the post-war economic boom. The economy was so productive that real median income doubled in 26 years between 1947 and 1973 from $21,000 to $42,000 (all figures here are in 1998 dollars).[5] But this came to a painful end as productivity growth began to slow in the late 1960s at the same time expenditures in treasury and manpower for the Vietnam war were making labor markets tight. Workers demanded more pay, and the slower productivity growth meant that higher wages were passed along as higher prices. With the harvest failures and OPEC oil embargo of the early 1970s, inflation became a real problem for the U.S. and British economies. By the middle of the decade inflation was imbedded in both economies, and growth in productivity and median family income nearly stopped altogether. These economic downturns triggered a middle class revolt against big government because people started to sense they were paying more in taxes and getting less in return.

Tough Times

If the 1970s was the decade of stagflation, economic slump, inflation, and energy crises for the United States, it was even worse for the United Kingdom. By 1975, according to the Pulitzer prize-winning author Daniel Yergin, "Inflation was running at 24 percent. The trade unions had just brought down the Conservative government of Edward Heath. Constant strikes gave unions a stranglehold on the economy and immobilized the nation. Marginal tax rates were high—up to 98 percent—destroying incentives. Britain was well along the road, people feared, to becoming the East Germany of the Western world, a corporatist state, ground down to a gray mediocrity, and one in which any kind of initiative was regarded as pathological behavior, to be stamped out. . . . The entire country was on the dole, forced to borrow money from the International Monetary Fund in 1976 in order to protect the pound and stay afloat. As a condition of its loan, the IMF required sizeable cuts in public expenditures, setting off a bitter rebellion in the Labor Party."[6]

England's problems, like those of the United States, were largely related to the failures of central economic planning, a bloated government, and an over-extended welfare state, all of which had grown steadily after World War II. Government planners had created large bureaucracies to support increased public expenditures on numerous programs for a wide variety of constituencies.[7]

To put the English political and economic crises of the 1970s into a proper perspective, it is important to make a point about culture. Where America's social conflicts often centered on racial and ethnic tensions over access to the country's wealth, England had a different sort of problem that hampered its ability to adjust to the changing economic realities of the 1970s. As economic growth in the 1960s increasingly became tied to personal consumption, most Americans literally bought into this as a positive phenomenon; many in England, especially the young, rebelled against both personal consumption and growth.

In attempting to explain England's economic decline, the Harvard professor of history and economics David Landes wrote in 1998 that scholars have "sought to explain Britain's retreat from hegemony by the triumph of an antibusiness, antimaterialist outlook and its negative consequences for recruitment. The teachers, poets, men and women of letters, and intellectuals—the people who set the tone and orchestrated the values—nurtured a sense of scorn for the shop and the office. The point was to rise above the material to higher things. Such pretensions found particular resonance among those older elites who found themselves jostled by grubby newcomers, and of course among the grubby newcomers who wanted to de-grub themselves. Snobbery is the revenge of the haughty and the humbug on the ambitious."[8]

A survey commissioned by *New Society* magazine in 1977 revealed an England "remarkably unambitious in a material sense. . . . Very few sincerely want to be rich. Most people in Britain neither want nor expect a great deal of money. Even if they could get it, the vast majority do not seem prepared to work harder for it: most of our respondents thought we should work only as much as we need to live a pleasant life. . . . It seems clear that the British today prefer economic stability to economic growth."[9] The problem with this attitude is that it doesn't lead to economic stability but to economic stagnation and decline. This fact was pointed out by the prime minister Edward Heath when he warned in 1973: "The alternative to expansion is not, as some occasionally seem to suppose, an England of quiet towns linked only by trains puffing slowly and peacefully through green meadows. The alternative is slums, dangerous roads, old factories, cramped schools, stunted lives."[10]

The Changing Economy and the Call for Lifelong Learners

As the post-war economic arrangements turned sour, the middle-class Americans and British started to feel increasingly insecure and uncertain about the direction their countries were moving. It was certainly not clear that society was marching progressively forward, and in fact many people were worried that the best days were behind them. As early as 1969 many middle class Americans felt: "The values we held so dear are being shot to hell. . . . Everything is being attacked—what you believed in and what you learned in school, in church, from your parents. So the middle class is sort of losing heart. They had their eyes on where they were going and suddenly it's all shifting sand."[11] By the second half of the decade, President Jimmy Carter spoke openly of an "economic malaise."

In this period of political, social, and economic instability, people began turning away from big ideas and started looking inward to discover values that gave their lives meaning and that helped them form strategies to address their individual needs and concerns. This turning inward opened the door for a Conservative revolution based on individual rights and opportunity in the United Kingdom and the United States. Many middle class voters had simply become fed up with things they felt they had little or no control over, and their anger was increasingly aimed at anything coined "big," "collective," "liberal" or "progressive." Faith in big governments' ability to solve problems dissipated and voter attitudes turned 180 degrees. As Ronald Reagan quipped to great effect, "Government was the problem."[12] Onto this fertile soil for change stepped Margaret Thatcher and her faithful tutor Keith Joseph along with Ronald Reagan and his free-market allies from the University of Chicago (notably Milton Friedman) and a growing number of right-wing think tanks.

To a number of economists and social historians writing in the late 1990s, the election of Margaret Thatcher as prime minister in 1979 and Ronald Reagan as President in 1980 marked the beginning of the end of the government's central position in a relatively autarkic (closed) national economy and the political consensus that supported it. Their elections, along with technological changes, opened the way for the acceptance of a more open post-industrial economy based on reducing barriers to the movement of goods and capital across national boundaries.[13] The term used to describe this economic openness in the 1990s was globalization. What this meant for national politicians was that they had to increasingly consider the reaction of the financial markets to economic policy decisions. Peter Drucker said the global economy "is shaped mainly by money flows rather than by trade in goods and services. These money flows have their own dynamics. The monetary and fiscal policies of sovereign national governments increasingly react to events in the transnational money and capital markets rather than actively shape them."[14] The market, rather than government planners, became the central decision maker.[15]

This shift in economic power away from central governments would have a tremendous influence on education systems and the political debates that would rage around them. No longer was education about great national crusades to help make the world safe for democracy. Nor was education about just helping young people develop the basic skills necessary for working successfully in factories or large bureaucracies seen as central to national survival. By the mid-1980s, education was seen in the context of economic competition between countries and individuals in increasingly de-industrialized employment, and this meant working not just harder but smarter. Employers started speaking about the need to attract workers who could think critically, who could innovate and solve problems without direct supervision, who had superior speaking and writing skills, and who could learn on the job. In short, they started looking for employees with higher-order skills who could use new technologies to come up with creative solutions to old processes and problems. This became the era of innovators and entrepreneurs. This represented a radical shift in educational goals for schools and education systems, but one that earlier progressives like Dewey, Froebel, and Montessori would have been comfortable with. There was now to be a premium on people who could think for themselves.

The term "lifelong learning" emerged as a key goal for education, although few people really expressed opinions on exactly what this change in "goal" would mean for systems of education. In fact, for many, it was assumed that lifelong learning simply meant lifelong access to schooling and training. It would mean expanding the education system downward and upward. In contrast, the authors of this book see "lifelong" as an attitude where people have faith in their own abilities to learn new skills and to judge when these will be needed. Learning isn't something done apart from the rest of life and work but is actually an integrated part of both. This may or may not entail going to a formal learning center. Those who make their living using computers understand this concept well. They rarely have time, or even the inclination, to go back to a formal classroom for a course on a new software package. They have the confidence to teach themselves on a need-to-know basis. Sometimes these learners go to workshops and training courses, but more often than not they use the Internet or the book shop to acquire the information they need and they work their problems out by themselves. Such learners excel in a dynamic economy because they do not simply react to changes but actually drive them. Why? Simply because it matters to them. Motivation drives learning.

A Dynamic Economy and the Need for "Higher-Order Skills"

A dynamic economy, in the words of the Austrian economist Joseph Schumpeter (1883–1950), is one that is equal parts destructive and constructive. Innovators challenge old ways of doing things and develop new methods of working. Since the early 1980s there has been a literal application of Schumpeter's notion in the United States of creative destruction with some 44 million jobs lost and 73 million private-sector jobs created.[16]

Obviously, such economic changes have an immense impact on individuals, their families, and what is expected of education systems. As noted above, this model of economics puts a premium on individual learning, responsibility, personal thinking skills, and creativity. The mental scaffold for these attitudes and skills is developed most rapidly in young children, and to think they can be easily developed in adults who weren't exposed to them in their youth is to misunderstand the workings of the human brain and how humans learn.

Yet, the education systems of North America and Europe were not, and never had been, designed for developing such "higher-order skills" in all young people. As the cognitive scientist John Bruer noted in 1993: "No educational system has ever tried to educate all its students to be higher-order thinkers. Improving our schools to educate everyone to this level, not just the select few, may not be possible if all we do is reaffirm past standards, raise graduation requirements, and apply existing methods and practices more rigorously."[17]

The tension Bruer was picking up on, and which is still very much with us at the beginning of the 21st century, is that education systems have been given radically different purposes. This shift in purpose is not the result of government dictates; rather, it is the outcome of economic and technological changes. Subsequently, we are living with education systems that were designed for a different era. Yet, to say this is to be seen by many to be heretical. The fact is that educational reform has become so politicized over the past couple of decades that to consider a new design for models of education based on how children actually learn is ridiculed by many in education and policy positions as "giving up on public education."

For many people education is synonymous with the teacher-dominated, school-based learning they know from their youth. Learning is seen as something that is highly sequential, orderly, and thoroughly quantifiable. Therefore only the professionals are held accountable for it. This institutionalized way of thinking misses out on the fact that children only spend about 20 percent of their waking hours in a classroom.

If learning is to be seen as a lifelong activity for all children, then what is now needed is a view of learning that incorporates an effective partnership between parents, the business community, teachers, and the power of information communication technologies. Learning is an inherently messy and interconnected activity that for many is triggered by experiences well beyond the formal setting of the classroom. This incongruity between the needs of learners and the cult of schooling can be dealt with by shifting the orientation of lifelong learning from schools and institutions to learners and learning. Such a significant shift in thinking is possible and would parallel the economic shift from a focus on large systems and bureaucratic control to that of personal responsibility, creativity, and entrepreneurship.

When Ideas Become Reality

Margaret Thatcher was elected British prime minister in 1979, and to an electorate fed up with the status quo, she personified a more positive and persuasive way out of a floundering and failing economy. She argued that post-war economists, politicians, and policymakers had promised much more from the national welfare state than government could actually control or deliver. Much of Thatcherism would be based on the carefully worked through ideas developed by Sir Keith Joseph during his years in opposition.

Joseph built on the free-market theories of F.A. Hayek and the monetarist theories of Milton Friedman at the University of Chicago. Thatcher and Joseph made the case that England needed an economy that offered greater risks and greater rewards because both were necessary to achieve a higher standard of living and a greater general prosperity for all. They wanted to liberate the economy from what they saw as the negative influences of government ownership, union domination, and regulation in order to release the personal drive and ambition of individual entrepreneurs.

During the mid-1970s, Sir Keith traveled around England delivering speeches on the moral case for capitalism. He argued: "The problem in any society is to reconcile the interests of people as workers with the interests of the same people and their dependants as consumers. The least ineffective way yet discovered to achieve this balance is by decentralized ownership and decision-making within the rule of law and subject to competition. We call this, for short, free enterprise or capitalism."[18] Joseph, like Hayek, understood the power of ideas and the inescapable link between the abstract world of theory and the real world of policy. Joseph used the bully pulpit of the shadow government to initiate a shift in how people thought about the way the world worked.

During Joseph's speeches he would often be heckled, but he never wavered from his argument that England was "over-governed, over-spent, over-taxed, over-borrowed, and over-manned." He explained that England needed to nurture its entrepreneurs. To Joseph, "The entrepreneur is the person who seeks to identify what consumers, at home or abroad or both, want and would be willing to buy at a profitable price. These entrepreneurs are the job-creators because it is they who gather the men and women, the material, the machinery and the money to turn the vision of the market into a reality. It is they, who, in the hope of profit but under the risk of bankruptcy, within the law—and subject, of course, to competition from every similar product or service and from every other use to which consumers can put their money—create the jobs. . . . We should not underrate the risks that even the less ambitious take: most have worries; some have great worries; some go bankrupt."[19] Joseph was as aware as anyone that academia largely did not understand entrepreneurs and they most certainly did not see the purpose of education as being related to helping develop such creative thinking and attitudes in the young.

In the polarized atmosphere Joseph's views generated, critics on the left argued that he and Thatcher wanted to glorify individualism at the expense of the collective good. Their enemies contended that Thatcherism, as their free-market policies became known, "challenged the notion that Britain could be a community; at a stroke people were to be relieved of any responsibility for one another, the Biblical maxim 'love thy neighbor' exposed as ill conceived post-war funk. . . . Thatcherite doctrines offered little encouragement to love anyone at all—anyone, that is, other than oneself. This was to be the masturbatory society, offering a solitary view of fulfillment, free of complications arising from tiresome moral demands by others,"[20] wrote John Kingdom, the left-wing social commentator, in 1992.

The Conservatives in England and the Republicans in the United States argued the exact opposite. They blamed big government for disempowering citizens and taking control from them other essential services of government, such as schools, welfare, roads, and even garbage collection. Ronald Reagan could have been speaking for the Tories when he argued in 1984 that government had "pre-empted those mitigating institutions like family, neighborhood, church, and school—organizations that act as both a buffer and a bridge between the individual and the naked power of the state."[21]

Privatization and the Entrepreneurial Society

In order to create the risk-taking entrepreneurial society that Thatcher and Joseph envisioned, "The Thatcherite agenda entailed nothing less than the death of what she herself termed 'socialism,' and what others termed 'social democracy,' as the price of national economic revival. The assault was to be directed at both the institutions and the culture which was held to sustain them."[22]

It would be a very bitter battle, and many still get rankled when they think about it. The central instrument used by Thatcher and her allies in this assault on government domination of the economy was privatization. State-owned enterprises such as British Telecom, British Gas, Britoil, the airports (with water and electricity to follow at the end of the 1980s), and others were all privatized. By 1992, some two-thirds of state-owned industries had moved into a private sector that had absorbed 46 businesses and 900,000 employees. The government's take was well over $30 billion,[23] and many industries that had sucked up public funds had been converted into sources of tax revenue.

Thatcher's goal was "to use privatization to achieve my ambition of a capital-owning democracy. This was a state in which people would own their own houses, shares, and have a stake in society, and in which they have wealth to pass on to future generations."[24] It became a world where ordinary individuals had to think responsibly and creatively about their life choices. There were no longer well-defined paths for young people to follow from school to the factory. Choices, opportunity, and insecurity had replaced certainty, stability, and guarantees. It was quickly becoming a thinking person's world.

Margaret Thatcher's political vision was imbued in the concept of individualism developed by the 17th, 18th, and 19th century philosophers like John Locke, David Hume, Adam Ferguson, Adam Smith, and Samuel Smiles. Thatcherism resonated in what Smiles termed the "spirit of self-help." According to Smiles's 1859 book *Self-Help*, "The spirit of self-help is the root of all genuine growth in the individual; and, exhibited in the lives of many, it constitutes the true source of national vigor and strength. Help from without is often enfeebling in its effects, but help from within invariably invigorates."[25] Along the lines of *Self-Help*, Margaret Thatcher was seeking to create an economy where people would be rewarded for taking control of their own destinies by making economic opportunities for themselves. Personal responsibility and drive became the pre-eminent social and economic values.

Her first challenge in this effort to remake England was presented by the power of the unions over the national economy, and in particular the National Union of Miners, which had brought England to a standstill during its strikes against the Conservative government of Edward Heath in 1974. Thatcher declared that the two great problems facing the British economy in the early 1980s were "the monopoly nationalized industries and the monopoly trade unions."[26] In other words, organized management and organized labor were both predominantly interested in their own immediate wellbeing. Against the nationalized industries she used the weapon of privatization and against the unions she used a well-publicized frontal assault. Though the education industry was not immediately identified as a target, it contained all the elements that Thatcher defined. The attack was only to be a matter of time.

The *Guardian's* Will Hutton described Thatcher's attack on the unions saying: "The miners' strike of 1984–85 was perhaps the seminal act in this drama of Labor decline; the union whose solidarity and industrial importance had made it seem invincible was beaten savagely. By building up coal stocks and outlawing secondary picketing, the government had some key strategic advantages over its opponent. Even so, it required all of Mrs. Thatcher's single-mindedness, above all in nurturing the Nottingham miners who worked through the strike, to win the victory she required.

The miners (after a year) returned to work having gained nothing and lost almost everything except their dignity."[27]

This was a devastating blow to union membership, which, as a result of lost battles against the Thatcher administration and the changing nature of the British economy "slumped from around 13 million in 1980 to 9 million in 1987 and below 7 million by 1999."[28] With the election of Ronald Reagan as president in 1980, the United States cemented the same free-market path toward breaking the hold of inflation and triggering economic recovery that Thatcher's government had started. In both countries there were similar winners and losers.

The significance of these changes for education systems on both sides of the Atlantic was captured a decade later when the president of the American Federation of Teachers told a gathering in England that: "When the factory was touted as the ideal organization for work and when most youngsters were headed for the assembly lines, making a public education system conform to the model of the factory seemed liked a great achievement. But the old fashioned factories are dead or dying and they will not be resurrected as we know them. The limitations of the traditional factory model of education have become manifest and they are crippling. The traditional model of schooling is, therefore, incompatible with the idea that students are workers, that learning must be active, and that children learn in different ways and at different rates."

These Changes Are Transnational

To appreciate the significance of these changes in the economic landscape and what it means for education systems, consider the 1997 comments of the former Japanese Prime Minister Kiichi Miyazawa: "The end of the long cold war has led to the defeat of centralized systems of bureaucratic control, one of which is Japan's system of bureaucracy-led cooperative administration. Today, with the nation plagued by economic stagnation, political indecision, lack of individuality and creativity, and a host of other problems, many Japanese have become acutely aware of the defects of the Japanese-style system of social and economic management and of the need for radical reform. In a worldwide trend, radical administrative and fiscal reform, from centralized to decentralized systems, is coming to be seen as the most effective way to break out of such an economic and social impasse and bring renewed vitality. An important means of decentralizing administrative and fiscal systems is the complete abolition of restrictive regulations."[29]

Change over the past two decades has been dramatic, and few Americans or Europeans in 1981 could have imagined hearing such a statement coming from representatives of the economic juggernaut Japan. What this has meant for education in Japan are calls "to shorten the compulsory academic school week to three days" in order for children to spend the "other two days for personal cultivation and specialized vocational education."[30] Some Japanese have come to the conclusion that in the 21st century, individuals and creativity will become central to the process of globalization, the Internet, and networking.

Education systems around the world are being called upon to help young people take personal responsibility for their own economic welfare and development. The old model of a career in which an employee worked his way up the ladder of success in a single company is becoming rarer. School teachers should be advised that instead of asking students what they want to be when they grow up, they should ask what type of skills they want to possess when they grow up. The key to success is no longer loyalty but flexibility. For better or worse, these economic changes mean all young people have to develop the skills and attitudes necessary to chart their own lives, and they must be able and willing to start and restart several careers over the course of their working years.

This is why lifelong learning is now such a critical concept for everyone concerned with education to appreciate. The essence of a "post-industrial society" is a shift in the structure of organizations from hierarchies to networks, from centralized compulsion to voluntary association. According to the Harvard law professor Anne-Marie Slaughter, "The engine of this transformation is the information technology revolution, a radically expanded communications capacity that empowers individuals and groups while diminishing traditional authority."[31] Certainty and security are being traded in for opportunity and choice. For these changes to be taken advantage of by most young people, there must be a shift in organized learning away from the hierarchical and largely closed systems of education that still predominate in most countries.

The Premium on Learning in the 1990s

In the United States and England, the 1990s was the decade of the long economic expansion, driven by globalization: the supremacy of open and free-markets, the culture of consumerism, and the power of transnational finance. The opening of international markets to goods, services, capital, and ideas; the centrality of the consumer in developed countries; and the freedom of finance to seek high returns around the world have all been facilitated by the revolution in information and communication technologies. The author Thomas L. Friedman writes "globalization[32] is inevitable and irreversible; the forward march of technology makes it so. Governments can

131

no longer control the flow of information now that the cell phone and satellite television have come to the most remote Indonesian village. Day-to-day economic decisions can no longer be decreed from above by corporate CEOs, much less government planning ministers, now that markets mutate with frightening speed. . . . Capital can no longer be bottled up within borders now that billions of dollars can be moved with the click of a key."[33]

We will not debate whether globalization is inevitable, or even generally positive, but the changing nature of the economy and the role of politics in it matters for those who are concerned about education. These changes challenge the traditional purposes of education systems: preparing young people for work in an industrial workplace and national citizenship. The industrial workplace is becoming a thing of the past for the vast majority of working people who know little about long term loyalty to one employer and a golden watch at retirement time. *The Economist* observed in late October of 1997 that "for good or ill, globalization has become the economic buzz-word of the 1990s. National economies are undoubtedly becoming steadily more integrated as cross-border flows of trade, investment and financial capital increase. Consumers are buying more foreign goods, a growing number of firms now operate across national borders, and savers are investing more than ever before in far-flung places."[34]

In 1999, Gordon Brown, the British chancellor of the exchequer, told the Council for Foreign Relations in New York: "The task in our generation is to put in place a new framework for global stability in a new economy. Our predecessors did this for the post-war world of distinct national economies. They created not just new international institutions—the IMF, the World Bank, the GATT, as well as the UN—and a whole set of new rules for a new international economy, but gave expression to a new public purpose based on high ideals, and a commitment to economic progress and social justice." In his conclusion, Brown told the Americans, "What we must create together is a new economic constitution for a global economy, born out of new realities, grounded in new rights and responsibilities, enshrined in codes of conduct that are agreed nationally and applied internationally, rediscovering public purpose in the international economy and bringing to life again the high ideals of 1945."[35]

To fully appreciate the impact of the economic changes alluded to by Brown—changes rooted in the conservative revolution of the 1980s—one need only look at how radically transformed domestic politics in the United States and the United Kingdom have become. President Clinton, the pragmatic democrat from Arkansas, is a political child of the Reagan Revolution. "Mr. Clinton's considerable achievements are ones that most centrist Republicans would be proud of—new free-trade agreements, eliminating the budget deficit, presiding over a period of steady growth with low inflation, cutting the size of government."[36] In England, the Emeritus Professor of the Science of Government at Harvard Samuel Beer has observed, "Mrs. Thatcher's assaults on nationalization and the privileged position of organized labor were immensely successful in preparing the way for New Labour."[37] New Labor's decisive victory over old Labor was largely fought over the acceptance that markets and private businesses are more efficient and productive than central planning and state owned enterprises. Keith Joseph could have scripted the centerpiece of New Labor's platform.

The "Third Way" in Politics

Yet, in fairness to Clinton's and Blair's administrations, they speak not of a ruthless self-centered version of laissez-faire capitalism but rather of a more humane "third-way." In theory the third-way accepts the competition and instability of the global economy but tempers it with what Tony Blair calls the "center-left's traditional values of solidarity, social justice, responsibility and opportunity."[38] A key difference, third-wayers would argue, between old Labor (or in the United States, old Liberals) and the new is that the old sought equality of outcomes while the new seeks equality of opportunity. Central to equality of opportunity, according to Blair and Clinton, is "education, education, education."

The third-way, to its leading intellectual advocate Professor Anthony Giddens of the London School of Economics, "rejects class politics, seeking a cross-class base of support." The third-way argues that what is necessary is to reconstruct the scope of state and government, and international institutions, "to go beyond those who say 'government is the problem' and those who say 'government is the answer'."[39] What's needed, Giddens argues, is "a new mixed economy. The new mixed economy, unlike the old one, doesn't refer primarily to a balance between state-owned and private industries. It refers to a balance between regulation and deregulation; and between the economic and the non-economic in the life of the society."[40] It is still much too early to assess the impact that these ideas are having. Critics of the right find in them little that is new and much that smacks of a mildly diluted socialism. Certainly they seem unlikely to lead to any lessening of central control over education—rather the reverse.

Nonetheless, Blair has written that the role of government in the new mixed economy "is to promote macroeconomic stability; develop tax and welfare policies that encourage independence, not dependence; to equip people for work by improving education and infrastructure; and to promote enterprise."[41] The point here is that thinking smarter about politics is rewarding politicians. The ideological politician is out, and the savvy pragmatic politician rules. Elections are increasingly about who can most effectively come across as being the "true centrist" politician. This means politics, of which education is a central part, is increasingly driven by short-term thinking based on what polls tell politicians people say they want.

As sad as this may sound to those who believe core convictions and positions matter in leaders, becoming a leader is increasingly synonymous with being poll-savvy: following what it appears most people say they want. This makes it difficult for politicians to develop innovative policies on an issue like educational reform where, in fact, they are rewarded for talking tough and doling out money while in practice doing little that is substantially new. If this is indeed the case, then reforms that seek to nurture the intelligence, imagination, and creativity of all young people will have to emerge from the bottom up. Parents, business people, community advocates, concerned citizens, and teachers will have to push the issues they see influencing their children before politicians will do anything differently. This is, in fact, the way a democracy should work, and it provides an opportunity to reconnect the learning needs of children with the larger interests of families and community. We would argue that in various places in North America and Europe this process is already underway, and such efforts may very well lead to a resurgence in people's interests in de Toqueville's notion of civil society.

Lessons of Successful Business: Think and Work Smarter from the Bottom Up

Mortimer Zuckerman, the editor of *US News and World Report*, in 1998 described the business revolution that took place in America in the 1980s as follows: "Business managers, shocked out of their smug parochialism, began years of restructuring, re-engineering, and cost-cutting that saw their companies become vastly more efficient. . . . To bring this about, American managers invested in new technologies [and] high-tech training to exploit these new advances, increased quality control, and improved information systems to adjust supply, prices and output more quickly to market conditions."[42]

Zuckerman points out that by the mid-1990s the private sector was making the overwhelming majority of strategic and tactical business decisions that drove the U.S. economy—not central government. In short, business leaders took charge and decided it was imperative to start working smarter. In thinking smarter business leaders discovered that they needed employees with skills and attitudes different from those of the industrial

134

age. Remember in the industrial age, the age of Taylorism, most work was organized top-down, and individual responsibility was replaced by systemic controls. Only the leaders and managers at the top needed to be creative, imaginative, and enterprising. Most workers could be successful by knowing how to perform highly precise, structured, and repetitive tasks that necessitated a high degree of discipline but little or no personal initiative. Understandings by employees of the total business process were deemed unnecessary and were in fact discouraged.

It is now obvious to those working in the fastest growing segments of our economy that work at the beginning of the 21st century is radically different. Today's successful businesses are highly decentralized and rely on continuous innovation and employee involvement and knowledge at all levels. In high-performance workplaces, individuals have to do a lot more critical thinking: analyzing problems, proposing solutions, troubleshooting, communicating with others, and managing their own time. Workers are rewarded for being able to adapt rapidly without waiting for external direction.

This is a significant shift in operating principles and has the potential of facilitating the democratic goal of freeing up the intelligence and creativity that has laid dormant in so many people since the introduction of mass industrialization. However, there is also a darker side to all this: the danger of an increased split between the haves (those who think and do for themselves responsibly), and the have nots (those who are told what to do.) Consider the fact that the United States already has close to 2 million of its citizens locked up in prisons with the number rising annually, while those on the other end of the spectrum have more choices and opportunities than any other group of people in human history. The problem facing many young people on the positive side of this divide is that they simply have too many choices and therefore often seem overwhelmed. On the other side, many people still see nothing but despair and hopelessness.

The U.S. writer Daniel Goleman captured the significance of these changes for the average worker when he wrote, "The rules for work are changing. . . . These [new] rules have little to do with what we were told was important in school; academic abilities are largely irrelevant to this standard. The new measure takes for granted having enough intellectual ability and technical know-how to do our jobs; it focuses instead on personal qualities, such as initiative and empathy, adaptability and persuasiveness. This is no passing fad, nor just the management nostrum of the moment. The data that argue for taking it seriously are based on studies of tens of thousands of working people, in callings of every kind."[43] Ponder the first few sentences of Goleman's words carefully: "These [new] rules have little to do with what we were told was important in school; academic abilities are largely irrelevant to this standard."

The OECD simply stated in their 1998 Education Policy Analysis, "Within the working world, a range of generic skills—communication, linguistic abilities, creativity, team-work, problem-solving, familiarity with new technologies—are [sic] emerging as key attributes for obtaining employment and for adapting rapidly to changing work requirements."[44] If these analysts are correct, what this means is that simply to equate educational success with "the basics for all children" is to prepare youngsters for a world on the wrong side of the divide.

But here's what is even scarier. Schools have found it difficult to educate children for the standards needed for success in the industrial age, let alone to a new higher standard incorporating both the basics and higher-order skills. In the state of Maryland, for example, figures released in late 1999 showed that "of its 1997 high school graduates who enrolled in college, 27 percent—4,240—needed remedial math. Fifteen percent had to take remedial English, and 17 percent remedial reading. (Some students take more than one course)."[45] This means over one-quarter of students going to college in the state of Maryland (which is known for having some of the best high schools in the United States) can barely do basic mathematical equations like adding and subtracting fractions. This is anecdotal evidence, but it provides some insight into the increasing gap between the needs of a post-industrial labor market and the skill levels of a large minority of young people.[46]

According to the English Department for Education and Employment, "An estimated seven million adults in England cannot locate the page reference for plumbers in the Yellow Pages. And one in three adults cannot calculate the area of a room that is 21 × 14 feet, even with the help of a calculator." It is such statistics as these about literacy and numeracy skills that politicians are responding to when they call for higher standards, the end to social promotion, and more accountability on the part of teachers. We argue that motivation plays a central role in learning the basics as well as advanced thinking skills. To have a real impact on children's ability to develop the skills for success in a knowledge society, educational reform needs to look closely at where motivation for learning originates and how it can be encouraged. For in the end, you can not force a person to learn. You can coerce them to show superficial understanding of information and concepts on tests, but in the final analysis individuals are in charge of their own learning and they will decide whether or not they want to work at it.

The point being almost entirely lost in discussions about school reform is that children need not only higher levels of basic literacy but also those collaborative skills described in Chapter 1. The stakes have been raised, but politicians and policy people are weary of dealing with the more significant issue of developing the higher-order skills of young people because, when they do, it becomes clear that the current models of schooling aren't up to the task by themselves. The agenda for such significant educational reform would go way beyond just schools, to all those other influences within society that impact on young people's learning. Such an inclusive agenda for learning would certainly go well beyond the authority and political life of most individual politicians. Why then, from the largely short-term perspective that keeps most politicians in office, would they advocate such an agenda?

Consequently, political leaders take the convenient way out and focus instead on those skills schools were designed over 100 years ago to instill in children, while ignoring or actually belittling the more advanced skills and attitudes that well paying jobs now require of all employees, and which increasingly complex democratic societies require of their citizens. There is a safety valve in the current economy for those who do not have the more advanced cognitive and learning skills referred to as higher-order skills and that is in the service sector. With the decline in manufacturing jobs (and their unions), the outlet for those without advanced skills is the vast service sector of low-paying and often times dead-end jobs. The safety valve for democracy seems to be apathy.

"Work harder" is the political logic behind educational reform when what is really needed is to start working smarter. The future is not a simple replay of the past where the debate around education and learning revolves around "teaching the basics," or "helping children to learn how to learn" in a classroom. To work smarter education must actively incorporate both, and this means expanding learning opportunities away from the school into a more equal and effective partnership with families and the larger community. Information communication technologies have the power to help facilitate and connect these larger and more open relationships. If this expanded partnership doesn't come about then we risk a continued growth in the number of people who are excluded from the full benefits of economic growth. Schools can't pick the slack up by themselves. You can't bring children up to be intelligent if the world is not intelligible to them.

9 England: A Case Study of a One-Size-Fits-All Education System

The power of vested interest is vastly exaggerated compared with the gradual encroachment of ideas.

JOHN MAYNARD KEYNES

I n the United Kingdom and the United States, reform was a constant in the area of public education for the last quarter of the 20th century. The seminal political acts initiating the era of reforms were the English 1988 Education Reform Act[1] and the 1983 presidential commission report "A Nation at Risk."[2] This chapter is a case study of the English experience. We make no apologies for this as so many countries seem to be following similar paths, and it should be helpful to see just how an education system has become increasingly centralized and controlling over the past quarter of a century. The great paradox in all this lies in the fact that this centralization has occurred while the rest of society—the economic sphere, the World Wide Web, and even much of government itself—has actually become more open, and less bureaucratic and rigid.

A National System Administered Locally

The 1944 Education Act, an intrinsic part of the legislation that comprised the welfare state in post-war England, was designed to create equality of educational opportunity by building "a national system administered locally." The Act had its theoretical origins in the Spens Report of 1938 that claimed, quite unequivocally, that it is possible at a very early age to predict with accuracy the ultimate level of a child's intellectual powers. Thus, the 11-plus examination became a test format that was "rooted in the then prevailing notion of the child as inheritor of its 'intelligence quotient.' This notion had, before the Second World War, generally been seen by its exponents as a progressive measure, favoring the 'naturally gifted' child over the rich child of modest intellect."[3] This thinking, that somehow each person was pre-ordained by nature to a set level of intellect, was all part of the greater scientific mind-set of the era, which, at its extremity, led to the theory of eugenics and the obscenities of the Nazi racial policy.

The social origins of the Butler Act were, however, essentially benign. Despite assurances in 1914–18 that post-war England would be "a land fit for heroes," this promise had been largely ignored between the two world wars. This was particularly true in education, where there was an enormous gulf between what was available to those (largely boys) able to attend grammar schools and those whose education terminated at 12, 13, or 14 in the upper classes of the elementary school. Even more enormous was the gap between the 2 or 3 percent of boys who attended the independent and fee-charging public schools, and those in most of the partially state-maintained grammar schools. The Butler Act was to define a national system of education that would provide access to secondary education to every 11-year old in the country. In practice this meant an academic grammar school for roughly the top quarter of the ability range, a technological education for the next 10 percent, and a general education for the remaining two-thirds of the population.

While the criteria for this system were to be set by central government, the delivery of schooling was to be the responsibility of the locally elected county and borough councils, numbering in total some 120 authorities. According to Professor John Tomlinson at the University of Warwick, the LEAs "were seen as the engine by which broad national policy could be adapted to local conditions and aspirations within a framework of local control. Officials could be held directly and locally accountable, and councilors could be turned out at election time."[4] It was a highly democratic model that was created by a cross-party determination not to concentrate power at one level of government.

Central government assigned to each authority a block grant based on a formula of defined statutory rights and special needs, funded directly by the Treasury, which local authorities were then allowed to supplement by the raising of additional moneys through the rates (local taxes). As years passed, the amount of money that came from the Treasury increased, and how this was administered became an increasingly contentious issue. There was a strictly moralistic tone underlying the 1944 Act. After lengthy negotiations with the churches, it was agreed that all Anglican and Roman Catholic schools that wished to become part of the state system of education should be allowed to do so. In exchange for contributing their "plant," such schools would have all their future running costs, and 90 percent of their capital costs, covered by the state. They would, however, retain the right to give priority allocation of places to pupils who, with their parents, were active members of that religious denomination (a matter of major controversy ever since).

All state schools (serving over 97 percent of the student population in the late 1940s) were required, by law, to start each day with an act of group worship, and every school was required to teach religious education to every age group.[5] In 1944, the consensus between church and state required that the purpose of education went well beyond the issues of the material world. In numerous ways, the Butler Act reflected the middle class values of the 1930s. The curriculum of the grammar school was strictly classical and humanitarian; it was about the development of thoughtful, historically knowledgeable, literate, and articulate pupils whose general intelligence would have been honed to create an officer mentality. Only the 10 percent defined as in need of a technological education were encouraged to apply their knowledge in useful, practical ways.

For the lower two-thirds of the population, the curriculum was geared toward the development of conformists. No one expected such "intellectually limited" young people either to be creative or to have the potential of improving their intelligence. Formal schooling was, for many, little more than the rote learning of basic functional skills and the acceptance of formal discipline. This form of schooling for the masses was not about developing responsible critical independent thinkers. The system encouraged and supported a society where people of higher educational achievement for life would direct the majority of citizens.

Nowhere were British class attitudes toward education more prevalent than in the roles expected of teachers and headteachers. The headteacher of a major independent public school was a social colossus. Two Archbishops of Canterbury had been such headmasters earlier in their careers. Headteachers of less significant schools held more subservient positions. Grammar school pupils tended to be taught by ex-grammar school pupils. There was an ill-defined but very clear code of conduct that recognized pupils and teachers were from the same stock. Both accepted the same values and discipline was relaxed and taken for granted. This collegiality didn't exist for the pupils in the technical and secondary modern schools. Their teachers were almost invariably ex-grammar school pupils who sought to maintain an unbridgeable distance between themselves and their pupils. In short, these teachers never expected their positions, or their ideas, to be challenged by pupils. Secondary modern schools were strictly about superiors delivering instruction and pupils doing as they were told.

The Tension Between Traditional England and the Emerging Welfare State

So, paradoxically, England moved into the more egalitarian post-war world of the welfare state with an education system that reflected the class-bias social arrangements of earlier decades. The education system was ill equipped to adjust to new and more open circumstances and was slowly being forced to play catch-up with where the rest of society thought it was moving. This was the case for the simple reason that vast sums of money had been spent on establishing buildings, which reflected the assumption that grammar schools should be built in residential areas where it was thought brighter pupils lived while the secondary modern schools were seen to be more appropriately located in working class areas.

For the most part education systems were to be administered for the first few decades after World War II by senior civil servants who had themselves been educated at public schools or at grammar schools. Many of these civil servants, however unconscious this might have been, held paternalistic attitudes towards a new system with whose values they did not personally identify. Both the successful grammar school and public school graduates, feeling they owed their success to the system, were by temperament traditionalists. "I am a pure scientist," the quote went, "you are applied, but he, poor fellow, is merely technological."

This ambiguous state of affairs was propagated by a steadily expanding economy that provided a feeling that all was well and by a general social confusion about the actual purpose of education. By the 1960s, the centrality of traditional religious attitudes and the development of gentlemanly people who knew their place in society clashed with the emergence of an increasingly secular, more egalitarian welfare state. Despite these tensions, the attitude held by many of those working in the English education system in the late 1950s and 1960s was that England would always do well for three basic reasons: there was enough coal to last English industry for at least 300 years, England's reservoir of technical skills meant that British industry would remain "the factory of the world," and the Empire gave England an unlimited market eager to gobble up its goods.

Such attitudes seem generalized, imprecise, and unquantifiable, but they were nevertheless very real. These were, the mind-sets that many teachers and pupils brought to the school, day after day, year after year. These attitudes influenced greatly the actions of politicians, and in fact it wasn't until the changes wrought by Margaret Thatcher in the 1980s that they were completely dismantled.

The first criticism of the assumptions that were behind the Butler Education Act arose in the late 1950s and early 1960s. Critics argued that it

141

was utterly inappropriate, and even damaging, to use intelligence testing at the age of 11. IQ tests were simply inaccurate predictors of future academic success, and they were so ineffective that many youngsters were scarred for life by being mislabeled. The criticism of the 11-plus exams was the first real challenge to the spirit of compromise and virtual bipartisanship of educational policy that marked the 20-year period after World War II. Yet Sir Edward Boyle, who served as the Conservative Minister of Education between 1962 and 1964, met the criticism with action. Boyle was broadly sympathetic to the ending of the 11-plus exam and the case for comprehensive education.

Thus, when the newly elected Labor government of Harold Wilson issued Circular 10/65 in July 1965, it did not reflect any great shift in educational policy. The Circular "declared the (Labor) government's objective of ending selection at 11-plus and eliminating separatism in secondary education. It requested LEAs (in the spirit of a national system administered locally) to prepare and submit to the Secretary of State plans for reorganizing secondary education on comprehensive lines, and offered guidance as to methods of achieving this."[6]

The relative ease with which politicians of both parties were able to make this change in educational policy was a result of the fact that for the most part public opinion in the country was ready for the change. It was generally accepted that selection at 11 had been shown to be manifestly unfair and was probably inhibiting both the economic and social life of the nation. Parents had made common cause with teachers in clamoring for the end of selection at 11-plus, but, as was to become quickly apparent, the organizational changes triggered by the Circular would have many unintended and far-reaching consequences.

Educational Reform as Social Engineering and the Backlash It Triggered

In the second half of the 1960s, what had been stimulated by a philosophic/theoretical consideration about the appropriate nature of intelligence and how it could be developed became quickly overwhelmed by the awesome administrative, logistical, and financial changes that administrators saw were necessary to create a fairer system of education. Facing increased political pressure, applied by central government and their own local constituents, the thinking of administrators in many of the 120 educational authorities in England went no further than the need to provide, in a single school, the kinds of education previously offered by three very different schools: grammar, technical, and secondary modern.

Policymakers believed this sort of class merger would help solve the problem of the "late developer" by providing more opportunities later in a person's educational experience. It was argued that this model of comprehensive schooling, based largely on experience in the United States, would give students the opportunity to "move up" later in their careers. This reordering of the education system was carried out in what a British social satirist contemptuously termed "the meritocratic" spirit of the times. Schooling was to help reorder society, and for those interested in fairness and social efficiency, this was a truly noble effort. However, the effort was limited from the start by the fact that it held the government sponsored schools as being the central players in the cause. From 1965 onward, schools and teachers were in the frontlines of an effort to socially re-engineer England. This increased responsibility and exposure for educators would have a political cost.

One utterly, yet unquantifiable, factor was ignored in this entire effort. England in the 1960s was a country riven by class pretensions and jealousies. As long as middle-class parents were able to send their children to a local grammar school, they were able to ignore the needs and interests of the working classes. Not surprisingly with such a history of class segregation, the reaction of many middle-class parents to the establishment of the more inclusive, comprehensive school was to send their children to independent boarding schools. "How could my son sit in a desk next to the child of my cleaning lady?" was an often heard comment. "That upsets the whole order of things!"

Despite the problems, the spirit of equality and opportunity that the removal of the 11-plus examination engendered released a burst of creativity and dedication among primary school teachers. For primary school pupils remained in the same school, and while some internal walls were knocked down to create open classrooms, the energy of teachers increasingly went into new ways of helping youngsters develop better learning skills. The more successful the primary sector became in helping children learn-how-to-learn, the more uncertain secondary teachers became as to how they should handle youngsters who, coming to them at the age of 11, expected to take greater control of their own learning. To more conventional secondary teachers, these independently thinking youngsters from the working classes were seen as threatening and out of place. For other secondary teachers, there was confusion about the proper relationship between teachers and students of mixed abilities and backgrounds. (Was it to be that of a colleague as in the grammar school, or as the instructor in the secondary modern school? A tutor or an instructor?)

In a naive burst of enthusiasm, aided and abetted by the central directives of the Department of Education, literally hundreds of schemes of secondary re-organization were pressed through simultaneously. Many old grammar schools were closed, and many children had to be bussed not twice, but four times a day. Extraordinarily convoluted timetables were constructed, and some of the ugliest schools ever designed appeared on the landscape. It made little difference which party held power. In an irony of the times, Margaret Thatcher, in her only cabinet post outside that of Prime Minister, approved in the early 1970s the closure of more traditional grammar schools than any other Minister before or since. The schemes she implemented replaced the traditional tripartite provision with the more socially egalitarian comprehensive schools.

All these tensions led to great uncertainty. Then, in what seemed the final irony, as the organizational reordering started to move into high gear, government was forced to make immediate and extensive cuts to local government expenditures on education in response to the economic crisis of the 1970s. Almost overnight, schools found their staffing quotas reduced, and educators found themselves teaching subjects to students of age groups they had never worked with before. It is not surprising that in such a stressful environment, many politicians and educators advocated the tried, true, and less-demanding route of extensive teacher-centered instruction.

In part as a response to such turbulence in their children's education, parental expectations of the independent schools changed dramatically during these turbulent years. When comprehensive primary schools were first introduced, a number of independent preparatory schools (for pupils up to the age of 13) actually faced closure as parents decided they wanted the courses and opportunities offered by a new generation of teachers and classrooms in the local village primary schools. This changed as uncertainty and confusion increased, and by the latter part of the 1970s, independent secondary schools were experiencing a field day as more and more parents from the state sector sought independent education for their children.

When in Doubt, Return to the Basics

It was James Callaghan, the Labor Prime Minister who replaced Harold Wilson in 1976, who was the first national leader to make the link between England's increasing economic problems, the chaotic state of the education system, and a marked loss in a sense of national direction and purpose. Speaking at Ruskin College Oxford in October 1976, Callaghan suggested that the public should investigate "the secret garden of the curriculum." His choice of language was picturesque and highly appropriate for the time. What he meant by this comment was that educators felt they understood what the curriculum was all about, but very few people outside of schooling actually did. He was inviting those on the outside of education to make sense of what was happening in the schools. Thirty years after the Butler Act, it was clear there no longer existed an assumed social cohesion within England or within education.

The social contract behind the Welfare States had started to come unglued. People felt increasingly justified in asking the schools what they were doing, even if these same people were totally confused themselves as to what they thought they should do for their own children. In the halcyon haze of the "anything goes generation," flower power parents were busy throwing away any sense of responsibility for the moral education of their own children. They defended this irresponsibility by arguing, "It's the school's job to give moral instruction to our children, not ours." Or, in the spirit of relativism they argued, "Kids should be allowed to find their own way of doing things." Many a senior educator would confide in a personal diary, "The blind are leading the blind."

Added to the moral and social ambiguity of the times, the expansion of comprehensive education demanded a considerable increase in staffing. Many young teachers, Panglossian in their idealism, were recruited. In the primary schools there was a reasonably well-thought through philosophy and sufficient good working practice of experiential learning methods as described in the Plowden Report. The situation in secondary education was very different. Secondary reorganization not only involved many more pupils and teachers, but, because of the economic pressures of the time, the reorganization involved merging teachers of a Grammar School background, with those of the Secondary Modern school. As mentioned earlier, these teachers came from vastly different experiences and were used to working with pupils of differing motivation and ability. When these two distinct types of teachers came together, the confusion about the actual purpose of the secondary curriculum in the comprehensive school became that much greater.

Very quickly, the comprehensive school became riddled with tensions, running strongest with the less academic pupils who saw their time in school as being a holding exercise before they were allowed into employment. These students saw little reason to invest any of their energies into a curriculum that seemed to have no application to their future work. Many teachers worked incredibly hard to try and develop a compromise position that would provide space for individual approaches to teaching and learning. The struggle for many, however, was too great, and there was a steady drift away from the profession of well-trained teachers—a trend that has

continued into the 21st century with as many as one-third of newly qualified teachers leaving the profession within three years.

What Callaghan said in 1976—and still more what he implied—put
educators on their guard. In speaking of preparation for the world of work
and the need to return to the basics, Callaghan was addressing the concerns of a worried and confused country, frightened by what many saw as
a decline in standards and confusion in education. To their chagrin, teachers, many of whom had been struggling for years to make a bewildering
system of ever-shifting priorities function, now saw themselves increasingly targeted as scapegoats for society's general economic and social
malaise. By the late 1970s, teachers, who in the spirit of the welfare state
had been told to take on more responsibilities so as to construct an increasingly egalitarian and open England, began taking a significant battering.

According to the account provided by the University of London Professor Clyde Chitty, Callaghan gave the obituary for the post-war consensus around education on that autumn day in 1976. The post-1976 effort
would, according to a Labor Prime Minister, involve "the construction of a
new educational consensus built around the more central control of the
school curriculum, create teacher accountability, and the direct subordina-
tion of the secondary curriculum to the 'needs' of the economy."[7] This was
indeed the beginning of a very changed world for those involved in education, if not as yet the parents beginning to appreciate the opportunities
and dangers of a more open and competitive global economy.

As the 1970s played out and England wallowed in economic stagnation, the leaders of both the Conservative and Labor Parties found it impossible to move beyond their traditional assumptions and constituencies.
The status quo was deeply entrenched. Yet, there was a group within the
Conservative Party who were dissatisfied with the situation in their own
party, and that of the country generally. Starting in 1965, and continuing
sporadically until 1977, these conservative radicals issued a series of Black
Papers on education that argued for a return to a primary education of formal instruction and a curriculum based on grammar school principles. In
1975, the authors of the Black Papers began extending their thinking to
the three C's: Choice, Competition, and parental Control of schools.

What the three C's represented was described powerfully by the Conservative MP Rhodes Boyson, himself a former headmaster, in his 1975
book *The Crisis in Education*: "The malaise in schools in Britain has followed from a breakdown in accepted curriculum and traditional values.
There was little concern about either political control or parental choice so
long as there was an 'understood' curriculum, which was followed by every
school. Schools may have differed in efficiency, but their common values

or curriculum were broadly acceptable. The present disillusionment of parents arises from their resentment that their children's education now depends upon the lottery of the school to which they are directed. Standards decline because both measurement and comparisons are impossible when aims and curriculum become widely divergent. . . . These problems can be solved only by making schools again accountable to some authority outside them. The necessary sanction is either a nationally enforced curriculum or parental choice or a combination of both."[8] This, added with a good dose of smashing the power of the Teacher Unions, was to become the platform for the Conservative Party's efforts at educational reform throughout the 1980s. The ideas expressed by Boyson in 1975 would culminate 13 years later in the 1988 Education Reform Act and would resonate with Labor policy into the 21st century.

Boyson and his fellow authors of the Black Papers were joined in 1975 by that other Conservative thinker, Sir Keith Joseph. Initially, few people in positions of authority took notice of their activities. After all, the Conservatives were the party of tradition and guardians of the establishment and all things English (which included traditional forms of schooling). It was the Labor Party that was given to radical proposals. It was the radicals on the Left whom the bureaucrats feared, not the radicals in right-wing think tanks.

This changed with the election, amid a plethora of strikes and high inflation, of Margaret Thatcher as Prime Minister in 1979. Sir Keith and his various allies found themselves at the very center of power. However, for the first three years of Margaret Thatcher's administration, education had a low profile, which, given the economic tensions of the time and the 1982 Falklands-Malvinas War, was hardly surprising. Mark Carlisle, an old-style Tory, was Minister of Education for the first two years of the Conservative's administration, and he did little to promote radical educational innovation. His one lasting accomplishment was the establishment of the Assisted Places Scheme in 1980, which offered scholarships for children wishing to go to private schools but whose parents could not afford the full fees. The independent schools were delighted with the scheme (more children could now afford fees so their market expanded); educators were affronted (by whose definition are independent schools necessarily better?); and the radical conservatives were furious (this was but a travesty of a dynamic free-market of educational choices they sought).

An Opportunity Lost

In September 1981, Sir Keith persuaded the Prime Minister that he should transfer as Minister of Trade and Industry to the Department of Education.

Such a move was unprecedented for the third most important Minister in the cabinet. The architect of the conservative economic revolution and tight money control running a department that had always seen itself as totally removed from economic theory, and had the least appreciation of accountability, seemed unthinkable. Joseph brought with him a powerful respect and admiration for the power of market forces to help solve problems of stagnation and inertia in both the private and public sectors.

Educational bureaucrats were incredulous, and this served the interests of Keith Joseph. As the Tories saw it, the conservative revolution would be stillborn if they could not find a way of controlling local authority expenditure. The biggest component of this public expenditure was on education. With the appointment of Sir Keith, radical educational organization and radical ideas on how education should be funded came together in the hands of one person.[9]

In practice, Joseph wanted essentially to alter where power and influence would reside in the education system, but his efforts were not guided by a credible underlying theory of learning. What Joseph had as informing principles for children's learning were the "academic basics" as first developed by Plato and as rehashed by the authors of the Black Papers. This pattern of shaking up the system, without basing the efforts on a theory of learning more coherent and developed than that of the ancient Greeks, would be repeated many times in the 1980s and 1990s on both sides of the Atlantic. In hindsight, this was unfortunate because Joseph's classical market liberalism—an economic and social theory based on opportunity, personal responsibility and community support—was highly congruent with what is now known about the dynamic, open, and supportive environment within which the brain thrives and learns. A model of open and dynamic learning that integrated economic opportunity, schooling, community interaction, home, and information communication technology would have been supportive of Joseph's economic and social arguments for an entrepreneurial society and vice-versa. But it was not to be.

These ideas about a community-owned model of learning were in the distinct minority in the early 1980s, but they were reflected powerfully by a diverse group of people who met for a week-long conference in 1983 to consider the nature of education for the 21st century. Education 2000, as it would later be known, was an influential, bipartisan group that included leading industrialists, community figures, academics, and private individuals. The members of this group, who first met under the patronage of the Duke of Edinburgh, were well aware of the numerous disconnected initiatives at the time in England that sought to improve individual aspects of education. The gathering was dismayed, however, by the fact so much energy was going into educational reform without any overall unifying set of principles as to what kind of world the reformers were hoping to create.

Education 2000 saw the need for the very broadest of thinking about economic, social, and technological issues to be drawn together in a way that would provide clarity and cohesiveness to necessary educational reform. Their report, "Education 2000: A Consultative Document on Hypotheses for Education in A.D. 2000," sought a consensus on the centrality of learning across society. They gave considerable attention to the way in which the new technologies of information and communication could be used to support a more open and dynamic form of learning. The group quickly understood that learning transcended the school.

They recognized that such open forms of learning would require profound changes not only in formal education, but also in the informal opportunities for learning provided by the community. This was a novel proposition at the time, but commended itself immediately to hardpressed business and commercial people who respected the energy of private sector initiatives but were confused as to their significance in the overall scheme of educational reform. "There are more educational pilots around than there are aircraft in the Royal Air Force," one cynical and confused business leader commented at the time.

In attempting to set out a broad, national agenda, the conference findings annoyed many sections of the educational establishment: "Change is not simply something which applies to other people; we all have to reconsider how new ideas also make our own accustomed way of doing things quite possibly out of date." As the activities of Education 2000 became better known throughout the 1980s, its very success antagonized other groups who, however much they may have identified with the message of consensus building, wanted to maintain the role of messenger for themselves.

This was particularly true of two influential groups: the School/Industry Liaison Officers of the major corporations and senior LEA officials. Despite the enthusiasm of chief executives from many of England's leading companies for a more coherent education strategy, Education 2000 received no support whatsoever from any company that had an official school liaison link. "The reason is clear," said Chris Marsden of British Petroleum. "We are backing the chief education officers. It is their job to do this, not yours. You are only clouding the issue." To the chief education officers, the emphasis that Education 2000 placed on the partnership between school and community was total anathema and weakened the authority's claim for more money for schools. The fact that Education 2000 was talking about a changed way of doing things rather than just lobbying for money was something that no one else wanted to understand.

At its inception, Education 2000 also annoyed, much to the conference participants' surprise, Sir Keith Joseph. The reason in hindsight was simple: The Conservative Government of Margaret Thatcher was no longer interested in consensus politics. An education policy based on choice, competition, and control was not interested in deeper thinking about how learning actually happens. Yet, it was because Sir Keith intuitively understood the connected nature of issues and believed in the central importance of an open and dynamic democratic society that he eventually became a supporter of the efforts of Education 2000. Upon retirement from the Department for Education, he actually became president of the Trust in 1988.

Power Resides in the System

Over time, however, the input of the Education 2000 Trust would be subverted by that of more politically connected and partisan interest groups within the educational establishment. The position that eventually emerged, and which would be solidified in the 1988 Education Act, was one that promised not compromise based on how children can best be helped to learn but "a national curriculum, rigorous national tests at seven, eleven, fourteen and sixteen. . . . [, including the] opportunity for schools to opt out of local authorities altogether, and the break-up of the largest LEA in the country."[10] As time would prove, the 1988 Education Act was driven by systemic issues of power and money rather than concentrating on how parents, businesspeople, concerned citizens, and schools could come together to facilitate children's learning. Because of this, the policies around the Education Act were riddled with paradoxes, confusion, and problems that have had to be addressed with new legislation in almost every year since 1988.

Joseph's experience as Minister of Education was to set the pace, not only for subsequent educational policy in England, but to ensure that the educational debate would be linked to the emergence of the global economy in many other countries as well. Here was a new global agenda. The primacy given the economic perspective around educational issues, especially global competition, as set out by Joseph was to be vastly influential. For example, in 1983 a U.S. presidential commission issued "A Nation at Risk," which argued, "Whether we like it or not, we are beginning to see that we are pitted against the world in a gigantic battle of brains and skill, with the markets of the world, work for our people, and internal peace and contentment as the prizes at stake."[11]

With the 20/20 vision of historical hindsight, it is unfortunate that the free-market arguments of Sir Keith were spun by politicians in his own party around the basis of fear and threat rather than that of opportunity. Joseph believed that a "free economy" supported a good society where all people had the opportunity to use and develop their talents and interests to the maximum of their potential. A good society was one based on opportunity, and support for children to help take control of their own lives. In contrast, fear encourages entrenchment and the attitude that we all must simply work harder or face the horrible prospects of falling permanently behind our international competitors. Fear invites deference to experts and systems.

An alternative political spin was available in 1983. This spin could have developed a more balanced responsibility for educational success, and it would have been an argument of new opportunities that required everyone to start working more imaginatively and in new and more effective partnerships. It was just this sort of "coordinated effort," based on shared values of excellence for all young people, between business, parents, community resource groups, and government that Education 2000 sought. In such an effort there is little room for scapegoats and blame.

It was in the spirit of opportunity and consensus that the founders of Education 2000 argued, "We are not taking up any party political stance—indeed we have probably taken ideas from most shades of political opinion; and the main practical reason for this is that, during the time-scale of the implementation of the changes we wish to see come about, there could well be four or five governments of different political character."[12] Not surprisingly, because of the intellectual support Education 2000 received from business, it is just these sorts of smarter and more coordinated efforts based on shared principles of excellence that successful businesses and organizations used to thrive in the 1990s.

As the 1980s played out, and this has extended through the 1990s, educators have largely not seen themselves as an integral part of a smarter system working to help all children take responsibility for their own learning and futures; rather, they have seen themselves as isolated and under siege by politicians running on take-charge election platforms. The Conservative Government, and after 1997 the Labor Government, increasingly centralized control of schooling at all levels. As the Chief Inspector of the Dudley LEA observed that year, "The Conservatives told us what to teach, and now the Labor Party is telling us how to teach. . . . Is there anything that could be more demoralizing and de-skilling of teachers than this incredible level of centralized direction, particularly when the best teachers know that there is never just one best way?"

Remember Frederick Winslow Taylor's comments from the close of the 19th century? "You do it my way, by my standards, at the speed I mandate, and in so doing achieve a level of output I ordain, and I'll pay you handsomely for it, beyond anything you might have imagined. All you have to do is take orders, and give up your way of doing the job for mine." It is in the spirit of Taylor's supremacy of the system that educational reforms in England, and increasingly across the United States, have been based since the 1980s. The essence of the move towards Taylorism in education was captured in a program that David Blunkett, the Education and Employment Secretary, announced in late 1998. He heralded a £1 billion package to provide performance-related pay to teachers, headteachers, and schools that raised standards. According to Mr. Blunkett, the program would "mean greater individual accountability, more flexibility and higher standards" with assessment validated by independent experts.[13] The scheme would create "a link between pay and children's results for the first time this century."[14]

It is just these sorts of government-mandated schemes that a columnist for *The Times of London* was referring to when she argued, "In the real world (a Tory-built world which new Labor shows no sign of challenging) heads of school departments are described as 'line managers' and teachers treated as mere shelf-stackers 'delivering the national curriculum'."[15] The problems with such an apparently straightforward scheme are many,[16] but the most significant one is that children's learning is not something that is measured as easily as the quality of widgets or car parts. *The Guardian* picked up on this theme when it observed of Blunkett's plan, "The idea of distributing bonuses to schools that do well is fine in principle, but everything once again hinges on how success is measured: there's a lot of progress yet to be made towards satisfactory measures of value added."[17]

The increased political emphasis placed on formal systems of learning has led schools and teachers to become the dominant players in children's overall learning and development. This has had the unintended consequence of making bureaucracies and their staffs the only factors in children's learning held fully accountable. As far as the public debate around education and learning goes, the role parents, fellow students, and the larger community play has become marginalized. It simply does not fit into the statistical equations used by the government. Yet research is increasingly arguing that this is where the greatest influence on children's development, in particular creativity, is to be found.[18]

The parameters of the debate are not around learning as a mental and social process but around issues related directly to institutional schooling. Whatever positive role adults play outside of classrooms is almost incidental to the "really important work of the professional education system." In the United States it is considered a success by those running the system if parents spend "20 minutes a day reading to their children." The fact is, and there are profound biological and cultural reasons for this, that the overwhelming majority of children who are successful in education are so successful because their parents, siblings, and the other peers and adults who care about them value education and learning. These children reside in a culture of learning, and they carry these attitudes into the school.

There is a riddle here that needs some unpacking. Parents often get confused about the role they are expected to play in their children's learning. Indeed, many educators actually work to maintain this gulf between school professionals and the general public. A European professor of education who was angered by the notion that the barriers between schools and the larger community should be broken down, wrote, "Those involved in school management draw a sharp boundary between the areas of education which are so-called professional areas, and therefore reserved for professionals (i.e., teachers), and those in which other members of the community (e.g., parents or retired people) can legitimately be involved. While many schools encourage the involvement of members of the community for certain activities, those activities are clearly separated from the 'professional' work of teachers. It is very difficult and indeed might well be foolhardy to try and blur this distinction."

Sir Keith Joseph, and many other like-minded thinkers, whose own education had benefited enormously from a range of extracurricular activities, intuitively understood the significance of family and community in learning. Yet, in the early and mid-1980s there was little "scientific" evidence as to why these informal sources of learning were important in children's overall intellectual and social development. Cognitive sciences and the breakthroughs in the brain and evolutionary sciences that offer a more rigorous and coherent understanding of the biology of learning were in their infancy in the early 1980s.

Policy debates centered primarily around the competing theories and experiences of educational philosophers (which were highly politicized) and the classroom experiences of teachers (which politicians had worked hard to tarnish). Many of the progressive ideas about learning had been discredited by Conservative politicians who dismissed these as "faddish educational ideas" advocated by Labor and which they argued had contributed greatly to the social and economic upheavals of the 1970s. It is one of the little understood ironies of history that just as cognitive science started to come of age by offering some very important insights into how it was children actually learned and developed creativity, these were being categorized and dismissed by political experts as "elitist tripe with no real scientific basis."

The experiences of Education 2000 offer important insights into why, in the case of education, politics really is local. Parents, when the case was presented to them in an open fashion, were quick to support Education 2000's suggestion that successful educational reform required community involvement. Parents accepted and supported the argument that groups of knowledgeable and enthusiastic people should, within their own communities, be actively encouraged to work with schools in finding new ways of supporting all aspects of children's learning. Scouts, Guides, church choirs, youth clubs, and especially homes, parents and business leaders argued, were as key to young people's development as were the schools. Communities that wanted to develop an environment in which all children would be taught to take control of their own learning needed to draw all these groups together into a single agenda.

What many people find surprising was that teachers in the Education 2000 projects really valued the input and support of the larger community. In fact, so great was teacher enthusiasm for the ideas behind Education 2000 that by 1990 there were nine communities in different parts of England—Bury, Coventry, Inner City Leeds, Loughborough, Ipswitch, Swindon, Tring, and Calderdale, and Letchworth—working to develop a community-wide approach to learning. The goal of these communities was to develop a fundamentally changed set of relationships between schools, home, and community facilitated by technology. These were powerful grassroots initiatives of the kind that any supporter of local community control over education would envy.[19]

The supporters of Education 2000 saw these projects as a way of demonstrating that new methods of organizing teaching and learning were essential if young people of all abilities were to develop genuine skills of creativity and personal enterprise. To the detriment of the values behind Education 2000, however, education minister after education minister since Keith Joseph has sought to move British government education policy ever further away from those people who know their children best. Educational policy in the 1990s became so dogmatic and partisan that alternative educational arrangements were treated if not as sedition, certainly as criticism to be responded to aggressively.

As the decade wore on, tension between what supporters of Education 2000 were striving for in the nine projects, and the ever increasingly centralized and prescriptive directives of central government, became too great for most to bear. Steadily, Education 2000 was squeezed out of the mainstream agenda of educational reform (which was now seen as being driven entirely from the center by ministerial mandates), and left with those self-contained projects that were good for individual children but did little to change the relationship of the school to the larger community.

The 1988 Education Reform Act

By early 1986, Keith Joseph retired from Parliament. His had been a thoughtful approach to policymaking, even though his intentions were radical. Within five years he had firmly placed economic arguments at the center of educational policy. He had effectively broken the power of the Local Education Authority ("a national system administered locally" became little more than a parody) and, through his dealings with the Manpower Services Commission, had found a way of fundamentally influencing the curriculum. He had also accomplished what no other former secretary of education had achieved: He had changed the examination system.

In terms of what was to follow, Keith Joseph must be seen as almost moderate in his policies, and certainly always thoughtful. While willing to be really radical when convinced this was right, he was a political pragmatist. (He had, for instance, rejected the voucher.) He had also been "at the creation" of the conservative revolution and as a result had a sense of authority and purpose that those who followed him would not have.

The ebullient, energetic, and ambitious Kenneth Baker who succeeded Sir Keith as Minister in 1986 was, in comparison to Joseph's deliberate and methodical approach to policy making, always in a great hurry. Margaret Thatcher had encouraged him in 1986 by arguing "something had to be done about the schools." Imbued with the new conservative ideology of choice, competition, and control, academic affairs intrigued him, and he enjoyed the company of intellectuals, at least when their political leanings were similar to his. Keith Joseph had opened an opportunity for radical reform, and Kenneth Baker saw himself as the man who could lead it and so further his own rise in the Conservative Party.

It is important to point out that Baker, and this applies to numerous other educational bureaucrats and policymakers, believed that by simply applying free-market principles (choice and competition) to a system, whether it be education, or the police or the postal service, that particular system would start working smarter. In the spirit of the survival of the fittest—competition breeds intelligence—you either get smarter or die. There are two problems with this notion when speaking about educational reform. The first is the fact that there was absolutely no thought, after Keith Joseph, given among free-marketers within the Conservative government that, for an increase in productivity, it is actually necessary to interject insights from research as well as integrate new ideas from information technologies. This required thoughtfulness that high-stakes politics did not allow. The second problem was that no matter how often people may have spoken of a free-market in education, England has never had such a thing. The failure of the voucher movement under Sir Keith assured this.

Baker, as well as being an ardent advocate of the free market, was also ardent in his support of information communication technologies. He never, however, made the connection between technology and learning theory that, with his dynamic energy, he could have used to really transform the relationship between teaching and learning. He felt the need to respond to the Right Wing of the party, which was becoming increasingly frustrated that the systemic reforms they sought just did not seem to be happening. He was convinced that to move fast was necessary to overcome the progressives in the educational establishment who were obstructing real change, or so his advisers told him.

In an effort to move more rapidly towards a free-market in education, extensive discussions were held at Downing Street in late 1986 and early 1987. The meeting was instigated by right wing pressure groups such as the Center for Policy Studies, the Hillgate Group, and others who wished the government's agenda to go far further and focus on the breaking up of the entire comprehensive system. Their views had been set out in the Black Papers of two decades earlier. They also wanted the eventual removal of all vestiges of local control, including the complete destruction of Local Education Authorities and their elected committees. Thus began the posturing for policies that were to result in the 1988 Education Act, which quickly became known as the Baker Act. In contrast to Butler, who had spent the better part of five years engineering the consensus that resulted in support of the 1944 Education Act, Baker pushed through his legislation ("the most radical of 50 years") within less than 18 months of preparation. He made no attempt to seek consensus among those in the system, let alone those of goodwill outside of the system. He did not have to. Joseph had created a new set of power relationships, and Baker exploited these to the full. He and the system were unassailable.

The Act was, wrote Peter Willby, "a gothic monstrosity of legislation." It increased the power of the Education Secretary to a quite alarming degree and returned to central government a control over the curriculum that had been surrendered in 1944. The Act was contentious from the very start. Her advisors persuaded Margaret Thatcher that government's assessment plans had been "hijacked" by the detested "professionals." In reality, Baker was discovering what Keith Joseph had learned before him: that to change educational systems successfully required altering power relationships.

156

Nick Davies of *The Guardian* gave an historical explanation of the Baker Act in 1999 when he observed, "A reform of schools would have to have, as its overriding priority, the welfare of children. Since this involved the construction of a new system to disseminate learning and knowledge, it would have to be built on a particularly strong intellectual foundation, a great deal of solid research and clear thinking. Not so. The most sweeping educational reform this century, it transpires, had just as much to do with guesswork, personal whim, and bare-knuckle politics."[20]

To Thatcher the Act was an abomination. What was needed, she said, was simply "the teaching of the six R's; reading, writing, arithmetic, religious education, and right and wrong." Her choice of language may seem quaint, but in her terms this was more of what young people needed than the complex academic prescriptions that Baker incorporated from the academic establishment. These intellectual instructions wrought havoc for teachers and others over the following years as the administrative load of these reforms became completely and utterly unmanageable. The Act did not open up new opportunities but stifled everyone with the mandates of the system.

In summary, the 1988 Education Act created a national curriculum for all state school pupils. Attainment targets were to be set for all children. Assessments would be linked to the publication of results in ways that would enable judgements to be made by parents about the "effectiveness" of individual schools. This was the free-market aspect of the law. Originally, assessment was to have been undertaken by the schools themselves but, in the words of the 1987 National Curriculum consultative document published by the Department of Education and Science, "at the heart of the assessment process there will be nationally prescribed tests done by all pupils to supplement the individual teacher's assessments."[21]

"Any Color You Want"

The message to teachers could not have been clearer. Whoever sets the tests conditions what is taught; one inevitably follows the other. However much individual teachers might have yearned for some common definition of what the curriculum was to offer, teachers feared the idea of central control of the curriculum even more than they feared the lack of clarity they had experienced within local government. Teachers were no longer to have the freedom, as they saw it, to develop curricula that responded to the needs of individual students. This power play by Government was seen by many teachers as an affront to their professional competence, and progressively increased the influence of bureaucrats over children's learning at the expense of teachers. As opposed to the business mantra of the 1990s that argues power should be dispersed throughout the system, in the case of the 1988 Education Reform Act, power moved up and away from those on the ground.

Secondly, the Act pitted schools against each other in a competition defined by rules that sought preconceived ends. The rules and the markers for success did not emerge to fit the needs of the market participants themselves as Education 2000 argued; rather, they were designed to apply monolithically across every school in the country. The Government basically told the consumer (parents) what to buy, and argued this was a free market because it let the consumer decide where to purchase the goods. This is akin to Henry Ford saying, "The customer can have any color he wants as long as it is black."

This emphasis on competition between schools to deliver one set of goods throughout the system effectively told local communities to stay out of education if they weren't willing to play by Government's rules. Such arrangements are antithetical to all those who believe learning requires collaboration, not only between the teachers of one school and another (in their continuous training processes and the development of curricula) but, even more importantly, between the formal provision of the classroom and the informal provision of the community. Successful communities don't simply split themselves up in hinterlands around individual schools; rather, they broadly identify with all their schools.

The changes in the United Kingdom have been mirrored, if not systemically in spirit, in many educational reform efforts around the world. In the United States, the steadily growing political influence over education in the 1990s has led to the rhetoric of "high standards," "accountability," and the culture of testing being central planks for any politician seeking office and for school administrators seeking big contracts to run large public school systems. The irony in all this, which the next chapter will unpack, is that the 1990s was a decade of major advances in understanding both the brain and how human learning takes place and can be most successfully facilitated. These new insights that build on many older theories and philosophies of learning blow apart the simplistic notion of successful education being driven by politicians and policy makers running on slogans of just high standards and accountability.

10 Making the Leap from Instruction and Schools to Learning and Community

There are always two parties—the party of the past and the party of the future, the establishment and the movement.

RALPH WALDO EMERSON

For good reasons this book is called *The Unfinished Revolution*. We are writing about a revolution in thinking about learning, human development, and community rejuvenation that has been simmering for well over a century. It is, quite simply, about developing learning arrangements that maximize human potential by "going with the grain of the brain." However compelling the new ideas are, in reality, they challenge the theoretical assumptions and mind-sets that have underpinned much of educational thought for more than a century and the institutional frameworks built up to support them.

Rigorous, compelling, ideas in and of themselves do not guarantee that change will occur. A clear strategy based on a clear set of core values and beliefs is necessary to win the intellectual and emotional support of a wide range of people. This is about community issues, not simply schooling. To successfully use the ideas in this book to develop new models of learning will require many people within the current educational systems, and outside of them, to forgo their immediate self-interest in favor of long-term gains for children. A cynic would say this will never happen, but humans have been making sacrifices for the younger generations for as long as we have roamed the earth. Adults have made sacrifices far greater than re-appraising how our time and money are spent in relationship to the needs of children.

There have been moments when this revolution seemed to be gathering momentum. For example, the followers of Froebel, Montessori, Pestalozzi, and Dewey thought they were beginning to make real progress toward building models of learning that helped all children take control of their own learning and talents. So, too, did those working in the English experiential elementary schools in the late 1960s and early 1970s. A few innovators have made a lasting impression on educational practice, but, like Montessori, they have maintained their convictions by keeping outside mainstream education. That is exactly what is now happening at the dawn of the 21st century to the children of successful entrepreneurs in the new digital industries. Such families are feeding the homeschool movement and the Montessori schools.

Most innovators are all too easily likened to bright, shooting stars: They are here for a short while, but once they have burned themselves out, the darkness returns. Nevertheless, there are reasons to believe that we are living at a moment of special opportunity. The nature of the world in which education exists has changed dramatically in the last generation. What young people need is qualitatively different than what was previously thought to be necessary.

Large numbers of people, including some politicians, in many different countries are beginning to realize that simply getting young people to work harder on developing basic academic skills will not be as significant as helping them work smarter in altogether different ways. This book has sought to identify a conjunction between these new approaches to learning with a better appreciation of the kinds of schools and communities that the challenges of the 21st century will demand. If this conjunction is to occur it will be because people are consciously, and systematically, working together to bring learning communities into being.

The changes these communities seek would go well beyond current school reform agendas. They would challenge people to rethink at a personal level their own commitment to young people and their commitment to establishing forms of community that have the intellectual, social, and even spiritual needs of young people at their very center. Such communities would force people to rethink the old adage: "Do we work to live or live to work?" This book has been about raising difficult, and controversial, questions in order to help you, the reader, decide if you want to take on the challenge of reinventing community around the learning needs of children. It is not a challenge for the meek, but such social change is certainly possible. The change is simply waiting for "us" to make it happen. "Us" means everyone, for if the challenge set forth here is to be taken up, it will require a massive grass-roots effort.

Evidence from science and the personal experience of vast numbers of ordinary human beings support those seeking learning arrangements that move well beyond what occurs just in an academic classroom. The education system of the future will need to actively permeate learning opportunities throughout the entire culture. This form of dynamic learning will probably not even be seen as a system but as a way of life. Learning will be something that we all recognize, encourage, and actively support through community participation and the power of the connected world of information communication technology.

Schools are only part of the equation for those interested in trying to determine how to best prepare young people for the opportunities and challenges of the 21st century. Thus, for those who define the debate around just school effectiveness, high standards, improving test scores, and accountability, we argue that you're missing many of the central issues that must inform learning policy. Or, more simply put, education reform is only a subcomponent of the more important issue of how we go about creating a learning society.

This final chapter will show that if the goal is to help all children develop the skills necessary to become creative and responsible lifelong learners, then we must move well beyond the mantras of reform swirling around current systems of education. It is now necessary to consider how communities can begin to actively build on young people's natural learning predispositions, their ability to learn how to learn, and the principle of weaning young people of their dependence on direct formal instruction.

The Role of Schools in a Learning Community

Formal schooling is an intrinsic part of lifelong learning, but it is only one part, critical though that part is. Schools need a new focus on pedagogic practice that openly and continuously emphasizes children's ability to understand their own thinking and learning. All this has to become more "visible." Because effective learning goes beyond the classroom to handling real-life challenges, subject content has to be presented in such a way that it (1) constantly enables even the youngest children to understand the skills they are developing and (2) helps them to identify which skills are appropriate to particular situations. Young learners need the opportunity to stand on their own feet. From this assertion of the importance of an intellectual weaning that parallels normal human development, it follows that maximum teacher support is needed when the student is very young. It is at this stage that the foundations for building both process understanding and content understanding begin.

Class size is important. To return to Figure 2.1 in Chapter 2, we recommend as a starting point for discussion the principle that class size should equal the age of the student times two: 5-year-olds in classes of 10, 6-year-olds in classes of 12, and so on. But class size alone is only part of the issue; it is class size that makes pedagogic change possible. Smaller classes give the teachers the space to help children develop metacognitive skills; it is in such smaller classes that teachers can help students "see" their own learning. It is at this early stage that genuine thoughtfulness develops. Children who learn how to do this at a young age do not expect so much teacher instruction later. This completely reverses the conventional role of the teacher where currently the largest class sizes are in the first years of primary education, with classes getting smaller as the pupils get older. We call reapportioning educational funding and its focus to better serve the instructional needs of children turning the system "upside down."

This argument is based on fully utilizing the learning predispositions and windows of opportunities of the youngest learners with the intention of ensuring adolescents are equipped with the basic skills and the ability to learn how to learn on their own. This would be the aim of primary education and the raison d'être for very small class sizes in the earliest years of education. If primary schools do their job correctly, then the express goal of secondary education would be to wean adolescents of their dependence on direct formal instruction for successful learning. A high school graduate should be a responsible, competent, and highly motivated lifelong learner who actively seeks to constantly build his or her own knowledge base and skills in order to overcome challenges and excel at taking advantage of opportunities.

This new emphasis on children becoming continuous learners—reflective practitioners—means that it is critical that teachers are also given the opportunity to be continuous learners. The professional development of teachers has to become a continuous process fully integrated into the whole life of the school, and it should be funded accordingly. Teachers need access to the same high-quality training programs that successful businesses use. Teachers need to understand the practices of nonacademic learning. For young people to become responsible lifelong learners, teachers need to be prepared to help children discriminate between faulty and valid information (their traditional role) and effective and ineffective learning strategies (key to the development of higher-order skills). Both how teachers will need to teach, and what they need to teach, have to be better understood.

The role of the teacher will change as pupils mature. Initially, the student-teacher relationship would be close, but teacher support would reduce as the pupil demonstrated increased confidence in the application of the initial skills. Teachers (to use the language of cognitive apprenticeship) would become expert in the application of both "scaffolding" and "fading." To develop their critical faculties, teachers would become more Socratic. As direct formal instruction decreases, so the use of learning resources (both within the school and outside of it) would of necessity increase in a genuinely open, on-demand way, and not as an alternative way.

This approach would also change the concept of class size for older students in a dramatic way. For example: If 34 17-year-olds need to be taught for each of eight periods in a day, and there is only one teacher available at any one time, then a class of 34 is the inevitable result. However, if some of these students are effectively working under their own direction for half the time (and for the previous 12 years have been prepared to do just that), then, certain timetable logistics permitting, they could effectively be taught in classes of 18 for each of four lessons in a day, or classes of 12 for each of three lessons, directing their own work for the remainder of the day.

There are examples, albeit exceedingly rare, of just this sort of arrangement working well in the United States. A 17-year-old student, largely studying the sciences and hoping to get into an Ivy League college to study medicine, works as a birthing assistant at the maternity ward in the local hospital. For two days a week she helps mothers who are in labor, and during the three days she is in class she carries a beeper to answer the call of the hospital. If the delivery room is short-staffed, they beep her for assistance. This student is taking on adult responsibilities and learning what her future life work is really all about. Such an experience also provides her with the motivation to do whatever it takes to attain her dream of being a doctor. The dream is tangible, and she will have met role models that have actually accomplished what she wants for herself.

The high school we are describing has two rules that govern this student's internship. First, whatever class-time she misses she has to make up in her own time. Second, if she behaves in a way that might bring disrespect on the school, she is reprimanded publicly in the presence of her peers and taken out of the program.[1] Such a model of learning offers adolescents immediate and meaningful ways to test their developing intellectual powers, to feel needed, and to be essential members of a community.

Once the emphasis in schools is more formally linked to the skills of managing lifelong learning, so the potential of information and communication technology becomes clearer. Word processing for older students releases the curriculum from the pace of paper and pencil technologies, and the Internet creates domestic gateways into knowledge to rival any library.

Students also benefit from Internet access to lectures, workshops, and educational materials. Such forms of distance learning are happening in many countries with university students taking courses with top scholars from their home computers.

George Washington University in the United States already offers an advanced degree in business management that is organized around the Internet, and students from around the world participate in the course. Both Indiana University and the University of Missouri have been granted accreditation to operate on-line high schools. When York University in England compared the overall academic performance of its Internet students, it found that when dropouts were removed from the equation: "Internet students achieved significantly higher grades than in-class students."[2] To those familiar with the growth of the British Open University over the past 35 years, this will come as no surprise. Motivated students, working at their own pace but with structured support as and when needed, have over many years made exceptional progress.

The potential significance for secondary education is immense. There is absolutely no reason why 14-, 15-, and 16-year-olds, who understand their own learning and have a rigorous base of knowledge on which to build would any longer need to take all their coursework in the confines of a teacher-directed classroom. Young people who have gone through the kind of education we are advocating would need, and want, a different form of education in the upper years of secondary education. This is where the most profound changes have to occur. Instead of education for older students being delivered almost entirely by teachers to confined students following the conventional academic curriculum, education could be a far more rigorous, far broader, and more connected affair, more related to what was earlier assumed to be appropriate only for the brightest pupils. This would also have the added benefit of offering new flexibility to school administrators dealing with shortages of qualified teachers. Key to doing this successfully would be seeing primary and secondary education as a seamless learning experience, not as two separate entities operating under differing political, pedagogic, professional, and economic concerns.

A truly "new economy" will be one in which creativity and personal enterprise are applied at all levels. Unfortunately, because formal education systems are still stuck thinking largely in terms of teachers and students, they encourage the idea that pupils are still not skilled or mature enough to act as mentors of younger pupils. In a model of learning that accepted the ability of adolescents to take responsibility for their own learning, it would be desirable if part of the experience of older adolescents also involved some commitment to working formally with younger children.

A recent illustration of this comes from Estonia. With money for only three years of information technology education, the education system concentrates on 14-, 15- and 16-year olds. Then it requires these students to spend five hours or more a week in each of the subsequent four years as teacher assistants in elementary schools, working with children four or six years younger than themselves. This is another example of adolescents learning from their experiences of being useful, and this approach actually allows youngsters to give something back to the community that's paying for their education. Though this approach was brought in for pragmatic reasons, it nevertheless addresses a basic need: You never really know something until you have had to teach it. In a properly worked-out scheme utilizing this principle, such teaching would be the result of careful tutoring of the older students and then the careful assessment of how well they assist the younger students.

The Clash: Unifying Understandings of Sustainable Expenditure and Intellectual Weaning

With the discussion above in mind, let us reconsider the two figures from Chapter 2 and superimpose them, uniting a biological model of learning and the current model of education dominant in the West.

It must again be stressed that the present arrangements for conventional schooling are a reflection of the assumptions about human nature and learning that emerged to support the needs of the industrial revolution. As Figure 10.1 (see p. 166) shows, this creates a dramatic clash. The clash reveals the desperately inappropriate educational provisions for the youngest children, and it goes far in explaining why, as they move into adolescence, many youth are so ill-equipped to handle the biological and social changes that then hit them. Over the years, teachers have come to fear the aimlessness and apparent reckless irresponsibility of so many adolescents. So the call has constantly been for more resources to control youngsters, who are already feeling increasingly sullen and misunderstood.

Adolescents' criticism of teachers and the system, not always well-articulated but always full of passion, is immediately thrown back on them: They are uncooperative! At the stage in which they are impelled by their natural predispositions to take responsibility, they are inhibited by their lack of early skill development. They become frustrated, disillusioned, and awkward. In ways that often seem incomprehensible to worried adults, their energies are expended in kicking the system. A century or so ago, girls married after menstruation at the age of 16 or so, while boys took up jobs by the age of 14 that eventually gave them the independence to

Figure 10.1 The Clash of Present Educational Arrangements with the Progression of Normal Human Intellectual Development

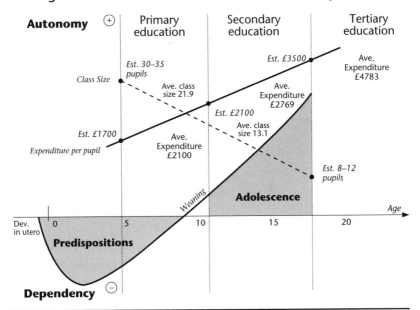

start a family. Now, not only does menstruation begin earlier (around 11) but in an effort to protect adult jobs, it is now almost impossible to begin a job that offers a living wage until the age of 22 or 23. For an extended period of 10 to 15 years, adolescents are neither children nor adults. The media glamorizes the 17-year-old beauty while moralists seeking family values call for a morality based on ever-longer periods of delayed gratification. The biological turmoil is real enough, but the cultural confusion is even greater.

Are We at an Evolutionary Crossroads?

Most conventional school reform has failed to realize its full potential because it attempted to mandate new structures without changing the rules throughout the system. Thus, vast numbers of educational reformers and innovators have seen their best thinking frustrated by the need to fit their innovations into the parameters of the existing system. Imaginative attempts to help children understand their own learning in elementary schools have almost invariably been minimized by the experience of the secondary school where the pedagogic tradition is different. The flip-side of this is when children attend traditional teacher-centered primary schools and then enter a high school that is based on open collaboration with peers, experiential learning, making connections between disciplines, and the extensive use of information communication technology. Students who are unprepared struggle to handle their intellectual freedom often flounder and risk becoming a problem.

An example of dealing with this disconnect between the primary school experience and the secondary school comes from the Illinois Mathematics and Science Academy (IMSA). IMSA accepts students from across the state of Illinois and consistently leads the state of 11 million people in academic achievement. The president of the academy, Stephanie Pace Marshall, observed in early 2000 that many students initially struggle in taking control of their own learning because for the first 10 years of their schooling, they were never expected to do so. Old habits are hard to eradicate. The academy compensates for this by providing extra support for first year students, support based on the premise of short-term scaffolding. Students are helped in taking control of their own learning.

What's even more disappointing than the initial transition many entering students face, Pace Marshall says, is that students who excell at IMSA often find the first couple years of university work stifling because they feel constrained by the teacher-dominated form of instruction. They have to tolerate this until near the end of their first degree, when they are allowed to start developing their own programs and artifacts. The freedom to do original research, or create new computer programs, isn't possible until the students enter graduate school. The game of schooling seems a waste of time when young people already know the power of taking control of their own learning, and the pride of creating new ideas, concepts, or technical know-how.

At all levels of the education system, it seems as if the system is simply reluctant to "let go" of students. It is as if they believe that no learning is taking place unless students are being taught. Rather than weaning youngsters, the system seems bent on playing down their ability to do something for themselves. In a variety of subtle, and not so subtle, ways, Western society has trivialized all levels of young people in the school. Is it any wonder teenagers say they feel bored, uninvolved, and conflicted in a world that tells them what to do instead of expecting them to work it out for themselves?

It is these discontinuities, together with the need to jump through all kinds of hoops, that has led to a call for reversing upside down and inside out systems of education. Without a consistent, integrated agenda that seeks coherent change across the learning experiences of children and young people, piecemeal change is always going to be disappointing, and the system will go on doing pretty much what it has for the last 100 years.

With the knowledge and experiences currently available, it is not an exaggeration to say that societies now stand at an exciting time in human history, at an evolutionary crossroads so to speak. Will we be able to capitalize on the many understandings about learning and brain development to harmonize our knowledge about learning with the rapidly changing economic and social needs of post-industrial societies? If we are to rise to the challenge, then the unit of change can no longer simply be schools but the larger community. Learning communities would have as their first priority the strengthening of families and providing for the learning needs of all their young people. All available resources, both formal and informal, would be used toward the goal of helping children become responsible adults who know how to function successfully within a community.

Learning would no longer simply be bound to the walls of a single institution; rather, it would be seen as a total community responsibility. Individual schools would be seen as responsible to the whole community, not just part of it. From this perspective it is not merely teachers who can teach; it is not just pupils who need to learn; and it is certainly not just the classroom that is any longer the major access point to a range of knowledge, information, and skills.

For example, within the community at large, there are an ever-increasing number of early retirees who are fit and strong and have many professional skills. At the moment they are largely wasted in terms of helping the young develop a motivation for learning, and understanding how what they learn in the classroom can actually be applied in the workplace, voting booth, or life in general. Many of these retirees don't want to become full-time certified teachers, but many would be interested in sharing their expertise with young people informally. These are just the individuals that adolescents need to be able to relate to, almost surrogate grandparents. These citizens need to be recruited to work with young people. This strategy of expanding the pool of people who have talents, skills, and experiences to offer young people would help communities deal with the impending teacher shortages that education systems across North America and the United Kingdom are beginning to face. It would also go a long way towards reconnecting the adult community with the needs of children.

Remember, the brain is an open biological system, and learning is a dynamic interaction between the environment and the individual brain.

The brain does not turn itself on and off to fit the school's hours of operation. That is why we argue turning systems of education not just "upside down" but, even more importantly, "inside out." Helping young people become lifelong learners requires the involvement of the whole community because this is the environment that provides children with the immediate feedback they need to make connections between academic learning and the happenings of the real world. This is why we argue the locus of learning now has to extend well beyond just the classroom.

Obstacles to Reform

If these discontinuities are so clear, then why are things so slow to change? There is no single answer to this question, and in any one person's understanding, there are many contrary messages. Additionally, some of the ideas and experiences discussed above are gaining credence and proponents, but there is little cohesion among programs or even between different levels of schools in the same system. Everything still pretty much happens in isolation. Yet, with that said, the problem, as with many good policy ideas that cross traditional boundaries, is that focusing on learning and the learner rather than schools, institutions, and teachers collides head on with what we identify as the "three I's": Ignorance, self-Interest, and Ideology.

Ignorance

First, there is ignorance, or, more precisely, lack of awareness, confusion, and misinformation. At a basic level, the general public, policymakers, and politicians do not yet know much about brain science, the evolutionary sciences, the history of education, or even innovative educational practice. Even fewer know how to relate such studies together in a synthesis. The evolutionary biologist Ernst Mayr lamented this lack of scientific knowledge in the policy making arena when he wrote in 1997: "An ignorance of the findings of biology is particularly damaging whenever humanists are forced to confront such political problems as global overpopulation . . . or the failures of our education system. None of these problems can be addressed without taking into account the findings of science, particularly biology, and yet too often politicians proceed in ignorance."[3]

In his Chief Inspector Report for the Office of Standards in Education, Chris Woodhead stated, "Why then is so much time and energy wasted in research that complicates what ought to be straight forward[?] . . . We already know what constitutes good teaching. We need to escape the emptiness of educational theorizing that obfuscates the classroom realities that

169

matter." Such comments by one of England's leading educational authorities epitomize the staying power of the vestigial concepts of behaviorism and scientific management. But Woodhead is not alone. There are few leaders in the world of education that have a background in the biological and medical sciences. It is not surprising, therefore, that one of those who does, Paul Cappon, the director general of the Canadian Council of Ministers of Education, is one of the most significant proponents of many of the ideas discussed in this book.

At times of great change, it has always been difficult for the layperson to evaluate new ideas. Writing in the late 19th century, the U.S. social commentator Josh Billings observed: "It's not people's ignorance you need to fear it's what they know which damned well ain't true any longer that causes all the problems." This was never truer than in the story which politicians on either side of the Atlantic daily recreate as the underlying cause of educational failure: teachers aren't good enough; teachers are largely distracted by the afterglow of the 1960s and willy-nilly progressivism; schools are not short of money (thanks to the politicians), but they are simply badly managed (due to the teachers); there is nothing "special" about learning; learning flows automatically from good teaching. The public almost swallows this false analysis—but not completely. In practice, it's an analysis that runs counter to people's own personal experiences.

The problem of lack of awareness is compounded by the speed at which new findings about the brain and learning are emerging from laboratories, universities, and research centers. Before the advent of big science during World War II, new findings of broad significance occurred with less frequency, and each discovery had a greater potential to generate a moment of amazement, excitement, or fear. For example: "The day after major newspapers reported to the world in 1919 that Arthur Eddington and his research team had discovered that light from stars appeared to bend as it brushed the sun, affirming a critical prediction of relativity, Einstein became a world hero."[4] A well-read person at the beginning of the 20th century could quite possibly keep up with these various new discoveries.

In our own time, rapidly advancing technologies have made the occurrence of equally stunning revelations far more commonplace. Added to the difficulty of keeping up with science generally is that scientists employ language, techniques, and ways of thinking that are powerful and effective in their field but are hard to articulate to nonspecialists. This means most people who read about new findings in science get their information through the filters of the mass media. We are drowning in a flood of semi-comprehensible ideas.

Confusion was widespread when new research on the brain and human learning came to the attention of policy people and the general public in the mid and late 1990s. The research, largely from the neurosciences, showed why the first few years of life were the most critical years to children's long-term cognitive development. *Time, Newsweek,* and many other parenting and educational journals told concerned readers that they could influence long-term brain structure by timely hugs and kisses, reading books to their toddlers 10 minutes a day, or playing Mozart to their infants. Educators and policymakers had no sooner started to excitedly discuss how to develop educational programs that could take advantage of the new understandings about the brain when voices such as John Bruer produced counter-arguments.

Bruer's book, *The Myth of the First Three Years,* asserted the neurosciences' research really wasn't that new, and in any case it really didn't support the contention that the first 3 years are any more critical than the next 7 or even 20 years of development. Conflicting messages led to a feeling of despair and even cynicism among those who were committed to doing better by children. To some this provided the justification for doing nothing, for fear that if they did something new they would risk having another group of experts tell them what they were doing was wrong or at least insignificant. This paralysis supported the status quo because those invested in the current arrangements for learning could use this episode as evidence for why those progressives seeking change were simply do-gooders infatuated with the latest fad, and therefore should not be taken seriously.

An extreme version of using scientific evidence selectively to make a political argument recently occurred in the United States when the religious right used disagreements and squabbles between evolutionary scientists as evidence that the theory of evolution was no more than just one of several equally plausible theories of human development. The critics of evolution used the debates between scientists such as Richard Dawkins, Stephen Jay Gould, and Daniel Dennett as evidence for why evolution and the Biblical story of creation should be held up as equal theories. Of course, the evolutionary scientists all agree on the most significant premises[5] and are really only debating side issues, which, in a sense, is what academics get paid to do. Yet political advocates picked up on these controversies and argued that the new discoveries and debates actually challenged the existing theory to the core. They were able to convince enough people of their case that they got the Kansas State School Board of Education to vote against the teaching of evolution in science classes.

With so many conflicting stories and media reports about science, it is not surprising that many people see science as interesting but something that shouldn't be trusted to inform really important social or cultural issues like how we educate children. Confusion and uncertainty cause many lay people to see science, especially the biological and behavioral sciences, as just a collection of theories and conjectures not much different from philosophy. The great paradox here is that such people can accept the validity of biological and behavioral research that gives ever greater insights into cancer, mental illness, or Alzheimer's disease, but they dismiss any biological explanations for how children learn and mature.

This confusion surrounding the state of knowledge about learning, human development, and what it means to be human is further amplified by the sheer amount of information and misinformation that is now available through the Web and in the general media. A plenitude of information leads to a poverty of attention, and, not surprisingly, capturing the attention of readers becomes highly problematic. Those organizations with name recognition—large publishers, major newspapers, national magazines, and journals—that can distinguish valuable information from white noise become increasingly influential. Jerome Kagan summed this up when he argued: "One unfortunate consequence of the rush of new facts is the temptation among a small number to hype an empirical discovery so that it might have a chance of being heard above the din. Darwin only had to whisper; contemporary scientists have to scream in order to be heard."[6]

An example of screaming to be heard was Richard Dawkins's *The Selfish Gene*, which really wasn't about humans being driven by a selfish gene at all. This fact didn't prevent the book's German publishers from producing a front cover showing a picture of a human puppet jerking on the end of strings descending from the word "Gen" (gene). Nor did this fact prevent the French publishers from using a picture of bowler-hatted, clockwork men with wind-up keys sticking out of their backs. "This is not what Dawkins's thought he meant at all. He had both covers changed, and lectured for a while using slides of the originals as illustrations of what he did not mean about genes."[7]

Research and new scientific understandings, from the perspective of publishers, have to be marketed in such a way as to make money, and this means capturing the attention of readers. Selling nonfiction books is difficult business because there really isn't a large number of readers for such books. In the United States, for example, a country of 260 million people, only about 4 million people consider themselves serious readers of nonfiction. "And the realistic maximum potential audience for a 'solidly written, well-promoted book' is probably no more than, say, 20 percent of that total, counting on both cloth and paperback sales—some 800,000 copies."[8]

Another difficulty is that much of science still seeks to solve complex problems by dealing with them in isolation. This reductionist approach has given rise to the cult of the specialist who has all the answers for everyone else and the psychological view that all habits are established through the administration of rewards and punishments. Our contemporary concepts and practices in politics, organizational change, and education are defined for the most part by this intellectual framework that began with the development of physical mechanics in the 17th century.

This mechanistic worldview supports the language of reforming systems of education by dealing with the inputs, processes, and outputs of instructional systems. This helps cloud the fact that the brain is a complex, self-organizing system, and the learning of children is a highly complex cognitive, emotional, and social phenomenon that struggles to fit into the rigid parameters of education systems. In discussions about educational reform, what seems to matter is the more mechanical concepts of professionals delivering prescribed knowledge to all students in the same prescribed manner. The fact that the brain of each individual learns by making connections meaningful to itself is largely ignored. Children are simply expected to react and adapt to the structure and contents of the curriculum. Some can adapt, but many do not. The ease with which many educational policymakers seem able to imagine disciplines being divorced from contact with nature, such as the biological workings of the brain, is extraordinarily dangerous in a world that is becoming increasingly interconnected and complex.

In 1944, as the era of big science got a grip on the collective imagination, the physicist Irwin Schroedinger (1887–1961) anticipated today's difficulty with synthesizing knowledge when he wrote, "A scientist is supposed to have a complete and thorough knowledge at first-hand of some subject, and therefore is usually expected not to write on any topic on which he is not a master. We have inherited from our forefathers the keen longing for unified, all-embracing knowledge . . . but the spread, in width and depth of the multifarious branches of knowledge, confronts us with a queer dilemma. It has become next to impossible for a single mind to fully command more than a small portion of it. I can see no other escape from this dilemma (lest our true aim be lost forever) than that some of us should embark on a synthesis of facts and theories, albeit with a secondhand and incomplete knowledge of some of them—at the risk of making fools of ourselves."[9]

Self-Interest

Although few people have gone as far as us in saying that current systems of education are upside down and inside out, awareness is growing

173

that a one-size-fits-all education system simply does not work in a pluralistic democratic society riding the wave of a dynamic economy. Some people in positions of influence over the current systems of education (elected officials, educational administrators, and teacher's unions) often see their role as managing the workings of the current system. They become preoccupied with the political rhetoric of the educational reform of the day. They are concerned with reform, not transformation. Therefore, they tend to defend the system from those who advocate changes that would seek to disperse power to those outside the control of the formal system.

Such people are more comfortable with incremental change rather than a systematic change. They are more comfortable with managing rather than leading. For them there is more security and less risk and exposure to controversy by not rocking the boat. Besides, why challenge a system that has been good to you personally? Fifteen or more years of increasingly prescriptive legislation has turned the job of headship (or principal in the United States) into that of a manager rather than a leader. Managers have rules to follow, not questions to ask. This philosophy denigrates the professional competence of thoughtful educators.

Managers work within the rules of the system and to the needs of the system. They tell subordinates what to do in order to make the system, as it is currently structured, more efficient. To those educators who are more managers than leaders, they see research about learning and the brain in two distinct ways: to be incorporated into the system or to be dismissed outright. Recent research that has been incorporated into various education systems includes, but is not limited to, smaller class sizes; integrating technology across the curriculum (while keeping it in the school); increasing teacher development (but only in assisting teachers in developing strategies for carrying out the orders of superiors); added graduation requirements (or GCSE requirements); and using research on early years learning to expand the formal education system downwards.

The research dismissed outright in some quarters includes, but is not limited to, seriously considering how the development of metacognitive skills can be used to alter the pedagogy (weaning) across the system; constructivism and how it calls for a coalition of learning among all those people who have an influence on children's learning; how information communication technology can actually alter the role of teachers and students (especially in the secondary school) and move learning beyond the walls of the school; or how to move the agenda from schools and institutions to learners and learning. In short, anything that actually challenges the workings of the system is ignored or ridiculed, and that which can be used to strengthen the power and efficiency of the system is incorporated accordingly.

Whether educational managers are elected or appointed, they face intense political pressure to show results and to show them quickly. For such officials, an agenda that goes beyond a one- or two-year time frame has little appeal for they know that long-term thinking will do little to protect their position, or increase their influence. The average length of a school superintendent's tenure in the United States is three years, and elected officials who stay on for more than four years are considered fortunate. Another factor that breeds short-term thinking in education is that an elected position to the local school board is seen by many as a first step toward a longer and more significant political career. It is not in the interest of political players to invest in and initiate a campaign for learning that requires commitment over the long haul.

Teachers and head teachers (principals) are on the front-lines of education systems, and, despite the bad press they have received in recent years, they actually keep things running. In some cases it is their sheer willpower and strength that keeps the system or at least individual schools from complete collapse. Good teachers understand it is in the interest of children to work in partnership with parents and the larger community. But they also realize it is not in their short-term interest to take on the burden of working in outreach programs with parents and business leaders when they are rewarded largely on exam results. Therefore, they focus not on explaining why the rules of the game should be changed but on maximizing the scores of their children. Bonus pay is increasingly related to one thing: improving test scores. Teachers see it as being in their interest to simply play the game of education as the rules tell them they should. For those teachers who do point out that they are actually limited in how much they can do for children by factors outside the school, their reward is to be dismissed by political leaders as belonging to what Prime Minister Tony Blair calls "the culture of excuses."

Parents and taxpayers could initiate real change in the arrangements their communities provide for children, but they are limited in their influence by many factors, not least of which is the ignorance of the issues described above. Parents, as mentioned several times in this book, are working more hours than ever before, and they simply do not have a lot of time to study the latest research on human learning. What they do read is often contradictory and presented in such a way as to seem utterly counter to their common sense. It might be in the interest of parents to advocate the development of more inclusive models of learning, but those with the resources already buy for their children much of what we've advocated in this book. Private schools, charter schools, and homeschooling all subsidized with plenty of extracurricular activities and access to home computers provide vast amounts of appropriate stimulation for successful learning, as does living in neighborhoods where most of the children come from households of well-educated parents.

Parents living in such neighborhoods may not be around much, but they can be fairly certain their children are running around with other children who know their parents value education and learning as much as they do. Parents who can afford it simply operate at a level well above where current education systems operate. Those parents who are caught in the current educational arrangements and dysfunctional neighborhoods are often times stuck, and they themselves feel trapped by a world of impersonal bureaucracies that appear largely impenetrable from the outside. It is these parents who clamor for new choices such as charter schools and voucher systems so they can take a more active role over their children's learning. They want to matter in their children's education.

Hopefully, this book will help these parents make the case for themselves as to why community regeneration is as important to the success of their children as is any sort of school reform. For those of us who currently reside on the fortunate side of the divide, it should be clear that if we want our children and grandchildren to live in prosperous and stable democracies, then we need to figure out how to provide all children with the learning environments advantaged children already experience.

Ideology

The issue of equity leads us into the last category of reasons for why too many children are still unsuccessfully prepared for a lifetime of responsible and successful learning. It was political ideology that overwhelmed the work of the early 20th century progressives in education. The progressive's view of education and learning was quickly subsumed as an integral part of the larger agenda of the political left. This political agenda sought to use schools as a vanguard in moving societies away from capricious capitalism toward what they saw as a more just society moderated by benevolent state control of the economy. This resulted in progressive ideas about child-centered education becoming part of a larger political movement that sought increased state influence over the raising of children.

In the spirit of scientific management, it was held that professional educators, because of their training and base of scientific knowledge, should play the central role in the raising and education of young people. Parents and the larger community were relegated to a support role, one that would emanate from the professional business of teaching. Teachers and schools were given roles larger than they could possibly hope to fill, and with the economic problems of the 1970s, conservative politicians pointed out that schools had lost sight of what they were supposed to be all about, which in their ideological perspective meant teaching the basics. What was seen as the chaos of youth running rampant was quickly blamed on left-leaning progressive educators who, it was argued by opponents, held an "anything goes" attitude toward children's learning and development. Progressive education, critics persuaded many, was nothing more than fun and games; it lacked rigor and dismissed the significance of cultural literacy.

With the ascent of the conservative movement epitomized by the elections of Margaret Thatcher and Ronald Reagan in the 1980s, education has been the most political of all social activities. As a result, over the last two decades, education has been stuck between competing political ideologies that argue learning is either experiential and progressive or strictly formal, disciplined, and logical. The former has been deemed to belong to the political left while the right has owned the latter. It was the enduring strength of this political dichotomy that a writer for *The Atlantic Monthly* was referring to in the summer of 2000 when he wrote, "In education politics, where ideology often reigns, logic is not always easy to come by."[10]

The territory between schools and the community where so much of our children's learning actually takes place presents difficulties for many policy makers and the general public on both sides of the ideological divide because it is largely uncharted territory. The term community means different things to different people, while the concept of school is literally concrete. Such difficulties aside, more people, especially those in the voluntary sector, now recognize that a dynamic form of learning we describe as constructivism requires strong partnerships among all those who help children learn and grow.

Yet few professional educators and community leaders have a well worked out understanding about the significance of this middle ground that incorporates the home, the school, and the community, sometimes facilitated by new technologies. The agenda is all around us, but the whole picture still remains fragmented. Put another way: As with an impressionist painting, the issues and experiences raised in this book require two kinds of vision—the ability to understand the interrelationship of individual blobs of color as well as the ability to stand back and appreciate the beauty and the significance of the whole. Only when we are able to do this, with earlier assumptions reassessed and a clearer perception of new opportunities, will viable solutions to what for too long have been seen to be intractable problems start to leap to mind.

Toward Dynamic Learning Communities

One person who has given more thought than most to this middle ground, although she would not call it that, is Stephanie Pace Marshall. A one-time teacher, superintendent, president of the Association for Supervision and Curriculum Development (ASCD), president and co-founder of the Illinois Mathematics and Science Academy, and director of two Fortune 500 companies, she argues that ideology goes well beyond conventional sectional polemics.

Pace Marshall calls for a new point of view when she argues: "We have to draw a sharp comparison between the current story that underpins educational assumptions as being a story I call the Culture of Acquisition, Independence and Competition, and a new story. I call this new story the Culture of Inquiry, Interdependence and Collaboration. These stories are grounded in very different ways of knowing and discovering who we are. It is in how we come to understand ourselves that we shape particular kinds of learning environments, and these shape the way our minds work . . . and that of course shapes our futures. It is my belief that the ultimate purpose of education is to liberate the goodness and genius of all children in the world. Learners of all ages need to be engaged fully, and in an interconnected way, around significant questions that matter to them, to the community, and concerns the most significant issues of our time. This would create a new mind for the new millennium (and of course this new mind also includes a new heart, soul and spirit)."[11]

Dee Hock, the founder of VISA International, gives a glimpse of what learning communities might look like when he contends: "Lifelong learning is essential to a just, equitable, peaceful society of free people in an abundant and enduring natural world. That innate, lifelong and unique to each person learning is influenced by intended and unintended processes inseparable from and shaped by both context and motivation. It cannot be separated from life itself. Individuals are in control of and responsible for both their learning and its application. Learning communities are intradependent, interdependent, and independent. Community learning deepens mutual understanding of, respect for, and trust in one another in the natural world; leading to more constructive relationships and the non-violent resolution of conflict."[12]

Partly through our familiarity with the emerging ideas discussed in this book, but mainly because of the pent-up energy of parents, teachers, and community figures in many countries, we believe that change is possible, and in fact is starting to bubble up in various communities around the world. The New York-based Public Agenda Foundation has identified seven stages for those seeking significant social change. These stages provide a useful barometer for those who feel compelled to push this learning community agenda forward. Readers may well wish to compare themselves and their colleagues or communities to this scale. The Public Agenda Foundation stages are:

1. People become aware of an issue, and consciousness-raising activities through media and grass-roots organizations call their attention to the concern.

2. People develop a sense of urgency as the gravity of the issue strikes close to home.

3. People begin to look for answers. They convert their free-floating concern into more specific proposals for action.

4. Resistance sets in! People are reluctant to face trade-offs coupled with choosing a specific course of action. They may understand, engage in narrow or wishful thinking, have difficulty balancing conflicting values, or offer personal reasons why change is not applicable to them or their sphere of influence.

5. People begin to weigh choices and seriously wrestle with the pros and cons of a particular course of action.

6. People undergo a basic change in values and intellectually accept the consequences of a particular course of action.

7. Full, emotional acceptance of the need to change follows in time, but it cannot be rushed.

Intellectual Acceptance Is Much Easier to Accomplish Than Emotional Acceptance

From the experience we have gathered in the five years we have worked with the 21st Century Learning Initiative, and the more than 15 years experience from Education 2000, we have added some further observations of our own that relate to the following questions. Where on this continuum are people currently involved in school reform, and at what stage do the ideas in this book start becoming highly relevant?

Stage 1: This is readily identified by noting the frequency that major journals such as *Newsweek, Time, The New Yorker, The Economist, New Statesmen, Prospect, The Guardian, Harper's,* and *The Atlantic Monthly* focus on a new topic related to education and learning. For example, brain research on children from birth to 3 years generated a mass of stories in these journals in the middle to late 1990s. This information created a general swell of concern that these "issues have to be addressed." It then became an acceptable topic for discussion. Policymakers were expected to have a view on what needed to happen, however ill-thought out such views might be. Simple explanations, however, increase the search for scapegoats. Around issues of education generally, this has been the stage of reform in the United States since the 1983 "Excellence Report" became available. England can certainly trace current discontent in education back to James Callaghan's speech in 1976.

At this stage, a few perceptive people start to see some basic discontinuity between opportunities and the direction in which the current system is heading. They argue for more radical change and stress learning and community rather than instruction and schooling. There is a general interest in the issues set out in this book, but the intellectual incentive to think more profoundly is overtaken by the need to do something "practical on Monday," something that shows results. Using the example of findings in brain research, the Governor of Georgia gave out CDS of Mozart to all new parents hoping to help build up the brains of infants. Inevitably at this stage, solutions are sought within the present institutional structure.

Stage 2: Impatience with the current system, and an unwillingness to ask profound questions about the system itself, lead to demands to "raise standards" and "to hold people accountable." To do this defined outcomes are then agreed upon, and curricula to support these are set out. Classically, the system is driven to "work harder." Even more than before the school is seen as the only factor that matters to children's learning. As the activities of the schools are pushed ever harder, links with the community become more tenuous ("There just isn't time to support them"). Those who would push for deeper questioning of the present system tend to be silenced or ridiculed as being "against public education." "We all need to be in this together!" enthusiastic advocates of school reform argue: "Given enough support and resource we don't need to do things differently, just harder." By and large, business leaders and community figures tend to unite behind the "work harder" scenario, mainly because there is still lack of clarity as to overall long-term objectives. For decades this has been the stuff of much educational politics.

In our work with various groups, we ask people to make a distinction between their immediate needs and responsibilities (operational issues) and the more significant long-term issues (strategic issues).[13] Figure 10.2 contains a table used by the 21st Century Learning Initiative to help educational leaders see the balance between the two efforts.

Stage 3: Steadily, school systems are forced to try and combine arrangements for "working harder" with a range of other initiatives, such as charter schools, computer-assisted learning, additional vocational and civics courses, homework contracts, and other school-based reforms. There are an increasing number of political directives from beyond the school, including accountability arrangements and even incentive payments for teachers who improve their pupils' examination results beyond the average. "School effectiveness" becomes a key concept. Is the system giving maximum payback for its investment? Schools are put into competition

Figure 10.2 Starting a Conversation About the Future of Education and Learning

Operational	Strategic
Focus	
Present Focus	Future Focus
Certainties	Possibilities
"Real"	"Play"
Nature of Knowledge	
Knowledge confirmation	Knowledge development
Static language	Dynamic language
Set within a system	Focused on creating opportunities
Implicit assumptions	Explicit assumptions
Conversational Rules	
Advocacy	Dialogue
Authoritative	Hypothetical
Reach for closure	Open new conversations
Need for specialists	Need for generalists
Get a decision	Keep learning

with each other for resources based on examination results, and in the course of this competition they become ever more isolated both from each other and from their communities.

School personnel develop a bunker mentality where they simply dig in and do what they can in their own classroom, and what happens outside of it is no longer their concern. Community and children are the real losers in all this because the interactions and experiences children have with adults outside the school are not seen as adding value on standardized tests. Students are encouraged to focus on examination results and see learning very much as something defined for them in advance by the teacher and the curriculum. They are living in an increasingly disconnected world fixed by "the game of schooling."

A significant number of teachers and administrators start to question whether this singular focus on schools is not making education so singleminded and conformist that it is failing to develop creativity, adaptability, and individual responsibility in their students. Teachers increasingly question their own roles, and the most creative among them become so frustrated and disillusioned that they leave education and enter the more dynamic world of free-enterprise. They then see the discontinuity between what is going on in the school and the rest of the world more clearly than before, and this often frightens them.

Stage 4: The mass of people who have gone along with the education reform agendas feels an increasing sense of exhaustion—and a diminished sense of that enjoyment of teaching that first brought them into education. Examination results have undoubtedly improved, but it has been at least partly at the cost of cutting back on fringe and out-of-school activities. The business community is no longer as satisfied as it was earlier. "Young people may be getting higher test scores," they say, "but their life skills such as creativity, adaptability, and the intrinsic desire to excel, as well as their willingness to work collaboratively, seem no better than before." Other commentators think they are actually worse off. "Youngsters expect everything on a plate and they don't know how to think for themselves," such people say. There are demands for a curriculum that "teaches" creativity and social responsibility. As larger numbers of students score top grades on exams, there are accusations that the exam itself is not tough enough and that young people are not studying enough subjects. This is very much the situation in England at the start of the new millennium.

Disillusionment among thoughtful teachers increases, and still more leave the profession. In particular, difficulties are experienced in appointing headteachers to schools in difficult areas. Those who are appointed are aware that their task is far more that of a managerial responsibility rather than genuine leadership. This is the fact despite the politicians' acknowledgment of the importance of leadership. Leadership implies the ability to make choices. Management is the effective running of an institution according to highly defined rules. Those people who have been involved in dealing with the current educational reform programs start to become far more thoughtful and focused on their expectations for the future. Numerous requests for information and for lectures on the ideas described in this book are given to headteacher conferences in many lands. The deeper these people get into the ideas, the more they realize that a stark choice has now to be made: Is it more of the same, or do we go back to first principles and think it through all over again?

It is at this stage that people recognize the validity of the challenging statement: "Education for what? Do we want our children to grow up as battery hens or free-range chickens? By default," such people say, "we have been accepting a view of learning that was so interdependent with mid-20th century views of the economy that we are damaging our social structures and impeding our possible economic development. What is now essential," they argue, "is that arrangements are made to help key policymakers understand how all these issues interrelate so that they begin to create space (freedom from the legislation that currently maintains the present system) for radical new arrangements to be set up." Only then, they argue, will it be possible to develop arrangements for learning that will create both the disciplined mind and the creative mind, all within the same person.

This certainly won't happen unless many more people have a far deeper appreciation both of what is needed and of why it is needed. Too many earlier innovations have failed because their advocates had only a shallow understanding of what they were really trying to help give birth to. The need for a transnational point of reference becomes obvious at this point if the immediate pragmatics of local politics is not to divert the reforms. It is a reality of globalization that these ideas cross national boundaries, as easily as they cross specialized academic disciplines, so innovators feel the need to band together. They do this by taking advantage of cheap telecommunications, airfares, and the power of the Internet. "We are all novices now. All of us are exploring new territory. As these ideas are even more novel to policy makers than they are to teachers, it would be good to be able to reference our proposed action to a clear exposition of what all this means," would-be innovators contend.

Stage 5: For those who have been involved with the Initiative, and for those who have come to similar conclusions by following similar routes, this is where the commentary has to move into the future tense. To support the numerous peoples in many different countries who are now seeking to develop agendas for change, plans are being formulated to establish an Institute for the Advanced Study of Human Learning and Community Development. This will be a transnational resource to stimulate radical transformation of formal and informal learning arrangements for young people. These efforts will be based on the most current understandings of effective learning strategies as determined by international research and "best practice." We recognize that as yet very few educational innovators or community activists feel sufficiently confident in making the complex arguments developed in this book.

If they are to integrate this evidence to expand their own activities, then they need a nonpolitical, transnational agency able to:

1. Help legitimize their efforts.

2. Provide an authoritative and up-to-date analysis of appropriate research, processes, and practice.

3. Provide several levels of intellectual and practical support.

4. Create a network of innovators worldwide able to help each other through an exchange of information and experiences.

The Institute would have four primary functions. First would be to share the Initiative's story that there are now new and more appropriate ways of supporting the learning needs of young people by expanding the boundaries of learning beyond the school. The Institute would provide the evidence for this claim and share widely the strategies and resource implications of more effective arrangements for learning.

Second, the Institute would provide an array of seminars and support programs for three specific groups of people. These are:

1. Educational innovators, from politicians to teachers currently working in school systems to focus people's attention away from systemic issues and school politics to learning and the developmental needs of children.

2. Community leaders working in cities and towns to focus the resources of businesses, local and state governments, and the nonprofit sector on the learning needs of children.

3. Young people between 17 and 20 whose interest could energize the current older generation with the significance of new ideas about learning and so provide an informed, knowledgeable group who would want to take increasing responsibility for the shape of the educational agenda over the next 10 or 20 years.

Third, there is the need to maintain the authority of the Institute's documentation and presentations by constantly vetting new research findings and evaluating the evidence from innovative practice. Fourth, all this evidence needs to be disseminated through a highly efficient and interactive exchange system: through the Internet, mass media, policy seminars, and public presentations.

Stage 6: This stage will be characterized by the way in which communities learn to work together to implement profound changes that will touch all parts of their corporate and individual lives. This will not be easy. For years communities will have to work a double agenda (the operational and the strategic), doing the best they can for the current generation of young people according to learning arrangements currently provided. At the same time these innovative community leaders will need to help individuals and groups not currently involved in formal education systems develop and implement new partnerships and programs. The transition will require a tremendous amount of trust, collaboration, and leadership. However, as these new opportunities become better understood, the significance of the emphasis on developing learning skills will start to regenerate the community and reinvigorate people who previously have "opted out" of any community involvement.

Stage 7: For those innovators and communities who have thought—if not fought—their way through stages four, five, and six the nature of stage seven as described by the New York-based Public Agenda Foundation becomes very obvious. The people dedicated to improving the lives of their children and community fully understand why change is needed, and they are committed to achieving their goals. The winning of intellectual support will be more easily accomplished than the gaining of full emotional acceptance. However, once communities gain the power of "full, pure, gut emotional acceptance," they will eventually break out of the old constraints and show just what a community of really determined, knowledgeable, dedicated, and caring people can actually do. When such communities become confident of flexing their muscles, then, but only then, does the unfinished revolution come to a conclusion worthy of a just and free society.

●   ●   ●

This book has been written to help people "seize the excitement and opportunity of the moment" in order to initiate a dialogue around community-based models of learning that take full advantage of current understandings about how children learn and take responsibility for lifelong learning. The ghosts that have walked through our history for 500 or more years are still strong and vocal. Without careful and rigorous thought, many of these ideas could be twisted to meet aims and goals different from those described here. Yet the time has never been better to complete the unfinished revolution that could transform our schools and reinvigorate our communities and natural environment.

The outcome of such efforts at educational transformation would be a society motivated by thoughtfulness, developed through a model of learning that genuinely extends our inherited learning capabilities. People will quickly recognize that, in developing the learning skills of the young, the lives of whole communities will be revitalized as they change and grow. This involves escaping from the 19th century assumption that learning and schooling are synonymous. Good schools alone will never be good enough. This is about communities that think differently, work differently, and are even designed and built differently. We have the opportunity to generate a more purposeful, more creative, and even more sacred place in the universe.

Endnotes

Chapter 1

1. Sylwester's comments were made at a 21st Century Learning Initiative Conference in November 1995.

2. Michael S. Gazzaniga, *The Mind's Past* (Berkeley: University of California Press, 1998), 6. The University of California researchers John Tooby and Leda Cosmides have argued that "because human and nonhuman brains are evolved systems, they are organized according to an underlying evolutionary logic. . . . Familiarity with the basics of modern evolutionary biology is, therefore, an important working tool for cognitive neuroscientists." In *The Cognitive Neurosciences*, ed., Michael S. Gazzaniga (Cambridge: MIT Press, 1995).

3. Jerome H. Barkow, Leda Cosmides, and John Tooby, *The Adapted Mind: Evolutionary Psychology and the Generation of Culture* (Oxford: Oxford University Press, 1992), 39.

4. Philip Tobias, *The Brain in Hominid Evolution* (New York: Columbia University Press, 1970).

5. Christopher Wills, *The Runaway Brain: The Evolution of Human Uniqueness* (London: HarperCollins, 1993), 310.

6. Patricia Kuhl, "The White House Conference on Early Childhood Development and Learning: What New Research on the Brain Tells Us About Our Youngest Children" (White House Information Office, April 17, 1997).

7. For an excellent review of man's cognitive history, refer to Steven Mithen, *The Prehistory of the Mind* (London: Thames and Hudson, 1996).

8. For details refer to Ian Tattersall, *Becoming Human: Evolution and Human Uniqueness* (New York: Harcourt Brace & Co., 1998).

9. Michael S. Gazzaniga took the concept of predispositions further when he argued in 1998 that, "Over the past 30 years, the mind sciences have developed a picture not only of how our brains are built, but also of what they were built to do. The emerging picture is wonderfully clear and pointed. Every newborn is armed with circuits that already compute information enabling the baby to function in the physical universe. The baby does not learn trigonometry, but knows it; it does not learn how to

distinguish figure from ground, but knows it; does not need to learn, but knows, that when one object hits another, it will move the object." *The Mind's Past.*

10. Luigi Luca Cavalli-Sforza, *Genes, Peoples, and Languages* (New York: North Point Press, 2000), II.

11. Kenneth Wexler, Richard Aslin, and Peter Jusczyk in a paper given to the American Association for the Advancement of Science (Philadelphia, February 1998).

12. Bénédicte de Boysson-Bardies, *How Language Comes to Children* (Cambridge: MIT Press, 1999), 8.

13. Luigi Luca Cavalli-Sforza, 60.

14. Ibid.

15. William F. Allman, *The Stone Age Present* (New York: Simon & Schuster, 1994), 70.

16. Refer to Jane Goodall, *In the Shadow of Man* (London: George Weidenfeld & Nicholson Limited, 1988); and Steve Jones, *In the Blood: God, Genes and Destiny* (London: HarperCollins, 1996).

17. Refer to Peter Laslett, *The World We Have Lost* (London: Routledge, 1983).

18. Judith Rich Harris, "How to Succeed in Childhood," in *The Nature-Nurture Debate*, Stephen J. Ceci and Wendy Williams, eds., (Malden, MA: Blackwell Publishers, 1999), 93.

19. Ibid., 95.

20. Ronald Kotulak, *Inside the Brain* (Kansas City: Andrews and McMeel, 1996).

21. "Children Living in Relative Poverty," *The Economist* (June 17–23, 2000), 144.

22. Catherine C. Lewis, *Educating Hearts and Minds* (Cambridge: Cambridge University Press, 1995), 1.

23. Refer to Stanislas Dehaene, *The Number Sense* (Oxford: Oxford University Press, 1997); and Brian Butterworth, *The Mathematical Brain* (London: Macmillan, 1999).

24. According to Michael Posner and Daniel Levitin, "There is already evidence of critical periods in the learning of skills. Weber-Fox and Neville (1996) studied the learning of English by immigrants from China who came to the United States at ages ranging from two years to adulthood. They found that the brain circuitry involved in understanding the meaning of lexical items was similar regardless of age of immigration. However, the circuitry underlying grammatical judgments resembled American natives for those who immigrated as young children, but was very different in those whose immigration was late. A similar critical period has now

been reported in learning the violin. Children who begin lessons prior to age 12 show changes in somatosensory cortical representations between the left and right hands that are not present even in expert violinists who began their lessons late." In Robert L. Solso, ed., *Mind and Brain Sciences in the 21st Century* (London: The MIT Press, 1997), 97.

25. Daniel Goleman, *Emotional Intelligence: Why It Can Matter More Than IQ* (London: Bloomsbury, 1996). The term would appear to have been originally coined in P. Salovey and J.D. Mayer, "Emotional Intelligence," *Imagination, Cognition and Personality* (1990), 9.

26. Beth Hennessey and Teresa Amabile, "The Conditions of Creativity," in Robert J. Sternberg, ed., *The Nature of Creativity* (Cambridge: Cambridge University Press, 1997) 11.

27. Linda Perlstein, "The Sweet Rewards of Learning," *The Washington Post* (November 14, 1999), A1.

28. Howard Gardner in *Educational Leadership* (Alexandria, VA: ASCD, April 1993).

29. Quote comes from John Abbott, *Learning Makes Sense* (Letchworth, UK: Education 2000, 1994), 22.

30. National Research Council, *How People Learn* (Washington: National Academy Press, 1999), 30.

31. Geoffrey Colvin, "What Money Makes You Do," *Fortune* (August 17, 1998), 213.

32. The work of Howard Gardner and others on the learning of very young children shows children's amazing capability to form "naive theories of everything." Gardner capitalized on this with the title of his seminal work: *The Unschooled Mind.* In this he argued that cognitive science demonstrates the surprising power and persistence of the young child's conceptions of the world.

33. David Perkins, *Smart Schools* (New York: The Free Press, 1992), 74–75.

34. Ibid., 77.

35. Lauren B. Resnick, ed., *Knowing, Learning and Instruction* (Pittsburgh: Laurence Erlbaum Associates, 1989), 3.

36. Roger C. Schank and John B. Cleave, "Natural Learning, Natural Teaching: Changing Human Memory." Harold J. Morowitz and Jerome L. Singer, *The Mind, The Brain and Complex Adaptive Systems* (Reading, MA: Addison-Wesley Publishing Company, 1995), 175.

37. Ibid., 181.

38. Lauren B. Resnick, "Learning In School and Out," *The Educational Researcher*, (December, 1987), 18.

39. Ibid., 15.

40. Allan Collins, John Seely Brown, and Ann Holum, "Cognitive Apprenticeship: Making Thinking Visible," *American Educator* (Winter, 1991), 9–10.

41. Ibid., 10.

42. The Institute for Research on Learning (Palo Alto, CA: IRL, 1995).

43. Etienne Wenger, "Communities of Practice: The Social Fabric of a Learning Organization," *Healthcare Forum Journal* (July/August, 1996), 2.

44. Ibid.

Chapter 2

1. Philip Webster, "Tailor Learning for All, Says Blair," *The Times of London* (December 3, 1999).

2. Centre for Educational Research and Innovation, Education Policy Analysis (Paris: OECD, 1998), 5.

3. Finn's comments come from a letter he wrote John Abbott in the summer of 1999.

4. David Gergen, "The Case for Quality," *U.S. News & World Report* (November 1, 1999), 104.

5. "The Use and Misuse of Test Scores in Reform Debate," (The RAND Corporation, 2000).

6. Peter Schrag, "High Stakes Are for Tomatoes," *The Atlantic Monthly* (August, 2000), 21.

7. Dan Eggen, "Tech-Savvy Private Schools Boom: Institutions Wired and Ready for Children of Dot.Com Parents," *The Washington Post* (January 30, 2000), A1.

8. Ken Robinson, "Our Future Must Be Creative," *The Times of London* (July 16, 1999).

9. "An Upbeat School Report: Primaries Turn a Crucial Corner," *The Guardian* (July 9, 1999), 21.

10. Ken Robinson, "A Stream of Inventive" (Learning Centre, July, 1999).

11. Barbara W. Tuchman, *The March of Folly: From Troy to Vietnam* (New York: Ballantine Books, 1984), 5.

12. Morton Egol, *Information Age Accounting: Catalyst and Enabler of the Self-Organizing Enterprise* (New York: Arthur Andersen, 1996).

13. Peter Drucker, *Post-Capitalist Society* (New York: HarperCollins, 1993).

14. Actor/Director Rob Reiner Speaks on Early Childhood Development. See www.hsph.harvard.edu/children/press/press4.html.

15. Rob Reiner, "The White House Conference on Early Childhood Development and Learning: What New Research on the Brain Tells Us

About Our Youngest Children" (White House Information Office, April 17, 1997).

16. Marian Diamond and Janet Hopson, *Magic Trees of the Mind* (New York: A Dutton Books, 1998), 1–2.

17. Joel Davis, *Mapping the Mind* (New York: Birch Lane Press, 1997), 64.

18. Ann B. Barnet and Richard J. Barnet, *The Youngest Minds* (New York: Simon & Schuster, 1998), p. 27.

19. John Bruer, *The Myth of the First Three Years* (New York: The Free Press, 1999), 8.

20. Bruer quotes Dr. Bruce Perry of the Baylor College of Medicine on p. 15.

21. John Bruer, p. 60.

22. Ibid.

23. Malcolm Gladwell, "Baby Steps," *The New Yorker* (January 10, 2000), 86.

24. OECD countries as a whole invest 18 percent of GDP per capita per primary student, 25 percent per secondary student, and 49 percent per tertiary student. Data come from the Centre for Educational Research and Innovation, *Education at a Glance* (Paris: OECD, 1998), 20.

25. Ibid.

26. Jerome Kagan, *Three Seductive Ideas* (Cambridge, MA: Harvard University Press, 1998), 91–92.

27. John Abbott, *Learning Makes Sense* (Letchworth: Education 2000, 1993).

Chapter 3

1. Gordon Brown concisely described the New Economy when he told a reporter for *The Washington Post*, "In Britain's past . . . expectations of boom and bust led to . . . a vicious circle of low investment, wage inflation, low growth. . . . The opportunity exists now in Britain for a new virtuous cycle of low inflation, high investment and high and stable levels of growth." T.R. Reid, "British Economy: All Boom, No Bust," *The Washington Post.* (September 20, 1999), A12.

2. Office of the Press Secretary, "1999 Economic Report of the President" (Council of Economic Advisors, The White House, February 4, 1999).

3. "What on Earth? A Weekly Look at Trends, People and Events Around the World," *The Washington Post* (September 11, 1999), A15.

4. Juliet Schor, *The Overspent American* (New York: Basic Books, 1998), 11–12.

5. Robert Gilpin, *The Challenge of Global Capitalism* (Princteon: Princeton University Press, 2000), 6.

6. James Twitchell, "Two Cheers for Materialism," *The Wilson Quarterly* (Spring, 1999), 25–26.

7. Christian Lutz in *Societies in Transition* (Paris: OECD, 1996), 102.

8. "All Consuming Passion: Waking Up from the American Dream," 3rd ed. (Seattle: New Road Map Foundation, 1998).

9. Kirstin Downey Grimsley and Jacqueline L. Salmon, "For Working Parents, Mixed News at Home," *The Washington Post* (September 27, 1999), A8.

10. The University of Michigan's Institute for Social Research reported in late 1998 that "free time left after going to school, eating and sleeping . . . has decreased from 40 percent of a child's day in 1981 to 25 percent [in 1997]. "Barbara Vobejda, More School, Structure Found in '90s Child's Life," *The Washington Post* (November 9, 1998), A2.

11. William J. Bennet, Chester E. Finn, Jr., and John T.E. Cribb, Jr., *The Educated Child* (New York: The Free Press, 1999), 8.

12. Mihaly Csikszentmihalyi and Reed Larson, *Being Adolescent* (New York: Basic Books, 1984), p. 73.

13. Public Agenda, "Kids These Days," at http://www.publicagenda.org/specials/Kids/kids7.htm.

14. Centre for Educational Research and Innovation, Children and Families at Risk (Paris: OECD, 1998), 23.

15. Deborah Yurgelun-Todd, "Physical Changes in Adolescent Brains May Account for Turbulent Teen Years," Press Release from McLean Hospital (Boston, June 11, 1998).

16. Patricia Hersch, *A Tribe Apart: A Journey into the Heart of American Adolescence* (New York: Fawcett Columbine, 1998).

17. Ibid., 19–20.

18. Philip N. Johnson-Laird, "Freed and Constraint in Creativity," Robert Sternberg, ed., *The Nature of Creativity* (Cambridge: Cambridge University Press, 1989), 208.

19. Kenneth J. Cooper, "Clinton, Governors Assess Efforts to Improve Education," *The Washington Post* (October 1, 1999), A13.

20. Arnold Langbo, "The White House Conference on Early Childhood Development and Learning," (Washington: The Office of the President, April 17, 1997).

21. For examples in the United States, refer to Daniel Patrick Moynihan's report, *The Negro Family: The Case for National Action* (1965); James Coleman's *Equality of Educational Opportunity* (1966); and, more recently, Laurence Steinberg's 10-year study entitled *Beyond the Classroom: Why School Reform Has Failed and What Parents Need to Do* (1996). Also refer to the success of homeschooling. For example, "A Home Run for Home Schooling:

Movement Can Point to High Test Scores in National Study," *The Washington Post* (March 29, 1999). In the United Kingdom, refer to Peter Mortimore's 1979 *Fifteen Thousand Hours and Their Effect on Children*.

22. A Report by the Council of Economic Advisors, "Families and the Labor Market, 1969–1999," (Washington: Office of the President, May 1999).

23. Barbara Vobejda, "Mother's Employment Works for Children; Study Finds No Long-Term Damage," *The Washington Post* (March 1, 1999), A1.

24. Kirstin Downey Grimsley and Jacqueline L. Salmon, "For Working Parents, Mixed News at Home," *The Washington Post*. (September 27, 1999), A1.

25. Lauren B. Resnick, "Learning In School and Out," *Educational Researcher* (December 1987), 15.

26. A Report from Public Agenda, "Necessary Compromises: How Parents, Employers, and Children's Advocates View Child Care Today" (New York: Public Agenda, 2000), 13.

27. Ibid.

28. In A Survey of Recent Articles, "The Battle Over Childcare," *The Wilson Quarterly* (Autumn, 1998), 116.

29. Ibid.

30. In 1997, President Clinton argued that daycare was not only beneficial for working parents but also a mechanism for getting welfare recipients into work. He argued, "Because states are getting money for welfare reform based on peak caseloads in welfare in 1994, and we've reduced the welfare rolls by 2.8 million since then[;] most states, for a period of time[,] . . . will have some extra funds that they can put into more child care. This gives states the opportunity they have never had before to train more childcare workers, to use funds to help even more people move from welfare to work and perhaps even to provide discounts to low-income workers to make child care more affordable for them. This welfare reform effort, if focused on child care, can train lots of people on welfare to be accredited child care workers and expand the availability of welfare in most states of the country." The White House Conference on Early Childhood Development and Learning: What New Research on the Brain Tells Us About Our Youngest Children (April 17, 1997).

31. Dr. Donald Cohen at the White House Conference on Early Childhood Development and Learning: What New Research on the Brain Tells Us About Our Youngest Children (April 17, 1997).

32. Penelope Leach, *Children First* (New York: Alfred Knopf, 1994), 78–79.

33. Ernst Mayr, *This Is Biology* (Cambridge, MA: The Belknap Press, 1997), 243.

34. Murat F. Iyigu and Ann L. Owen, "Risk, Entrepreneurship and Human Capital Accumulation" (Board of Governors of the Federal Reserve System, July, 1997), 2.

35. Arie P. De Geus, "The Living Company: A Recipe for Success," *The Washington Quarterly* (Winter, 1998), 184.

36. To appreciate the relationship of openness to why some countries are rich and others poor, refer to David S. Landes, *The Wealth and Poverty of Nations: Why Some Are So Rich and Some So Poor* (New York: W.W. Norton and Company, 1998).

37. John Cleveland, "Learning at the Edge of Chaos," *The Chaos Network Newsletter* (August, 1994), 2.

38. Research Reports, *The Wilson Quarterly* (Spring, 1999), 121.

39. Peter Drucker captured the essence of this issue when he wrote for the *Harvard Business Review*, "The developed world is in the process of committing collective suicide. Its citizens are not having enough babies to reproduce themselves. . . . For the next 25 years, the underpopulation of the developed countries is an accomplished fact and has the following implication. . . . Economic growth can no longer come either from putting more people to work—that is, from more resource input, as much of it has come in the past—or from an increase in consumers' demands. It can come only from a very sharp and continuing increase in the productivity of the one resource in which the developed countries still have a competitive edge (and which they are likely to maintain for a few more decades): knowledge work and knowledge workers." Peter F. Drucker, "The Future That Has Already Happened," *Harvard Business Review* (September/October, 1997), 20.

40. Nikolaus Lobkowicz, "The Vice of Tolerance," *New Perspectives Quarterly* (Winter, 1998), 56–57.

41. Rebecca Smithers, "Poor Marks for Homework," *The Guardian* (July 2, 1999), 4.

42. Dalya Alberge, "Author Brings 'Stifling' School System to Book," *The Times of London* (September 15, 1999).

43. John Carvel and Rebecca Smithers, "Blunkett and Blair Rail at 'Elitist' Critics," *The Guardian* (July 20, 1999), 10.

44. Ibid.

45. Ibid.

46. "Schools Chief Attacks Elitist Liberal," *The Independent* (July 20, 1999). From www.independent.co.uk.

Chapter 4

1. Lauren B. Resnick, ed., *Knowing, Learning and Instruction* (Pittsburgh: Laurence Erlbaum, 1989), 1.

2. Steven Quartz and Terrence Sejnowski, "The Neural Basis of Cognitive Development: A Constructivist Manifesto," *Behavioral and Brain Sciences* (1997), 539.

3. Ian Tattersall, *Becoming Human: Evolution and Human Uniqueness* (New York: Harcourt Brace & Company, 1998), 6.

4. Andy Green, *Education and State Formation* (London: Macmillan Press Ltd., 1991), 1.

5. David B. Tyack, *The One Best System* (Cambridge: Harvard University Press, 1974), 33.

6. Noah Webster, "On the Education of Youth in America" in Frederick Rudolph, ed., *Essays on Education in the Early Republic* (Cambridge: Harvard University Press, 1965).

7. Benjamin Rush, *Plan for the Establishment of Public Schools* (1786) in Michael J. Sandel, *Democracy's Discontent* (Cambridge, MA: The Belknap Press, 1996), 129.

8. Joel Spring, *The American School: 1642–1996* (New York: The McGraw-Hill Companies, 1997), 96.

9. Donald Mackinnon, June Statham, and Margaret Hales, *Education in the UK: Facts and Figures* (London: The Open University, 1999), 47.

10. Green, 4.

11. Green, 31.

12. Michael Katz, "The Origins of Public Education: A Reassessment," *History of Education Quarterly* (Winter, 1976), 383.

13. Green, 61.

14. Green, 62.

15. Lionel Rose, *The Erosion of Childhood: Child Oppression in Britain 1860–1918* (London: Routledge, 1991), 6.

16. Adam Smith, *An Inquiry into the Nature and Causes of the Wealth of Nations, Book 5* (1785), 305.

17. Green, 80.

18. Martin J. Weiner, *English Culture and the Decline of the Industrial Spirit: 1850–1980* (Cambridge: Cambridge University Press, 1981).

19. Ian Marshall and Danah Zohar, *Who's Afraid of Schrödinger's Cat?* (New York: William Morrow and Company, Inc., 1997), XX–XXI.

20. Arthur Schlesinger, Jr., "Has Democracy a Future?" *Foreign Affairs* (September/October, 1997), 3.

21. Barbara Tuchman, *The Guns of August* (New York: Ballantine Books, 1962), 10.

22. Ernst Mayr, *This Is Biology: The Science of the Living World* (Cambridge: Harvard University Press, 1997), 206.

23. Mayr, 177–178.

24. *The Mind,* edited by Daniel Robinson (Oxford: Oxford University Press, 1998), 229.

25. Tuchman, 11.

26. Lee Smolin, *The Life of the Cosmos* (New York: Oxford University Press, 1997), 223.

27. Ian Marshall and Danah Zohar, 62.

Chapter 5

1. Norman Brosterman, *Inventing Kindergarten* (New York: Harry N. Abrams, 1997), 102.

2. Steven Pinker, *The Language Instinct: The New Science of Language and Mind* (London: The Penguin Press, 1994), 406–407.

3. Henry Plotkin, *Evolution in Mind* (London: The Penguin Press, 1997), 33.

4. Plotkin, 28.

5. Robert Foley, *Humans Before Humanity* (Oxford: Blackwell Publishers, 1997), 3.

6. Peter F. Drucker, *Post-Capitalist Society* (New York: HarperBusiness, 1993).

7. Neil Postman, *Technopoly: The Surrender of Culture to Technology* (New York: Vintage Books, 1992), 51.

8. Transferable skills are defined as the ability "to learn something in one situation and then apply it in another, significantly different one—for instance, putting the math you learn in school to work in physics class or the supermarket." David Perkins, *Smart Schools* (New York: The Free Press, 1992).

9. Michael Gazzaniga, *The Mind's Past* (Berkeley, CA: University of California Press, 1998), 6.

10. Luigi Luca Cavalli-Sforza, *Genes, Peoples, and Languages* (New York: North Point Press, 2000), VII.

11. Cavalli-Sforza, VIII.

12. Carl Bereiter and Marlene Scardamalia, *Surpassing Ourselves: An Inquiry into the Nature and Implications of Expertise* (Chicago: Open Court, 1993), 182.

13. Ernst Mayr, *This Is Biology* (Cambridge, MA: Harvard University Press, 1997), 44.

14. Robert Kanigel, *The One Best Way* (New York: Viking Penguin, 1997), 19.

15. Shoshana Zuboff, *In the Age of the Smart Machine* (New York: Heinemann Publishing, 1988), 46.

16. Robert Kanigel, 19.

17. Peter F. Drucker, *The New Realities* (London: Mandarin, 1989), 182.

18. Robert Kanigel, 539.

19. Robert Kanigel, 18.

20. Robert Kanigel, 438–439.

21. Raymond Callahan, *Education and the Cult of Efficiency* (Chicago: University of Chicago Press, 1962), 18.

22. David F. Labaree, *How to Succeed in School Without Really Learning* (London: Yale University Press, 1997), 113.

23. Ibid., 114.

24. Daniel J. Boorstin, *The Americans: The Democratic Experience* (New York: Vintage Books, 1973), 491.

25. Diane Ravitch and Joseph P. Viteritti, "Introduction," in *New Schools for a New Century: The Redesign of Urban Education,* D. Ravitch and J.P. Viteritti, eds. (New Haven: Yale University Press, 1997).

26. David Wardle, *English Popular Education,* 1780–1975 (1976), 87.

27. Arthur Schlesinger, Jr., "Has Democracy a Future?" *Foreign Affairs* (September/October, 1997), 5–6.

28. U.S. Department of Education, *Digest of Education Statistics 1997* (Washington: OERI, 1997), 3.

29. Center for Educational Research and Innovation, *Education at a Glance: OECD Indicators 1998* (Paris: OECD, 1998), 17.

30. Michelle Cottle, "Too Well Endowed? Are Top Universities More Concerned About Money Than About Educating Students?" *The Washington Monthly* (September, 1998), 2.

Chapter 6

1. Aristotle, building on the work of Plato, observed "the citizen should be molded to suit the form of government under which he lives. For each government has a peculiar character which originally formed and which continues to preserve it." Aristotle, *Politics* (Book VIII), Chapter I.

2. Kieran Egan, *The Educated Mind: How Cognitive Tools Shape Our Understanding* (Chicago: The University of Chicago Press, 1997), 13.

3. In fact this belief is well expressed in the contemporary writings of E.D. Hirsch, Jr.

4. Kieran Egan, 20.

5. Jane M. Dewey, ed., "Biography of John Dewey," in Paul Arthur Schilpp and Lewis Edwin Hahn, eds., *The Philosophy of John Dewey,* 3rd ed. (La Salle, IL: Open Court, 1989), 9.

6. Ibid., 420.

7. Richard Wightman Fox and James T. Kloppenberg, *A Companion to American Thought* (Malden, MA: Blackwell Publishers, 1997), 536.

8. Paul Arthur Schilpp and Lewis Edwin Hahn, eds., 428–429.

9. E.M. Standing, *Maria Montessori: Her Life and Work* (New York: A Plume Book, 1984), XVI.

10. John Abbott, *The Child Is Father of the Man: How Humans Learn and Why* (Bath: Bath Press, 1999).

11. John Dewey, "The School and Society," in Martin Dworkin, ed., *Dewey on Education: Selections* (New York: Teachers College Press, 1959), 36.

12. John Dewey, *Individualism Old and New* (Amherst, NY: Prometheus Books, 1999), 6.

13. Sylvia Farnham-Diggory, *Schooling* (London: Harvard University Press, 1990), 24.

14. Joel Spring, *The American School—1642–1996* (New York: McGraw-Hill, 1997), 215–216.

15. Sylvia Farnham-Diggory, p. 27.

16. John Dewey, *How We Think* (Amherst, NY: Prometheus Books, 1991), 52.

17. The Book of Ecclesiastes, The Bible.

18. The American John Bruer argued in 1993 that "we should be as concerned with how we teach as we traditionally have been concerned with what we teach." John Bruer, *Schools for Thought* (London: MIT Press, 1993).

19. Ibid.

20. Richard F. Elmore and Milbrey W. McLaughlin, *Steady Work* (Santa Monica, CA: RAND, 1988), 5.

21. Robert J. Sternberg, "How Intelligent Is Intelligence Testing?" *Scientific American* (February, 1999 Special Edition Exploring Intelligence), 12–13.

22. Stephen Jay Gould, *The Mismeasure of Man* (New York: W.W. Norton and Company, 1996), 184.

23. Ibid.

24. Howard Gardner, *Multiple Intelligences: The Theory in Practice* (New York: Basic Books, 1993).

25. David Perkins, *Outsmarting IQ* (New York: Free Press, 1995).

26. This statement was made by David Perkins at a conference sponsored by the 21st Century Learning Initiative at Wingspread (Racine, WI: The Johnson Foundation, 1996).

27. David Perkins, *Smart Schools* (New York: Free Press, 1992).

28. Danah Zohar and Ian Marshall, *Spiritual Intelligence: The Ultimate Intelligence* (London: Bloomsbury, 2000).

29. Robert William Fogel, *The Fourth Great Awakening and the Future of Egalitarianism* (Chicago: The University of Chicago Press, 2000), 4.

30. Gould, 208.

31. Gould, 210.

32. The OECD observed in 1998 that "OECD countries as a whole invest 18 percent of GDP per capita per primary student, 25 percent per secondary student, and 49 percent per tertiary student." Centre for Educational Research and Innovation, *Education at a Glance: OECD Indicators 1998* (Paris: OECD, 1998), 20.

Chapter 7

1. Paul Krugman, *Pop Internationalism* (Cambridge: MIT Press, 1996), 35.

2. For a review of "progress and regress" in U.S. education, refer to David Tyack and Larry Cuban, *Tinkering Toward Utopia* (Cambridge, MA: Harvard University Press, 1995), and David Tyack, *The One Best System* (Cambridge, MA: Harvard University Press, 1974).

3. David Tyack and Larry Cuban, *Tinkering Toward Utopia* (Cambridge: Harvard University Press, 1995), 13.

4. Alexis de Tocqueville, *Democracy in America: Volume One*, trans. Henry Reeve (New York: Knopf, 1945), 6.

5. Charles K. Rowley, "On the Nature of Civil Society," *The Independent Review* (Winter, 1998), 402.

6. Social Capital can be defined simply as "a set of informal values or norms shared among members of a group that permit cooperation among them. If members of a group come to expect that others will behave reliably and honestly, then they will come to trust one another. Trust is like a lubricant that makes the running of any group or organization more efficient." Francis Fukuyama, *The Great Disruption* (New York: The Free Press, 1999), 16.

7. David Tyack, *The One Best System*, 275.

8. Richard Goodwin, *Remembering America: A Voice from the Sixties* (Boston: Little and Brown, 1988), 258.

9. Robert B. Reich, *The Work of Nations* (New York: Vintage Books, 1992), 46.

10. Ibid., 55.

11. David Farber, *The Sixties: From Memory to History* (Chapel Hill: The University of North Carolina Press, 1994), 13.

12. John Kenneth Galbraith, *A Journey Through Economic Time* (Boston: Houghton Mifflin Press, 1994), 136.

13. Daniel Yergin and Joseph Stanislaw, *The Commanding Heights* (New York: Simon & Schuster, 1998), 11.

14. Robert B. Reich, 68.

15. Daniel Yergin and Joseph Stanislaw, 24.

16. William H. Whyte, Jr., *The Organization Man* (New York: Doubleday Anchor Books, 1956), 7–8.

17. Norman F. Cantor, *The American Century* (New York: HarperPerennial, 1997), 408.

18. William H. Whyte, Jr., 245.

19. For an excellent review of modularity, refer to Carliss Y. Baldwin and Kim B. Clark, "Managing in an Age of Modularity," *Harvard Business Review* (September/October, 1997), 84.

20. David Tyack and Larry Cuban, 21.

21. Valerie Strauss, "A Case for Smaller Schools," *The Washington Post* (August 8, 2000), A10.

22. Larry Cuban, *How Teachers Taught* (New York: Teachers College Press, 1993), 152.

23. Donald Mackinnon, June Statham, and Margaret Hales, *Education in the UK: Facts and Figures* (London: The Open University, 1995), 26.

24. Francis Fukuyama, "Reconstructing America's Moral Order," *The Wilson Quarterly* (Summer, 1999), 34.

25. James S. Coleman, "Families and Schools," *Educational Researcher* (August-September, 1987), 50.

26. Ibid., 51.

27. Ibid., 52.

28. Nick Davies, "Mixture of Talent Makes or Breaks a School," *The Guardian* (September 14, 1999).

29. Robert Putnam. White House Publications. *Remarks by the President and the Participants in First Session of Economic Summit.* The East Room, April 5, 2000. (Washington, DC: The White House Office of the Press Secretary).

30. Larry Cuban, *How Teachers Taught*, 155.

31. David B. Tyack, *Turning Points in American Educational History* (Waltham, MA: Blaisdell Publishing Co., 1967), 321.

32. John Dewey, *How We Think*, 43–44.

33. F.A. Hayek, *The Road to Serfdom* (Chicago: The University of Chicago Press, 1944), xxxix.

34. Fritz Schumacher, *Small Is Beautiful: Economics as If People Mattered* (London: Blond and Briggs Ltd., 1973), 39.

35. David Farber, 270.

36. Francis Fukuyama, "Reconstructing America's Moral Order," 35.

37. Libby Purves, "The Family's Value," *The Times of London* (February, 2000).

Chapter 8

1. For a good review, refer to David R. Colburn and George E. Pozzetta, "Race, Ethnicity, and the Evolution of Political Legitimacy," in David Farber, ed., *The Sixties: From Memory to History* (Chapel Hill, NC: UNC Press, 1994).

2. David B. Tyack, *The One Best System*, 284.

3. Ibid., 287–289.

4. Milton and Rose Friedman, *Free to Choose* (New York: Harcourt Brace Jovanovich, 1979), 151.

5. Frank Levy, "Rhetoric and Reality: Making Sense of the Income Gap," *Harvard Business Review* (September–October, 1999), 164.

6. Daniel Yergin and Joseph Stanislaw, 92, 104.

7. As *The Economist* observed in its 1997 World Economy Survey, government spending, as a percentage of gross domestic product, from 1937 to 1980 increased in the United States from 8.6 percent to 31.8 percent and in England 30.0 percent to 43 percent. "The World Economic Survey," *The Economist* (September 20–27, 1997), 11.

8. David Landes, *The Wealth and Poverty of Nations* (New York: W.W. Norton & Company, 1998), 458.

9. Martin J. Wiener, *English Culture and the Decline of the Industrial Spirit 1850–1980* (Cambridge: Cambridge University Press, 1981), 163.

10. Ibid., 162.

11. *Newsweek*, "The Troubled America: A Special Report on the White Majority" (October 6, 1969), p. 31.

12. Quote taken from Ronald Reagan's first inaugural address.

13. This economic shift from the national to the transnational was initiated by the oil shocks of the 1970s and President Nixon's decision in August of 1971 to let the dollar "float." "Without consulting his allies, President Richard Nixon announced that the American dollar was no longer freely convertible. The decision to close the gold window ended the era of fixed exchange rates and ushered in a new period of floating rates, with the financial instability that has ever since been an inherent part of the world economy. . . . Globalization in its contemporary form was really launched on that fateful day in August. By allowing exchange rates to float, currencies themselves became the object of intense speculation, creating entirely new markets." Ethan B. Kapstein, "The Global Third Way," *World Policy Journal* (Winter, 1998/99), 29–30.

14. Peter Drucker, *The New Realities* (London: Mandarin, 1989), 109.

15. The former CEO and Chairman of Citicorp/Citibank, Walter Wriston, sums up the power of globalized financial markets over governments as follows, "Today the market is $1 trillion, and central bank intervention in foreign exchange becomes an expensive exercise in futility. The market is a giant voting machine that records in real time the judgment of traders all over the world about American diplomatic, fiscal and monetary policy . . . . Moments after a president announces a policy in the Rose Garden, the market's judgment is reflected in the price of the dollar." Walter Wriston, "Bits, Bytes and Diplomacy," *Foreign Affairs* (September/October, 1997), 176.

16. Mortimer Zuckerman, "A Second American Century," *Foreign Affairs* (May/June, 1998), 18.

17. John T. Bruer, *Schools for Thought* (Cambridge, MA: A Bradford Book, 1993), 7.

18. Introduction by Sir Keith Joseph. Samuel Smiles, *Self-Help* (London: Penguin Books, 1986), 12.

19. Ibid., 13.

20. John Kingdom, *No Such Thing As Society?* (Buckingham: Open University Press, 1992), 2.

21. Michael J. Sandel, *Democracy's Discontent* (Cambridge, MA: Harvard University Press, 1996), 312.

22. John Kingdom, 1.

23. Daniel Yergin and Joseph Stanislaw, 123.

24. Daniel Yergin and Joseph Stanislaw, 115.

25. Samuel Smiles, 19.

26. Daniel Yergin and Joseph Stanislaw, 109.

27. Will Hutton, *The State We're In* (London: Jonathan Cape, 1995), 94.

28. Kenneth O. Morgan, ed., *The Oxford History of Britain* (Oxford: Oxford University Press, 1999), 657.

29. Kiichi Miyazawa, "Deliberations and Conclusions on Deregulation," *The Washington Quarterly* (Winter, 1998), 143–144.

30. Doug Struck, "Japanese Panel Advises a Move to the West," *The Washington Post* (January 20, 2000), A1.

31. Anne-Marie Slaughter, "The Real New World Order," *Foreign Affairs* (September/October, 1997), 184.

32. To be candid, there is debate among economists as to how global the economy has actually become, with Paul Krugman of MIT arguing that globalization is actually "globaloney." Krugman states emphatically, "The idea that a country's economic fortunes are largely determined by its success on world markets is a hypothesis, not a necessary truth; and as a practical, empirical matter, that hypothesis is flatly wrong." For Krugman the rhetoric of globalization is more influential (and potentially more disruptive) than the facts of globalization, at least within the larger economies of the United States and Western Europe. The authors will not argue this point, but will simply note that globalization is real because it has undoubtedly influenced government policies and private industry in the 1990s. Because of the political nature of education, and the fact it is the producer of raw materials for the job market, economic globalization impacts on the way young people are raised, educated and prepared for the future. Paul Krugman, *Pop Internationalism* (Cambridge: The MIT Press, 1996), 5.

33. Barry Eichengreen, "One Economy, Ready or Not: Thomas Friedman's Jaunt Through Globalization," *Foreign Affairs* (May/June, 1999), 119.

34. Schools Brief, "One World?" *The Economist* (October 18–24, 1997), 79.

35. HM Treasury News Release, "Speech by the Chancellor of the Exchequer Gordon Brown at the Council of Foreign Relations," (September 16, 1999). www.hm-treasury.gov.uk.

36. "Mr. Blair Goes to Washington," *The Economist* (February 7–13, 1998), 16.

37. Samuel Beer, "Liberalism Rediscovered," *The Economist* (February 7–13, 1998), 23.

38. Tony Blair, "Third Way, Better Way," *The Washington Post* (September 27, 1998), C7.

39. Anthony Giddens, "After the Left's Paralysis," *New Statesman* (May 1, 1998), 20.

40. Ibid., 19.

41. Tony Blair, "Third Way, Better Way," *The Washington Post* (September 27, 1998), C7.

42. Mortimer Zuckerman, "A Second American Century," *Foreign Affairs* (May/June, 1998), 20.

43. Daniel Goleman, *Working with Emotional Intelligence* (New York: Bantam Books, 1998), 3.

44. Centre for Educational Research and Innovation, *Education Policy Analysis 1998* (Paris: OECD, 1998), 9.

45. Steve Twomey, "Moving on to College, Going Back to Basics," *The Washington Post* (September 23, 1999), A1.

46. The U.S. economist Frank Levy caught the essence of this gap when he observed in the *Harvard Business Review,* "About half of all 17-year-olds [in the United States] still read below a ninth-grade level, yet most well-paying jobs now demand a much higher level of literacy." Frank Levy, 167.

Chapter 9

1. For a thorough review of the 1988 Education Act, refer to Clyde Chitty, *The Education System Transformed*, 2nd ed. (Wiltshire: Baseline Book Company, 1999).

2. Refer to the National Commission on Excellence in Education, *A Nation at Risk* (Washington, DC: U.S. Government Printing Office, 1983).

3. Stephen Wagg, "Don't Try to Understand Them: Politics, Childhood, and the New Education Market," in *Thatcher's Children*, Jane Pilcher and Stephen Wagg, eds. (London: Falmer Press, 1996), 9.

4. John Tomlinson, "Limits to the Autonomous School: The Case for the LEA or Comparable Body," *Education: Putting the Record Straight* (Stafford: Network Educational Press, 1992), 69.

5. In fact the Butler Act described only two necessities for the curriculum: religious education and physical education.

6. Donald Mackinnon, June Statham, and Margaret Hales, *Education in the UK: Facts and Figures* (London: Open University, 1996), 53.

7. Clyde Chitty, 18.

8. Rhode Boyson, *The Crisis in Education* (London: Woburn Press, 1975), 141.

9. For a detailed description of activities at this time, refer to John Abbott, *The Father Is Child of the Man.*

10. Michael Barber, *The Learning Game* (London: Indigo, 1996), 36.

11. David Tyack and Larry Cuban, *Tinkering Toward Utopia* (Cambridge, MA: Harvard University Press, 1995), 141.

12. Education 2000 under the co-chairmanship of Bryan Thwaites and Christopher Wysock-Wright, *A Consultative Document on Hypotheses for Education in A.D. 2000* (Cambridge: Cambridge University Press, 1983), ix.

13. *The Guardian*, "£1 billion plan for teaching 'revolution'," (December 4, 1998).

14. John O'Leary, "Blunkett Offers Bonuses for Results," *The Times of London* (December 4, 1998).

15. Libby Purves, "Beleagured Children," *The Times of London* (October 15, 1997).

16. According to *The Guardian*'s Kathryn Riley, "Kentucky decided to reward teachers for improvements in the performance of their pupils. High-performing schools were given a sum of money and told to distribute this among staff. It was an administrative nightmare. What about the teachers who had already left the school but had contributed to its success? Could high test score results, in say English, be attributed solely to the English teacher? Hadn't other teachers also contributed to improved literacy? The approach was hugely unpopular. It led to lower teacher morale and pushed the school reform agenda off the rails." Kathryn Riley, "And the Winner Is. . . . " *The Guardian* (December 8, 1998).

17. *The Guardian*, "Teachers' Pay Through Blunkett's Gate," (December 4, 1998).

18. For a discussion on creativity, refer to *All Our Futures: Creativity, Culture and Education* by the English Department for Education and Employment in 1999. For a discussion on the role of peers in adolescent learning refer to Judith Rich Harris's *The Nurture Assumption* (New York: The Free Press, 1998).

19. For details on the Education 2000 projects, refer to John Abbott's *The Child Is Father of the Man* and Paul Fisher, *Education 2000: Educational Change with Consent* (London: Cassell, 1990).

20. Nick Davies, "Political Coup Bred Educational Disaster," *The Guardian* (September 16, 1999).

21. Clyde Chitty, 37.

Chapter 10

1. For a detailed description of this program from Princeton High School in the United States, refer to John Abbott's book *The Child Is the Father of the Man.*

2. Virginia Galt, "York Study Gives On-Line Courses A+," *Globe & Mail* (July 14, 1999), A5.

3. Ernst Mayr, *This Is Biology*, 39.

4. Jerome Kagan, *Three Seductive Ideas* (Cambridge: Harvard University Press, 1998), 97.

5. According to Ernst Mayr, "The basic theories of science, many of them as much as 50 or even 150 years old, are being confirmed again and again. Even in a field as controversial as evolutionary biology, the basic conceptual framework established by Darwin in 1859 has turned out to be remarkably robust. All attempts in the last 130 years to invalidate Darwinism (and there have been hundreds) have been unsuccessful, and the same is true for most other areas of biology." Ernst Mayr, 47.

6. Jerome Kagan, 98.

7. Andrew Brown, *The Darwin Wars* (New York: Simon & Schuster, 1999), 30.

8. The Periodical Observer, "Who Reads?" *The Wilson Quarterly* (Spring, 1999), 116.

9. Irwin Schroedinger, *What Is Life?* (Cambridge: Cambridge University Press, 1944).

10. Peter Schrag, "High Stakes Are for Tomatoes," *The Atlantic Monthly* (August, 2000), 21.

11. Stephanie Pace Marshall shared her comments at a 21st Century Learning Initiative conference at the Johnson Foundation's Wingspread Conference Center in Racine, Wisconsin (1996).

12. Dee Hock shared his comments at a 21st Century Learning Initiative conference at the Johnson Foundation's Wingspread Conference Center in Racine, Wisconsin (1996).

13. The concept for this table comes from Gary Hamel, *Leading the Revolution* (Boston: Harvard Business School Press, 2000).

Index

Note: An *f* after a page number indicates a reference to a figure.

Index

About the Authors

John Abbott is president of the 21st Century Learning Initiative, a transnational association of researchers and practitioners. He was a teacher of geography and religious studies at Manchester Grammar School, headmaster of Alleyne's School in Stevenage, chairman of the Royal Geographical Society's Expeditionary Advisory Centre, and director of Education 2000, with nine community-wide projects in the United Kingdom. Over the last six years he has lectured around the world on new understandings about learning. He and his family lived in Reston, Virginia, from 1995 to 1999.

He is the author of *The Iranians: How They Live and Work, The Earth's Changing Surface, Learning Makes Sense,* and *The Child Is the Father of the Man: How Humans Learn and Why.* Abbott is happily married and the father of three college-age sons.

Terry Ryan has served as a researcher for the 21st Century Learning Initiative since its founding in late 1995. In 1997 he became senior researcher. As senior researcher, Ryan has worked closely with a number of researchers, policymakers, academics, and businesspeople from many countries in developing the Initiative's training programs, documentation, public presentations, and Web site. Ryan has given public presentations on the work of the Initiative to groups in several countries.

Upon receiving his master's degree in political economy, Ryan received a fellowship from the American Federation of Teachers to work with educational reformers and students in Poland in 1994–95. His mentor in Poland was the former Solidarity leader and member of Parliament Wiktor Kulerski. Ryan and Kulerski have collaborated on a book looking at 20th century Polish history through the eyes of one of Poland's most politically active families, *The Shadows of the Past.* Ryan is happily married and the father of a 1-year-old daughter.